The Dong Language
in Guizhou Province, China

Summer Institute of Linguistics and
The University of Texas at Arlington
Publications in Linguistics

Publication 126

Publications in Linguistics is a series published jointly by the Summer Institute of Linguistics and the University of Texas at Arlington. The series is a venue for works covering a broad range of topics in linguistics, especially the analytical treatment of minority languages from all parts of the world. While most volumes are authored by members of the Institute, suitable works by others will also form part of the series.

Series Editors

Mildred L. Larson
Summer Institute of Linguistics

Volume Editors

Eugene Loos
Rhonda Hartell

Production Staff

Laurie Nelson, Production Manager
Hazel Shorey, Graphic Arts

The Dong Language in Guizhou Province, China

Long Yaohong (龙耀宏) and Zheng Guoqiao (郑国乔)

translated from Chinese by
D. Norman Geary (Ji Zhiyi, 吉志义)

A Publication of
The Summer Institute of Linguistics
and
The University of Texas at Arlington
1998

©1998 by the Summer Institute of Linguistics, Inc.
Library of Congress Catalog No: 97-62497
ISBN: 1-55671-051-8
ISSN: 1040-0850

Printed in the United States of America
All Rights Reserved

08 07 06 05 04 03 02 01 00 99   10 9 8 7 6 5 4 3 2 1

No part of this publication may be reproduced, stored in a retrieval system, or transmitted in any form or by any means—electronic, mechanical, photocopy, recording, or otherwise—without the express permission of the Summer Institute of Linguistics, with the exception of brief excerpts in journal articles or reviews.

Copies of this and other publications of the Summer Institute of Linguistics may be obtained from

International Academic Bookstore
Summer Institute of Linguistics
7500 W. Camp Wisdom Rd.
Dallas, TX 75236-5699

Voice: 972-708-7404
Fax: 972-708-7433
Email: academic_books@sil.org
Internet: http://www.sil.org

Contents

Abbreviations vii
Foreword ix
Preface xiii
Translator's Acknowledgements xv

1 Introduction 1
  1.1 The Dong nationality's name and origin 1
  1.2 Culture 6
  1.3 Language 9
  1.4 The influence of the Chinese language on the Dong language . 14

2 Phonology 19
  2.1 Syllable initials 19
  2.2 Syllable rhymes 23
  2.3 Tones 30
  2.4 Differences within standard Dong 33
  2.5 Pronunciation of Chinese loan words 34
    2.5.1 Pronunciation of Ancient Chinese loans 35
    2.5.2 Pronunciation of Modern Chinese loans 47

3 Lexicon 51
  3.1 Syllable structure 51
  3.2 Word structure 51
  3.3 Homophones, polysemic words, and synonyms 65
  3.4 Cognate words 71
  3.5 Loan words 73

4 Grammar ... 77
4.1 Lexical categories ... 77
4.1.1 Nouns ... 77
4.1.2 Classifiers ... 91
4.1.3 Numerals ... 100
4.1.4 Pronouns ... 110
4.1.5 Verbs ... 120
4.1.6 Adjectives ... 127
4.1.7 Adverbs ... 132
4.1.8 Sound descriptive words ... 138
4.1.9 Prepositions ... 141
4.1.10 Conjunctions ... 144
4.1.11 Auxiliary words ... 146
4.1.12 Interjections ... 153
4.2 Phrases ... 154
4.3 Sentence composition ... 163
4.4 Sentence structure ... 171
4.5 Sentence types ... 175

5 Dialects ... 181
5.1 Differentiation and distribution of dialects ... 181
5.2 Differences in pronunciation between lects ... 182
5.3 Differences in vocabulary between lects ... 195
5.4 Differences in grammar between dialects ... 201

6 Orthography ... 205
6.1 Language survey and the Dong orthography ... 205
6.2 Implementation and use of the Dong orthography ... 208
6.3 Using Chinese characters to record Dong ... 211

Appendix 1. Vocabulary of the Two Dong Dialects ... 215
Appendix 2. Co-occurrence of Dong Initials, Rhymes, and Tones ... 245
Appendix 3. Cognate Words ... 263

Postscript ... 267

Abbreviations

1	first person
2	second person
3	third person
a	adjective
CLF	classifier
CONT	continuous tense marker
EBs	Earthly Branches
EX	exclamation
exc	exclusive
IMP	imperative marker
inc	inclusive
INT	interjection
LIST	list marker
n	noun
NEG^STM	negative-statement marker
p	plural
PASS	passive marker
PAST	past tense marker
PTC	particle
Q	question marker
REL	relational marker
RMB	Rénmínbì (人民币, currency of the People's Republic of China)
s	singular
SD	sound descriptive word
STM	statement marker
v	verb

Foreword

The Dong Language in Guizhou Province, China, written by Lóng Yàohóng (龙耀宏) and Zhèng Guóqiáo (郑国乔), is being published in English. To those of us involved in linguistics, this is worth celebrating.

As indicated in the authors' postscript, this book was originally planned as one of a series of books on the minority languages of Guìzhōu (贵州), an item on the agenda of the seventh five-year plan of the Philosophical and Scientific Society of Guìzhōu Province. Its purpose was to provide a comprehensive introduction to the Dong language in Guìzhōu Province, thus laying a foundation for future research on the language. The earliest draft of the book was completed in February 1990. At that time, Mr. Lóng was my research student at the Central Institute of Nationalities (now the Central University of Nationalities) in Běijīng (北京). The two authors brought the draft to me for my suggestions, and I had the enjoyable privilege of becoming the book's first reader. For me there was much to be gained in reading it. We held discussions and reached general agreement about certain questions arising from the draft. In 1994 Mr. Lóng revised the original draft.

It is now 1997, and the two authors are both scholars of high standing in the field of Dong language research. Mr. Lóng has been engaged in such research at the Guìzhōu Institute of Nationalities since his graduation in 1984. He has a good command of both the southern and northern dialects of Dong, lecturing mainly on the subjects of modern Dong, Dong grammar, dialects, history, and culture. His published research has had a significant impact on the field of Dong research. He has wide-ranging interest and expertise in Dong language, history, society, folk customs, and culture and has published many articles on these subjects.

Mr. Zhèng is of Hàn nationality. He was a colleague of mine for nearly forty years and has been one of the most influential experts on the Dong language inside and outside of China. Together we began the work of teaching and researching Dong in 1953. He participated in the large survey of the language in 1956, taking responsibility for four counties: Róngjiāng (榕江), Lípíng (黎平), and Cóngjiāng (从江) in Guìzhōu Province, and Sānjiāng (三江) in Guǎngxī (广西) Province. He was also involved in the work of planning the Dong orthography in the late 1950s. His survey work led to a large body of good quality data, establishing a firm foundation for research of the language. His own research focussed on exploring Dong dialects and phonology, with research papers such as "Dong Tones" and "The Phonetic System of Róngjiāng Speech", and teaching material such as *A Comparison of Dong Dialect Pronunciations*. Such publications were the academic distillation of many years' teaching and researching the Dong language.

This book is divided into six chapters: introduction, phonology, lexicon, grammar, dialects, and orthography. In the introduction, the population distribution and cultural characteristics of the Dong nationality are presented. Documentary evidence is cited in a thorough examination of the origin of the Dong people. In addition, the language family and branch of the family to which the Dong language belongs is introduced.

The chapter on phonology, apart from describing the phonological system of the standard (southern) Dong dialect of Róngjiāng Zhānglǔ (榕江章鲁), also presents phonological phenomena associated with the northern dialect. Attention is paid to some particular phonological features which have been the subject of detailed research and analysis: for example, tone splitting, simplification and merging of syllable initials and syllable rhymes, the gradual disappearance of contrast between long and short vowels, and the effect of Chinese loan words on the phonology.

The chapter on lexicon has a section on cognate words. Apart from discussing cognate words among different lects of the Dong language, it also considers cognate words among different languages from the same language family and branch as the Dong language. The section on loan words points out that the majority of loan words in Dong are borrowed from Chinese. There are different ways in which words have been borrowed, according to the point in time at which they were borrowed, and four different styles of borrowing are indicated. The various borrowed words reflect different aspects of the history of relations between the Dong and the Hàn Chinese nationalities.

The chapter on grammar focusses on presentation of the grammar of speech from Róngjiāng Zhānglǔ of the southern dialect area. This is used as a basis for comparing the northern dialect speech of Tiānzhù Shídòng (天柱石洞), illustrating major differences. Many special features are highlighted and thoroughly discussed: for example, the phenomenon of phonetic change in nouns, classifiers, and numerals of the northern dialect; and the function of suffixes on adjectives. Research on Dong grammar has traditionally been rather weak, but the grammar chapter of this book accounts for almost half of the book's contents. The chapter reflects a welcome emphasis by the authors on the area of grammar research.

The three appendices at the end of the book are significant and useful. One is a table comparing vocabulary of the two Dong dialects. The second relates to the chapter on phonology, showing co-occurrence of Dong initials, rhymes, and tones. The third relates to the chapter on lexicon, with more extensive lists of cognate words.

All the data quoted in the book, for example referring to population distribution, language use, and implementation of the orthography, are based on the most up-to-date available statistics. This is the first time the Shídòng data have been published, and this no doubt greatly enhances the value of the book.

In writing the book the two authors agreed on an excellent division of labor. Mr. Lóng took responsibility for the introduction and grammar chapters, while the phonology, lexicon, and orthography chapters were written by Mr. Zhèng. Mr. Lóng is himself a Dong person from Tiānzhù County in the northern dialect area and has been teaching Dong grammar for many years in the Guìzhōu Institute of Nationalities. He has many natural advantages in researching the grammar of his own native language. Mr. Zhèng has researched Dong phonology for many years and is a leading authority on this within China.

Nowadays, writing a book does not seem that difficult; but writing a scientifically respectable treatise on a minority language is really a formidable task. Detailed and accurate language data are called for, and obtaining such data requires survey research incorporating an understanding of the society, history, culture, and customs of the minority people who speak the language. *The Dong Language in Guìzhōu Province, China* attained to these high standards in its writing. It is the culmination of many years of painstaking teaching and research by both authors.

The history of survey research of the Dong language can be said to fall into four stages. The first was in 1941–42, when Professor Lǐ Fānggùi (李方桂) surveyed the Shuǐ language in Guìzhōu Province and at the same time investigated the Dong language in some areas. He formally established the nomenclature for the Dòng-Shuǐ (侗水) branch of the Dòng-Tái (侗台) language family, opening up the field of Dong language research. The second stage was in 1953, after the creation of the People's Republic of China. At that time, Mr. Zhèng and I together surveyed the Dong spoken in the Tōngdào (通道) Dong Autonomous County in Húnán (湖南) Province. We used the Dong spoken in Píngtǎn (坪坦) as a basis for designing a roman-based orthography for Dong, compiling a Dong language textbook. The third stage was in 1956–57, when the Dong Section of the First Working Group of the Chinese Academy of Science's Minority Language Survey Team conducted a large national survey of the Dong language. Twenty-two Dong language points were surveyed, and the Dong orthography was designed using the speech in Róngjiāng Zhānglǔ as standard. The final stage has been the investigation and research that has been done since 1980. For example in 1980, Xíng Gōngwǎn (邢公畹) and colleagues of Nánkāi (南开) University in Tiānjīn (天津) organized a Dong language survey in Línxī (林溪) in the Sānjiāng Dong Autonomous County in Guǎngxī. In 1987, Mr. Zhèng and I surveyed the Dong language of Pìndòng (聘洞) in Róngshuǐ (融水) County in Guǎngxī.

The various Dong surveys led to the following publications: *The Conference on Scholarly Approaches to Questions of a Writing System for the Dong Language* (Guìyáng, 1959), *A Brief Description of the Dong Language* (Běijīng, 1980), and *The Dong Language in Sanjiang* (Tiānjīn, 1985). The publication of this volume will undoubtedly greatly facilitate future Dong language research. It is likely to attract interest in the wider realm of Sino-Tibetan language research.

Before concluding, I wish to introduce the book's translator Mr. Norman Geary (吉志义) and his wife Mrs. Ruth Geary (孔瑞贤). They are my former students and have become my friends. Mr. Geary is from Northern Ireland and has a doctorate from Oxford University. Mrs. Geary is Swiss. They studied the Chinese language in Běijīng for two and a half years, attaining a good level of competence in the language. Aspiring to study and research the language and culture of the Dong nationality, they went twice to live in the Róngjiāng countryside, staying nearly three months each time. They can already converse simply in Dong and we feel pleased about the good progress they have made.

This book may well push the subject of the Dong language onto a new platform of international research. Writing as one of an older generation of Dong teachers and researchers, I feel immensely gratified by this. Publication of such work is warmly welcome, and it is my pleasure to commend the book.

> Professor Yáng Quán (杨权)
> Central University of Nationalities, Běijīng
> April 2, 1997

Preface

The Dong language is the language of the Dong people, used in the Dong areas where the three provinces Guìzhōu (贵州), Húnán (湖南), and Guǎngxī (广西) have common boundaries. Owing to historical and population factors, and especially to some features of the language itself, the Dong language occupies an important position in the Dòng-Tái (侗台) family of the Sino-Tibetan phylum.

In the early 1940s, the renowned linguist Lǐ Fāngguì (李方桂) investigated the Dong language. (His findings were never published.) After Professor Lǐ put forward the names "Dòng-Tái family" and "Dòng-Shuǐ (侗水) branch," scholars in and outside of China all paid greater attention to the Dong language. However, because of poor transport facilities and for various societal and political reasons, hardly anyone conducted serious study of the Dong language before the establishment of the People's Republic of China (1949), and hardly any published work on Dong existed.

After 1949, the government responded to the need to help minority nationalities create their own orthographies where none had existed previously. In the summer of 1956, a Dong Language Survey Team conducted a comprehensive survey of the dialects of Dong. After three months' work, Dong language data and some cultural information had been collected from twenty-two Dong areas. At that time, Zhèng Guóqiáo (郑国乔) was responsible for collecting data from four counties: Róngjiāng (榕江), Lípíng (黎平), and Cóngjiāng (从江) in Guìzhōu Province, and Sānjiāng (三江) in Guǎngxī Province. In 1957, after the survey work had finished, Zhèng Guóqiáo and others arranged the data as the "Report on the Dong Dialect Survey." In October 1959, this was published in Guìyáng as part of *The Conference on Scholarly Approaches to Questions of a Writing System for the Dong Language*, and it became the foundational work for Dong language research. Later, Mr. Liáng Mǐn (梁敏) used the Róngjiāng Zhānglǔ (章鲁) survey data recorded by his predecessors to write *A Brief Description of the*

Dong Language, published in Běijīng in 1980. This became the first ever openly available publication on the Dong language in or outside of China.

Over the last forty years, there has never been a survey of the Dong language on the same scale as the one of 1956. Since 1980, however, theoretical research has been progressing by leaps and bounds. In particular, since 1985, minority language departments or Dòng-Tái language research units have been established in the Central Institute (now University) of Nationalities, the Guìzhōu Institute of Nationalities, and Nánkāi University in Tiānjīn. These have had an intake of students specializing in and researching the Dong language, and courses are offered in modern Dong, comparison of Dong dialects, Dong grammar, and so on. We became responsible for developing and teaching such courses. This book integrates our years of experience in teaching and in scientific research, and is written from the foundation of teaching materials for the above-mentioned courses.

The Dong Language in Guizhou Province, China describes and analyzes the Dong language as spoken in Guìzhōu Province. Fifty-six percent of all Dong people reside in Guìzhōu. In analyzing the language, we endeavoured to start from the six lects of the southern and northern dialects which exist in Guìzhōu and to conduct a comprehensive analysis and comparison of phonological, lexical, grammatical, societal, and historical aspects of these lects. The book first gives a brief account of the history and origin of the Dong nationality, the population distribution, the social customs, and language affiliation and use. This should help readers to understand the history of development of the Dong language and to understand the position of the Dong language within the Dòng-Shuǐ branch of the Dòng-Tái family of the Sino-Tibetan phylum. To facilitate more thorough research into dialects of Dong in future, we add a table of basic vocabulary as appendix 1.

The language data used in the book are robust and plentiful. The southern dialect data were mainly the result of survey work conducted by Zhèng Guóqiáo in Dong areas over a long period of time. Shídòng (石洞) speech of the northern dialect is the mother tongue of Lóng Yàohóng (龙耀宏). Wherever the work or data of other people are cited in the book, the source is individually indicated.

We hope that the publication of this book may lead to vigorous development of Dong language research, in and outside of China. The book provides source material for research of the Sino-Tibetan phylum and supplies linguistic data for research of matters relating to the society, history, and culture of the Dong nationality.

Lóng Yàohóng (龙耀宏)
Zhèng Guóqiáo (郑国乔)
April 1997

Translator's Acknowledgements

Our first teacher of Dong was Professor Yáng Quán (杨权) in Běijīng. He was very kind to teach two complete beginners, and his help was a great encouragement. He also introduced us to the best possible teacher of Dong in Guìyáng, Mr. Lóng Yàohóng (龙耀宏).

Mr. Lóng has now been our teacher for two years. When he mentioned the unpublished manuscript of this book, we were immediately interested, as our goal was to research the Dong language. We are very grateful to Mr. Lóng and Mr. Zhèng for permission to translate the book into English.

We have never met Mr. Zhèng Guóqiáo (郑国乔). Unlike Mr. Lóng, he is not a native speaker of Dong. He is, however, not only a respected authority on Dong language research, but also a fluent speaker of the language.

Professor Jerry Edmondson (艾杰瑞) of the University of Texas at Arlington encouraged us to proceed with this translation and we are pleased to acknowledge his support.

Thanks to Mr. Máo Jiànlín (毛健林) and his staff at the Foreign Affairs Office of Guìzhōu University, who have been excellent hosts to us, facilitating our study of Dong. Thanks to Ms. Xiè Míngyīng (谢明英) from the Office for help with checking the tones on some Chinese pīnyīn in the book.

Thanks to my wife Ruth (孔瑞贤) for her help and input on many aspects of the translation.

Thanks to Wú Róngxiān (吴荣先), Shí Fāguāng (石发光), and Chén Mèngxīn (陈梦心) for help in typing tables and interpreting Chinese.

Thanks to Bryan Allen (艾磊), Dottie Martin (马多恩), Donna Snyder (辛亚宁), my father David Geary, Douglas Humphreys, and Philip and Cecilia Brassett (白丰霖 and 廖乔婧) for their comments on various parts of the manuscript. Thanks to Rhonda Hartell, an editor of the SIL/UTA series, who made detailed and useful comments on the whole manuscript.

Thanks to Wil Snyder (辛维) for making available his draft translation of a description of Dong grammar, which contained material very similar to chapter 4 of this book, and for providing both the Dong IPA and the Chinese pīnyīn fonts originally used in typing the manuscript. Thanks also to Laurie Nelson of SIL for compiling the fonts finally used in the book and for miscellaneous help in preparing the book for publication.

Thanks to David Landin for help in formatting the text for publication, to Richard and Jean Rowland and to Irene Tucker for help in producing the dialect map, to Tom Pinson (孙堂茂) for help in creating new characters with Chinese Star, to Ian Wallace for help with photocopying, and to friends in Knoxville, Tennessee, for a grant towards the book's publication.

Translation errors remain the responsibility of the translator.

Norman Geary (吉志义)
Heiden, Switzerland
December 23, 1997

1
Introduction

1.1 The Dong nationality's name and origin

Origin and historical overview. The Dòng (侗)[1] nationality developed from a branch of the ancient Bǎiyuè (百越) nationality. After the Wèi (魏, AD 220–265),[2] Jìn (晋, AD 265–420), and Nán Běi (南北, AD 420–589) dynasties, this branch was generally known as the Liáo (僚). According to *Suí Shū. Nán Mán Zhuàn* (隋书. 南蛮传, AD 1120–1164),[3] "There are many kinds of *nán mán* (南蛮 'uneducated people living in the south'), and they mix freely with the Hàn (汉) people. They are known as Yán (蜒), Ráng (儴), Lǐ (俚), Liáo (僚), or Xiē (㐌). None of these peoples has a paramount leader. They live in caves, cut their hair short, and tattoo their bodies. Their ancestors were the so-called Bǎiyuè."

Gù Yánwǔ (顾炎武) in *Tiān Xià Jùn Guó Lì Bìng Shū* (天下郡国利病书, 1613–1682) says "The Dòng Liáo people, the ordinary people living in the river valley near Lǐngbiǎo (岭表) mountain, used to be called the mountain Yuè (越). They have been developing fast ever since the Táng (唐, AD 618–907) and Sòng (宋, AD 960–1279) dynasties." In *Sòng Shǐ. Xī Nán Xī Dòng Zhū Mán Zhuàn* (宋史. 西南溪洞诸蛮传, AD 1314–1355) it is noted that "In AD 1039 Chénzhōu's Jílliáo (辰州佶僚) had more than 3,000 residents

---

[1]The first time a nationality, person, or place name is mentioned, the corresponding Chinese characters will follow in parentheses.

[2]The first time a dynasty is mentioned, its corresponding Chinese characters and dates will follow in parentheses. For reference, dynasties referred to are listed here: Qín (秦, 221–206 BC), Hàn (汉, 206 BC–AD 220), Wèi (魏, AD 220–265), Jìn (晋, AD 265–420), Nán Běi (南北, AD 420–589), Táng (唐, AD 618–907), Sòng (宋, AD 960–1279), Míng (明, AD 1368–1644), and Qīng (清, AD 1616–1911).

[3]Dates given here are dates of main author's birth and death. Throughout this chapter, when a book is referred to, either the dates between which the main author lived are presented or the date of publication is given.

willing to be centrally governed." (Before, they had always been independent.) In *Chì Yǎ* (赤雅, 1604–1650) written at the end of the Míng (明, AD 1368–1644) dynasty, Kuàng Lù (邝露) states that "The Dòng are a subgroup of the Liáo." So here we can see the line of inheritance between the Yuè, Liáo, and Dòng: the Liáo evolved from the Yuè, and the Dòng evolved from the Liáo.

In the Míng and the Qīng (清, AD 1616–1911) dynasties, the Dòng were often known as 'Dòng Liáo' (峒僚), 'Dòng people' (峒人 or 侗人), 'Dòng Mán' (峒蛮), or 'Dòng Miáo' (峒苗); or they were lumped together with other peoples and called 'Miáo' (苗), 'Yí' (夷), and so on. From 1911 to 1949 local Hàn Chinese mostly called the Dòng people 'Dòng Jiā' (侗家); since Liberation (1949), they have been called simply the Dòng (侗) nationality.

Dòng autonym. Dòng people refer to themselves as $kəm^{55}$. There are local variations on this; some say $təm^{55}$ or $toŋ^{55}$, and there are further names according to place of abode, e.g., $təm^{55}$ $ʔao^{31}$, $təm^{55}$ tau^{31}, or $təm^{55}$ tan^{31}.

The Dòng autonym, as it appeared originally in the Sòng dynasty's historical records, was written down as 'Gēlíng' (仡伶) or 'Gēlàn' (仡儑), using the *fǎn qiè* (反切)[4] form. According to *Sòng Shǐ. Xī Nán Xī Dòng Zhū Mán Zhuàn*, "In AD 1171, Jìngzhōu (靖州) had Gēlíng people with the surname Yáng (杨), and Yuánzhōu (沅州) had a Gēlíng vice-governor of the areas not ruled by the Hàn Chinese, named Wú Zìyóu (吴自由)." In *Lǎo Xué Ān Bǐ Jì* (老学庵笔记, AD 1125–1210), it is noted that "There are Gēlíng and Gēlàn in Chénzhōu, Yuánzhōu, and Jìngzhōu"; "If a man has not yet taken a wife, he sticks a pheasant feather in his hair"; and "At times when there's no work to be done, one or two hundred men get together, hold hands and sing, with some men at the front leading the music on the *lúshēng* (芦笙)." These quotations evidently refer to the Dòng people.[5] Studies of Chénzhōu, Yuánzhōu, and Jìngzhōu show that for many generations right up to the present day these areas have been occupied by Dòng people. In *Míng Shǐ Jì Shì Běn Mò Bǔ Biān* (明史纪事本末补编, 1644–1723) it says that "Dòng (峒 or 洞) people live scattered in the areas of Zāngkē (牂牁) and Wǔxī (潕溪); they are especially numerous in Chénzhōu and Yuánzhōu." The areas just referred to are today's Xīnhuàng (新晃), Zhījiāng (芷江), Huìtóng (会同), Yùpíng (玉屏), Sānsuì (三穗), Tiānzhù (天柱), Jǐnpíng (锦屏), and Lípíng (黎平) Counties. It can be deduced then that Gēlíng and Gēlàn are just transcriptions of the Dòng sound $kəm^{55}$ or $təm^{55}$ (there is no syllable-final *m* sound in Chinese). Judging from these transcriptions,

---

[4] *Fǎn qiè* is a traditional method of indicating the pronunciation of a Chinese character by using two other Chinese characters, the first having the same initial consonant as the given character and the second having the same vowel (with or without final nasal) and tone.

[5] See *Qiǎntán Dòngzú Yǔ Gēlíng Hé Líng* (浅谈侗族与仡伶和伶) by Zhāng Mín (张民), published in *Guìzhōu Mínzú Yánjiū* (贵州民族研究), 1983, Volume 1.

Introduction

however, the Dòng may originally have called themselves *klam*. Later, the *l* in the initial consonant cluster disappeared, and the word became today's *kɐm⁵⁵*. So we can be sure that by the time of the Sòng dynasty, the Dòng people had already become a distinctive minority community as recorded in the annals of the time; and they have a history of at least 1,000 years of living and working in the territories referred to above.

In the Dòng language, *kɐm⁵⁵* can be a noun or a verb. As a noun, it is used for example, in the expression *nən²¹² kɐm⁵⁵* to mean Dòng person or Dòng nationality. As a verb, it usually means to use branches or sticks to fence off, cover, isolate, or keep free from intruders, as seen in (1).

(1)   *kɐm⁵⁵ khwən³⁵*   set up a road barrier (to monitor movements)
       kɐm⁵⁵ ɕai³³   make a fence around a village
       kɐm⁵⁵ tam⁵⁵   build a fish pond
       kɐm⁵⁵ pa⁵⁵   make a home for the fish in a pond
       kɐm⁵⁵ jan³⁵   fence round a garden (to keep animals out)

The autonym *kɐm⁵⁵* is thus probably associated with the idea of 'surrounding and protecting'.

Original meaning of *kɐm⁵⁵*. It seems that *kɐm⁵⁵* originally indicated a certain kind of natural environment. In Hàn literature dating from before the Qín (秦, 221–206 BC) dynasty, there was a kind of environment referred to as Qián (黔), and the old pronunciation of 黔 was *gyəm*.[6] According to Xú Zhōngshū (徐中舒), "Qián was used historically to indicate the natural environment inhabited by the southern peoples."[7] After Emperor Qín Shǐhuáng (秦始皇) united China in 210 BC, the administrative system of Jùn/Xiàn (郡/县) was established throughout the country, and in areas labelled Qián, Qián Zhōng Jùn (黔中郡) were established. Before the Qín dynasty, Qián Zhōng areas were called 'Chǔ Shāng Yū Dì' (楚商於地). In *Huá Yáng Guó Zhì. Bā Zhì* (华阳国志. 巴志, AD 317–369), Qián Zhōng areas are repeatedly referred to as 'Chǔ Shāng Yū Dì'. The old words *yū* (於) and *yuè* (越) were the same in meaning and pronunciation. Thus *shāng yū* was the same as *shāng yuè*. Now the people living at that time in the Qián Zhōng areas were Yuè people and not Chǔ people. This branch of the Yuè people at the time probably called themselves Qián (*gyəm*). The Qián Zhōng Jùn regions of the Qín dynasty were vast. According to *Zhōngguó Gǔjīn*

---

[6] This follows Wáng Lì (王力). In his book *Tóngyuán Zìdiǎn* (同源字典), 1987, Wáng Lì takes *Qián* (黔) as coming from the syllable initial pronunciation of 群 (pronounced *gē* in Ancient Chinese) and the syllable coda pronunciation of 侵 (pronounced *qīm* in Ancient Chinese) leading to the sound *gyəm*.

[7] See *Lùn Bā Shǔ Wénhuà* (论巴蜀文化) by Xú Zhōngshū (徐中舒), published by Sìchuān Rénmín Chūbǎnshè (四川人民出版社), 1987.

Dìmíng Cídiǎn (中国古今地名词典, 1982), former Qián Zhōng cities were located in the west of present-day Húnán's Yuánlíng (沅陵) County. These governed a huge area encompassing today's western Húnán, northeastern Guìzhōu, southwestern Sìchuān, and southwestern Húběi. The areas occupied today by the Dòng people are an exact subset of the old Qián Zhōng Jùn areas.

Qián originally indicated a kind of natural environment. The environment was such that the people were naturally segregated into many countryside communes. The people were called, or called themselves, Qián and used mountain ranges, forests, or rivers to serve as boundaries between communes. For example, *Hàn Shū. Yán Zhù Zhuàn* (汉书. 严助传, AD 32–92) states that "Yuè people don't live in cities or large towns, but rather live in the river valleys or in the woods." Zhū Fǔ (朱辅) of the Sòng dynasty, in *Xī Mán Cóng Xiào. Ài Kǒu* (溪蛮丛笑.隘口, AD 1245–1279), says "Everywhere around there are mountains. On the mountains there are thousands of trees; and there is just one natural pass for coming and going. In the past, people turned these valleys into settlements, and the mountains into barriers; the entrance was called *ài kǒu* (隘口 'narrow mountain pass')." The kind of environment lending itself to "living in the river valleys or in the woods" or "turning the valleys into settlements and the mountains into barriers" was just the ancient Qián and is also today's kem^{55}.

Present-day Dòng villages are still surrounded by many large, old trees. These are known as wind and rain trees and they symbolize protection and well-being. They are not permitted to be cut or burned down. Sometimes they are used to establish a gate through which people enter and leave the community.

This kind of living environment has been passed on from generation to generation. It illustrates kem^{55}'s earliest meaning: to use mountains and trees to surround, isolate, and protect.

Evolution of the name Dòng. Qián (黔) originated as a word of the southern minorities, not as an Ancient Chinese word. The word Qián in the literature probably originated in the Qín and Hàn (汉, 206 BC–AD 220) dynasties as a transcription of the word's sound. At the same time, the Qín established Qián Zhōng Jùn. Qián thus evolved from meaning a kind of natural environment to representing a class of people in society. This group developed until the Táng and Sòng dynasties, when the name Qián disappeared and was replaced by Dòng (峒 or 洞).

The name Dòng also indicated the 'surrounded by trees' kind of environment. In *Xī Mán Cóng Xiào. Ài Kǒu* it is observed that "just outside the Dòng environment conditions are pretty rugged and precarious, but inside it is vast and for miles around there is fertile land." According to *Tài Píng Huán Yǔ Jì* (太平寰宇记, ~AD 976) "Everywhere in the Dòng area is cultivated and people don't go elsewhere to work the land." It seems that the

Introduction

kind of natural environment indicated by Dòng is not much different from Qián. The main condition for such an environment was that "for miles around there is fertile land." Residents called this kind of land Píng Tǎn (平坦; level, even) or Dòng (峒 or 洞, cave or hole), and cultivated it intensively.

By the time of the Táng dynasty, Dòng (峒) came to refer to a societal structure that had been established, known as Jī Mí Zhōu Dòng (羁縻州峒). In *Guì Hǎi Yú Héng Zhì* (桂海虞衡志, AD 1126–1193) it is noted that "Jī Mí Zhōu Dòng have been administrative units since the Táng dynasty. The big settlements were called provinces (Zhōu, 州), small ones counties (Xiàn, 县) and yet smaller ones Dòng (峒)." *Yán Jiào Jì Wén* (炎徼纪闻, ~AD 1550) states that "People living together in a village became Dòng, and their leaders became Dòng government officials." The kind of natural environment indicated by Dòng was identical with the places where Dòng people lived: big and small communities alike chose flat areas to live in, near rivers in mountain valleys, with mountains crowding round, and cultivated the land for miles around. Thus the Chinese name $toŋ^{53}$ for the Dòng people arose from the administrative unit 峒.

Parallels with Hǎinán's *kom*. So the Dòng autonym $kɐm^{55}$ and the Chinese word $toŋ^{53}$ are closely related, with similar meanings. The words perhaps have the same origin. Their pronunciations are also related, as illustrated by the history of Hǎinán Island's Lí (黎) nationality people.

Before Liberation, Hǎinán's Lí people still retained a primitive social and political organization called *kom*. The original meaning of *kom* was 'flat land surrounded by mountains and inhabited by people'. The Chinese transliteration of *kom* was *gōng* (弓) or *dòng* (峒) or *lídòng* (黎峒). The *kom* people together had a fixed area of land, commonly owned land being an indispensable feature of their existence. Boundaries for the *kom* territories were usually mountain ridges or rivers, and, in addition, the people erected monuments, stacked rocks, planted trees, grew bamboo, built wooden fences, or buried cow horns to act as boundaries. Thus the different *kom* communities were clearly delineated, and the lines were established way back in history. Once the *kom* areas had been determined, they couldn't be violated at will, and it was the common duty of all the *kom* people to defend the territory.[8] It can be seen that the Lí nationality's *kom* and the Dòng people's autonym $kɐm^{55}$ have the same origin.

Names used for the Dòng by the Shuǐ (水) and the Miáo (苗) nationalities. Relationships between Shuǐ and Dòng nationalities are very

---

[8]See *Lízú Jiǎnshǐ* (黎族简史), Guǎngdōng Rénmín Chūbǎnshè (广东人民出版社), May, 1982.

close. Their respective languages are from the same language branch. The Shuǐ refer to the Dòng as kem^{35}, the meaning of which is the same as that of the Dòng kem^{55}, i.e., to shelter, bar the way, and protect.

The Miáo people from the Qián Dōng (黔东) district in Guìzhōu call the Dòng ku^{35}. The word ku^{35} in the Miáo language has no other meaning apart from 'Dòng'. According to some researchers of the Miáo language, ku^{35} is borrowed from the Dòng's autonym kem^{55}; the Miáo language does not have the syllable coda *m*.

1.2 Culture

The Dong[9] areas enjoy a temperate climate with abundant rainfall and fertile land; good natural conditions for developing agriculture and forestry. The Dong people have been engaged in agriculture for many generations, and agricultural technology has reached a high standard. The people are adept at planting paddy rice. Formerly, they planted mainly glutinous rice and it became their speciality food. Glutinous rice still occupies an important position in the life and culture of the Dong people. It is not only an indispensable food, but also an appropriate gift for expressing romantic intention. The yield from growing glutinous rice is not great, however, and currently areas planted in ordinary rice far outstrip those planted in glutinous rice, making glutinous rice appear all the more precious.

The Dong mountain area is one of the eight largest forestry areas in the whole of China. The trees grown are predominantly China fir. They grow quickly and are tall and straight-grained, facilitating machine processing. The timber is durable and good for building, providing high-quality raw material for the outstanding building culture of the Dong people. The Dong have an age-old tradition of cultivating forests and have developed some fine varieties, e.g., 'eighteen-year China fir'.

Traditional Dong architecture includes Dong homes, drum towers, and bridges of various styles.

Small Dong settlements may have twenty or thirty homes, large settlements five or six hundred. Some settlements have more than 1,000 homes; and there are also occasional households living alone, isolated from other Dong people. Usually the homes are two or more storeys high and are built in the Gānlán (干栏) style.[10]

Most southern villages have a drum tower, the larger settlements having up to three or four. Drum towers are the greatest distinguishing feature of

---

[9]The sign for the tone in the word Dòng is omitted here and generally omitted hereafter.

[10]A style of building wooden homes, with the ground floor occupied by domestic animals and the upper floor(s) inhabited by people.

Dong architecture, the mark of a Dong settlement and the center of cultural activity for that settlement.

The Dong generally live near rivers and as a result, different Dong settlements feature different kinds of bridges. Wind and rain bridges are the only kind unique to the Dong people. They are wooden bridges in the style of The Long Corridor (in Běijīng's Summer Palace) and enjoy high prestige because of their artistic structure and skillful construction. Lípíng County's Dìpíng (地坪) wind and rain bridge is famous for its peaceful and beautiful natural setting and for its magnificent architecture. It stretches more than seventy meters across the Nánjiāng (南江) river and is eight meters tall. Building was begun in 1894, in the twentieth year of Emperor Guāng Xù (光绪) of the Qīng dynasty. The bridge has three pagodas. Except for supporting stone pillars fixed in the river bed, the whole structure is made of China fir. The bridge is a protected cultural heritage in Guìzhōu.

In the southern areas, the people believe in the goddess Sà (萨), and a special feature of many villages in the south is the altar to Sà, which lends a special sense of national identity to such places.

Most Dong clothing uses home-grown cotton and is hand-spun, hand-woven, and hand-dyed. The people favor black, shiny purple, and light-blue clothing. There are obvious regional differences in women's attire, but it can basically be divided into two types: skirts and trousers. Dong women like to wear jewelry, including silver neck rings, necklaces, bracelets, earrings, silver flowers, and so on. Men's dress is usually similar to that of Hàn Chinese men. In the southern mountain areas, the men have short collarless jackets that are tightened up on the left side, and they wear baggy trousers, large head cloths, and cloth shoes with toes curled up. In some places, when men dress up, they wear feathers on their heads (cf. quotation from *Lǎo Xué Ān Bǐ Jì* (AD 1125–1210) on page 2: "If a man has not yet taken a wife, he sticks a pheasant feather in his hair").

Generations of hard physical labor have seen the Dong people creating not only an abundant material culture but also a rich spiritual heritage; a kind of literature, which is sometimes unwritten. This literature has wide-ranging themes and various forms of expression, including folk songs, mythology, fairy tales, traditional opera, proverbs, and speeches encapsulating traditional regulations and judgments. Of these, folk songs are the most prolific. Dong areas have been heralded as 'centers of poetry, oceans of song'. Most Dong folk songs come in complete sets; for example, the historical poem "Zǔ Gōng Shàng Hé" (祖公上河). This is a 1,700-line song describing the genesis of the Dong people, including creation, the origin of all earthly things, the great flood, Zhāng Liáng (张良) catching the thunder witch, brother and sister marrying, the ancestors moving up to the rivers, the conference of the ninety-nine old men, and legal rules about how punishment should be meted out.

The proportion of love songs among Dong songs is high; many of them are outstanding. They extol the virtues of sincere love. They helped to mobilize public opinion in the struggle for freedom of marital choice. Examples are the beautiful popular songs handed down in the Dong areas, "Qín Niángméi" (秦娘梅), "Xiù Yínjí Mèi" (秀银吉妹), and "Mǎng Xìliú Mèi" (莽细刘妹).

Many Dong songs have been handed down by word of mouth from generation to generation. In Dong society, old people teach songs and young people sing them. Learning songs in one's youth has long been a national tradition. Irrespective of being male or female, those who sing much and sing well are highly respected in society. Appropriate environments for singing in Dong society are still many: out working in the fields, gathering for a meeting, courting, and visiting friends and relatives. People sometimes use singing as a primary means of communication. Among the Dong there is this popular saying: "The full meaning of a matter cannot be adequately expressed through speaking, only through singing." This illustrates the place in society of singing. Dong villages have popular artisans known as *xiāng gā* (相嘎, song teachers). They live among the people and are familiar with their people's cultural heritage. They are authors and propagators of Dong songs; they are also grand masters of the Dong language.

The language of Dong songs is succinct and the rhyme is harmonious. These are important prerequisites for the creation of Dong music. Dong popular music is particularly prolific, as seen, for example, from the choral songs "Dòng Zú Dà Gē" (侗族大歌), "Cǎi Táng Gē" (踩堂歌), "Lán Lù Gē" (拦路歌), and from many solo songs, including storytelling songs, with instrumental accompaniment. Among all of these, the choral songs are the most outstanding in terms of artistic quality.

The composition and development of Dong music is inextricably linked to the customs of the Dong people. The people enjoy collective singing and amusement. Traditionally they like to interact and move about in large groups. At the same time, their social events have music at their core. This makes for a good environment for singing in parts. The Dong people call their *dà gē* (大歌) '*gā lǎo*' (嘎老). These are songs for which many people get together and sing in chorus. Usually there are two parts (high and low), sometimes three. The high part is generally sung by one person, the low part by everyone together. The songs have many sections. Usually after the leader sings one or two lines of a section, everyone joins in.

Around Cóngjiāng County's Gāozēng (高增) and Xiǎohuáng (小黄) there is a special kind of song for male voices, straightforward but very lively. Such songs are usually accompanied by Dong folk instruments, such as the *pí pá* (琵琶, large stringed instruments with fretted fingerboards), which give the songs an even richer folk flavor. Before Liberation, Dong men and women did not sing together in choirs. In 1958, a choir organized in Lípíng broke with this convention, paving the way for musical progress. Dong mixed choirs are impressive, more appropriate in modern days for reflecting the people's way of life.

1.3 Language

Language affiliation. The Dong language belongs to the Dòng-Shuǐ (侗水) branch of the Dòng-Tái (侗台) family[11] (in China referred to as the Zhuàng-Dòng (壮侗) family). The Dòng-Tái family is also known as the Qián-Tái (黔台) family. Presently there is still no unanimity among the international research establishment with regard to the affiliation of the Dòng-Tái family of languages. In keeping with traditional interpretation, the present authors take Dòng-Tái to be a Sino-Tibetan subgroup. The languages in Dòng-Tái are distributed over a large area. They incorporate ten or more languages in China alone. Dòng-Shuǐ is a branch of Dòng-Tái, including Dòng, Shuǐ (水), Mùlǎo (仫佬), Máonán (毛南), Lājiā (拉珈), and Mò (莫). The existence of the Dòng-Shuǐ branch was first postulated by Professor Lǐ Fānguì (李方桂). Professor Lǐ wrote a series of articles about the relationships between the languages of Dòng-Shuǐ and those of the larger family Dòng-Tái. This theme is particularly highlighted in "The Tai and the Kam-Sui Languages," 1965. Lǐ Fānguì's analysis of Dòng-Shuǐ as a sub-branch of the Dòng-Tái family is now generally accepted in the international linguistic community.

Common origin of languages in the Dòng-Tái family. The Dòng-Tái family is divided into three branches: Dòng-Shuǐ, Tái, and Lí. The common origin of Dòng and its sister languages may be observed from (2) (where tones are given as tone categories, not as phonetic values; note that Dòng, Shuǐ, and Mùlǎo are Dòng-Shuǐ languages, and Zhuàng and Dǎi are Tái languages).

---

[11] Outside China the Dòng-Shuǐ branch is referred to as the Kam-Sui branch and the Dòng-Tái family is referred to as the Kam-Tai family. The word Kam comes from the Dong people's self-appellation.

(2)

Dòng 侗	Shuǐ 水	Mùlǎo 仫佬	Zhuàng 壮	Dǎi 傣	Lí 黎	
ləm²	zum¹	ləm²	yŭm²	lom²	hwiu⁴	wind
pjən¹	fən¹	kwən¹	fun¹	fun¹	fun¹	rain
pui¹	vi¹	fi¹	fei²	fãi³	fei¹	fire
ja⁵	ʔya⁵	ya⁵	na²	na²	ta²	field
nɐm⁴	năm	nəm³	yăm⁴	năm⁴	năm³	water
ta¹	ⁿda¹	la¹	ta¹	ta¹	tsha¹	eye
ma²	ma²	ma²	lin⁴	lin⁴	ɬin³	tongue
mɐi⁴	măi⁴	măi⁴	fãi⁴	măi⁴	tshăi¹	tree
pa⁵	va⁵	fa⁵	bău¹	băi¹	beu¹	leaf
kuŋ²	kuŋ²	kyuŋ²	lai¹	lai¹	ɬoi¹	many
na¹	ʔna¹	na¹	na¹	na¹	na¹	thick

Origin of the Dong language. The forerunner of Dòng was the ancient Yuè language. Liáo evolved from Yuè, and Dòng evolved from Liáo. We no longer have any way of knowing much about the Yuè language, but there are still a few manuscripts in Chinese where it is possible to search for clues. For instance, Yáng Xióng (杨雄) of the Hàn dynasty, in *Fāng Yán* (方言, 53–18 BC), noted some Yuè language; and Liú Xiàng (刘向) in *Shuō Yuàn* (说苑, 77–16 BC) collected some Yuè Rén Gē (越人歌). Although these writings are from an earlier era and the structure of the language recorded is far removed from present-day language, we can still deduce from them the ancestor-descendant relationship of Yuè and Dòng. In recent years, Zhāng Mín (张民), Dèng Mǐnwén (邓敏文), and colleagues conducted thorough research into Yuè Rén Gē in regard to the relationship between the Dòng language and songs of the Yuè people. This is useful reference material for establishing the lineage of Dòng from Yuè.

The relationship between the Dòng and Liáo languages is even clearer and stronger. The *Guǎngxī Tōngzhì* (广西通志), revised during the Jiā Qìng (嘉庆, 1796–1820) period of the Qīng dynasty, quoted all the Liáo language recorded in *Qìng Yuǎn Fǔ Zhì* (庆远府志, 1796–1820). Some of these Liáo words are presented in (3).

(3) | Liáo in 广西通志 | Liáo pīnyīn | Modern Dòng | |
|---|---|---|---|
| 爸 | bà | pu³¹ | father |
| 奶 | nǎi | nɐi³¹ | mother |
| 怀 | huái | tai³¹ | older sibling |
| 浓 | nóng | noŋ³¹ | younger sibling |
| 馋佽 | zhǎn kāo | tan⁵⁵ ʔɐu³¹ | eat rice |
| 馋南 | zhǎn nán | tan⁵⁵ nan³¹ | eat meat |
| 馋考 | zhǎn kǎo | tan⁵⁵ khwau¹³ | drink alcohol |
| 登谷 | dēng gǔ | tɐn³²³ ʔuk³²³ | put on clothes |

Liáo's consonant in 'older sibling' in (3) is not the same as Dòng's but is the same as Shuǐ's, Máonán's, and Gēlǎo's. Liáo's vowel in 'father' is different from Dòng's. Other Liáo and Dòng words in (3), however, are very similar. These words clearly suggest that Liáo belonged to the Dòng-Shuǐ branch.

Guǎngxī's Líng (伶) language recorded in *Lóngshèng Tīngzhì* (龙胜厅志, 1821–1851) is also similar to Dòng.

(4) | Líng in 龙胜厅志 | Líng pīnyīn | Modern Dòng | |
|---|---|---|---|
| 扪 | mén | mən⁵⁵ | sky |
| 脸 | liǎn | ɲan⁵⁵ | moon |
| 令 | lìng | ləm²¹² | wind |
| 丙 | bǐng | pjən⁵⁵ | rain |
| 捏 | niē | ti³³ | earth |
| 不 | bù | pu³¹ | father |
| 扪 | mén | mɐn⁵⁵ | day |
| 拣考 | jiǎn kǎo | tan⁵⁵ ʔɐu³¹ | eat rice |
| 拣南 | jiǎn nán | tan⁵⁵ nan³¹ | eat meat |
| 拣窖 | jiǎn jiào | tan⁵⁵ khwau¹³ | drink alcohol |

Apart from the words for 'earth', the Líng and Dòng words listed in (4) are very similar. The Líng language in Lóngshèng (龙胜) County was actually what we now call Dòng. Today over twenty-five percent of the people in Lóngshèng are of Dòng nationality.

Population. According to the national census of 1990, the Dong population is 2.5 million, mainly residing in four provinces: Guìzhōu (贵州), Húnán (湖南), Guǎngxī (广西), and Húběi (湖北). Guìzhōu has the largest Dong population, with more than 1,410,000 people living in the Qián Dōng

Nán (黔东南) Miáo Dòng Autonomous Region's Lípíng (黎平), Róngjiāng (榕江), Cóngjiāng (从江), Tiānzhù (天柱), Jǐnpíng (锦屏), Sānsuì (三穗), Jiànhé (剑河), and Zhènyuǎn (镇远) Counties; Tóngrén (铜仁) prefecture's Yùpíng (玉屏) Dòng Autonomous County; and the Wànshān (万山) Special District. Húnán province has 750,000 Dong people, the Guǎngxī Zhuàng Autonomous Region has 290,000, and Húběi province's Èxī (鄂西) Tǔjiā Miáo Autonomous Region's Ēnshī (恩施) and Xuānēn (宣恩) Counties also have 50,000.

The Dong population is not widely dispersed, with Dong areas merging into one another. Dong people generally get on well with one another. Other nationalities live side by side with the Dong, including Hàn (汉), Zhuàng (壮), Yáo (瑶), Shuǐ (水), Mùlǎo (仫佬), Bùyī (布依), Gēlǎo (仡佬), and Tǔjiā (土家). For a long time these various nationalities have been cooperating well, together developing their mountain-river territories.

Dialects. Within Dong there are two dialects, southern and northern. The boundary is taken as the southern part of Guìzhōu's Jǐnpíng County, where Dòng, Hàn, and Miáo nationalities live together. The formation of the two dialects has been strongly influenced by Chinese. The dialects are further divided into four and three subdialects, respectively.

Generally speaking, the northern Dong people have closer contacts with Hàn Chinese and are more likely to speak and read Chinese than the southern Dong; they generally attain to a higher level in Chinese education than their southern counterparts. In addition, the northern Dong language has extensively assimilated many Chinese words and phrases and much Chinese grammar. Its pronunciation has undergone simplification; for example, the distinction between long and short vowels has disappeared and stop codas have begun to drop away or to merge. In contrast, the southern dialect still maintains features of the ancient language relatively well; for example, vowels are still differentiated by length and there is still a complete set of stop codas.

Language use. With regard to modern-day usage of Dong, the Dong people in Guìzhōu can roughly be divided into three groups. Firstly, there are those who can only speak Dong and cannot speak Chinese or other languages. Most of these live in the southern dialect area or are old people, women, and children living in the mountain villages of the northern area, far from Hàn Chinese centers. There are also some young men from these remote northern mountain areas who have never attended school, seldom leave their homes, and rarely come in contact with the outside world. They, too, cannot speak Chinese. Probably over fifty percent of all Dong people are in this group.

The second group comprises Dong people who cannot speak the Dong language or other minority languages and can only speak Chinese. Most of these live in the northern dialect area: for example, in the Yùpíng Dòng Autonomous County and the Wànshān Special District, or in Zhènyuǎn, Sānsuì, Tiānzhù, or Jǐnpíng Counties. Something under twenty-five percent of Dong people fall into this category. There are some differences within the group. In some areas, although people do not often use Dong, they still understand it, and some older people can still speak a little. In other areas, people really do not understand the language. Some only renewed their status as members of the Dong nationality after Liberation, by which time they had forgotten the language.

The third group among the Dong people are those who can speak both Dong and Chinese or other nationality languages. The great majority of these left home and received an education. They include civil servants, teachers, and educated country-folk. Something over twenty-five percent of Dong people are in this category. They are bilingual and have an important role to play in disseminating government policy, popularizing Dong culture, and learning from other nationalities. In some areas Dong people live together with Miáo, Yáo, Shuǐ, and others. Because relationships between the minorities in these areas are close, the Dong of certain areas can speak other minority languages and vice-versa. In different situations they use different languages. For example, in Dàtóng (大同), Qǐméng (启蒙), and Xiùdòng (秀洞) of Jǐnpíng County, Dong and Miáo nationalities all speak Dong, Miáo, and Chinese, and people choose the language according to the occasion. From outward appearances, it is difficult to say who belongs to which nationality. A different scenario arises among the Yáo people around Lòngbō (弄播) in Lípíng County. They normally speak the Yáo language among themselves, but when they sing they use Dong. In certain areas in the northern dialect area, young ladies who basically cannot speak Chinese can, however, sing Chinese songs and use these to express love in courtship. Around Yàhǎn (亚罕) in Lípíng County, the Miáo people (Dong people in that area call them miu^{55} $ȵaŋ^{13}$, namely Grass Miáo) only use the Dong language, a version very similar to that of the northern dialect. The majority of civil servants and teachers working in the Dong areas speak Dong as well as Chinese, and civil servants use Dong when they visit the countryside. Teachers often use both Chinese and Dong; Dong is used to explain obscurities in Chinese.

Development. Since Liberation, under the Party's leadership, the Dong people, together with all the other nationalities, have experienced rapid changes in society. Hand in hand with continuous exchanges with other nationalities has come enrichment and development of the Dong language. During the process of developing socialism and achieving the Four Modernizations, Dong vocabulary has borrowed more and more Chinese words. This borrowing has served to enhance the vitality and power of expression of the language.

The bilingual population among the Dong people is ever increasing. But the language is still the mother tongue of the people, their most basic resource in communication. Thus in most Dong areas the language could not possibly be usurped by any other language.

1.4 The influence of the Chinese language on the Dong language

For centuries the Dong people have been living side by side with other nationalities. Near neighbors naturally learned and influenced one another's languages. The greatest influence on Dong has come from Chinese. The Hàn people are in the great majority in China, with relatively advanced systems of government, economics, and education. Formerly, the Dong people did not have their own writing system and used Chinese characters to communicate in writing (cf. §6.3). Thus Chinese texts were used in schools as the main means of education, and Chinese had a tremendous impact on the development of Dong. The influence is evident in vocabulary, pronunciation, and grammar.

Vocabulary. The main means whereby Dong vocabulary is augmented is by assimilation of Chinese words and phrases. As society has developed and changed, Dong vocabulary has been continuously expanding. Apart from a few compound words made from pure Dong roots, most of the new words have been borrowed from Chinese. Practically all new technical terms which have appeared since Liberation have been adopted from Chinese. Moreover, many words that have become foundational in Dong were originally borrowed from Chinese and are now near-synonyms of Chinese words. This is especially true in the context of what might be called the spiritual songs of the Dong people. In order to preserve the requirements of rhyme and rhetoric, these songs often imported Chinese loan words which expressed practically the same meaning as their Dong counterparts.

The absorption of Chinese loan words not only increases Dong vocabulary, it also impels the language in the direction of modern Chinese which has many disyllabic words. The basic building blocks for modern Dong are still single syllables, but signs of disyllabification are evident in certain locative words, time words, and demonstrative pronouns in the southern dialect.

(5) Monosyllabic Dong   Disyllabic Dong   Chinese

    ʔun⁵³   maŋ⁵³ʔun⁵³   前面   front
    lən²¹²   maŋ⁵³lən²¹²   后面   behind
    ʔu⁵⁵   maŋ⁵³ʔu⁵⁵   上面   up
    te³²³   maŋ⁵³te³²³   下面   down
    ȵɐm⁵³   ʔɐn⁵⁵ȵɐm⁵³   晚上   evening
    hət³⁵   ʔɐn⁵⁵hət³⁵   早晨   (early) morning
    ʈan⁵⁵   ʔɐn⁵⁵ʈan⁵⁵   夜间   at night
    nai³³   ʔi⁵⁵nai³³   这样   this way
    ʈa⁵³   ʔi⁵⁵ʈa⁵³   那样   that way
    nu³⁵   ʔi⁵⁵nu³⁵   怎样   how

Although the monosyllabic and disyllabic forms in (5) can both be used, spoken Dong more commonly uses the disyllabic forms.

There are also various animal and plant names, for example, which can either be monosyllabic or add the generic term and become disyllabic.

(6) Monosyllabic Dong   Disyllabic Dong   Chinese

    ljai¹³   mok²¹ljai¹³   麻雀   sparrow
    ʔa⁵⁵   mok²¹ʔa⁵⁵   乌鸦   crow
    mjɐi³¹   pa⁵⁵mjɐi³¹   鲤鱼   carp
    pik³¹   pa⁵⁵pik³¹   鲫鱼   crucian carp
    jau³⁵   mɐi³¹jau³⁵   枫树   maple
    phak¹³   mɐi³¹phak¹³   杉树   China fir
    ʈup³²³   pu²¹²ʈup³²³   冬瓜   white gourd

Animal names in the northern dialect are all preceded by the classifier to²².

(7) Northern Dong   Chinese

    to²²to²²   牛   ox
    to²²məm³¹   老虎   tiger
    to²²ljai¹³   麻雀   sparrow
    to²²ta³⁵   鱼   fish

Again the vast majority of northern dialect place names are disyllabic, unlike most southern names which are still monosyllabic. In the north, names which were originally monosyllabic have been preceded by ʔo²² 'place' or ɕai³³ 'town', as in (8).

(8)　　Northern Dong　　Chinese

ʔo²²han²⁵　　汉寨 Hànzhài
ɕai⁴⁴han²⁵　　汉寨 Hànzhài
ʔo²²paŋ³⁵　　邦洞 Bāngdòng
ɕai⁴⁴koŋ³⁵　　邦寨 Bāngzhài

Pronunciation. Following the introduction of Chinese loan words, some words with Chinese pronunciations have been assimilated into Dong, thereby adding new phonemes to the phonology of Dong. For example, because of Chinese loan words, the phonology of the language of Róngjiāng's Chējiāng (车江) includes consonants *f*, *z*, *wj*, and *ts* and vowels *ɿ* and *ə*.

As well as increasing the number of phonemes, loan words break Dong's intrinsic rules of constraint between tones and syllable initials. Except for a few onomatopoeic words, aspirated initials in Dong only appear with odd-numbered (Yīn, 阴) tones, not with even-numbered (Yáng, 阳) tones. The odd-numbered tones in most areas are divided into two types according to whether or not the word-initial consonant is aspirated; because of the relationship between tone and aspiration, an unaspirated consonant merges with its aspirated counterpart to give one phoneme. But Chinese loan words don't strictly follow this rule. Chinese Yáng Píng (阳平) and Yáng Shàng (阳上) correspond to even-numbered tones 2 and 4, respectively, and with each of these tones there are both unaspirated and aspirated word-initial consonants.

(9)　　Dong　　Chinese

toŋ²　　铜 tóng　　copper
thoŋ²　　同 tóng　　similar
pu⁴　　父 fù　　father
phu⁴　　普 pǔ　　universal

As a result, the aspirated stops which were formerly allophones of their unaspirated counterparts become independent phonemes, further increasing the number of consonants in the phoneme inventory.

Some changes in the dialect pronunciations of Dong closely parallel the historical evolution of Chinese pronunciation, demonstrating the tendency for Dong to develop in the wake of Chinese. The development of Chinese from ancient to modern times has been a process of simplification: devoicing of voiced consonants, extinction of Rù Shēng (入声) codas (*p*, *t*, and *k*), merging of Yáng Shēng (阳声) codas (*m*, *n*, and *ŋ*), convergence of similar vowels, and so on. Except for tone-splitting, Dong has also experienced a gradual simplification in pronunciation. Voiced stops are already extinct (except in Guǎngxī's Róngshuǐ Pìndòng, 融水聘洞). The contrast between long and short vowels is in the process of change: in the northern dialect there is no longer any contrasting length and in most of the southern areas there is a length contrast only with the vowel *a*. Rù Shēng codas are still preserved intact in the southern dialect. In some northern dialect areas, however, the syllable coda *k* has dropped out to be replaced by Yīn Shēng (i.e., vowel) codas; in other areas the Rù Shēng codas are merging. In some parts, the Yáng Shēng codas are also merging: *m* becomes *n*, or in rare cases *ŋ*. No two areas develop in exactly the same way. In general though, it can be inferred that the gradual expansion of the influence of Chinese will continue to affect the development of pronunciation of Dong, causing the sound system of Dong to draw even closer to that of Chinese.

Grammar. Dong and Chinese are both analytic languages. Their grammars are mainly typified by word order and function words.

The word order of Dong is essentially the same as that of Chinese, with one clear exception: in Dong, adjectives come after nouns while in Chinese they come before.

For example, in the northern dialect of Dong, *wa^{11}* 'flower' + *ja^{25}* 'red' becomes *wa^{11} ja^{25}* 'red flower'. Note that the adjective can also be preposed, as in *ja^{25} ti^{33} wa^{11}*, where *ti^{33}* corresponds to the Chinese 的 *de*. Also, in certain cases of possession, the adjective must be preposed without insertion of *ti^{33}*, as in *ṯau^{35}* 'we/our' + *noŋ^{31}* 'younger brother' becoming *ṯau^{35} noŋ^{31}* 'our younger brother'. These examples are from northern Dong, where the phenomenon of preposing adjectives is spreading. It has also spread to the southern dialect, but in the south the basic form is still noun followed by adjective.

Dong has very few of its own function words. They have all evolved from content words and most have still not completely lost their semantic meaning. Many have been borrowed from Chinese, including those in (10).

(10)   Dong   Chinese

       wi^{33}   为 *wèi*   because, for
       jan^{55} jui^{33}   因为 *yīn wèi*   because
       ljen^{212}   连 *lián*   even
       so^{31} ji^{31}   所以 *suǒ yǐ*   therefore
       səi^{33} lan^{212}   虽然 *suī rán*   although
       tan^{55} si^{35}   但是 *dàn shì*   but

In socialist countries, a gradual decrease of differences among different nationalities within the countries tends to accompany the continuous development that flows from socialism and from the daily consolidation of unity among the different nationalities. In China, Chinese enjoys the status of the language of the majority people and in the course of time has become the common language of communication for all the different nationalities. Chinese benefits the languages of all nationalities in China by promoting the minority languages' enrichment and by accelerating the inevitable trend of increasing the language which is common to both Chinese and minority languages.

2
Phonology

Róngjiāng (榕江) County's Chējiāng (车江) Dong from the southern dialect area is taken as the standard from which the Dong orthography is derived. Chējiāng encompasses several villages which start at Róngjiāng county town and run south along a river for several miles. Zhānglǔ (章鲁) is one of those villages. In this chapter, the sound system of Chējiāng's Zhānglǔ Dong is introduced.

2.1 Syllable initials

Relationship between syllable initials and tones. Zhānglǔ Dong has two classes of syllable initial: one is the class of stops—*p*, *t*, *ţ*, *k*, *ʔ*, *pj*, and *kw*—each with its aspirated counterpart; the other is the class of nasals, laterals, and fricatives, none of which is differentiated by presence or absence of aspiration.

There are nine different tone values among the tones of Zhānglǔ Dong. (Here, tones from checked and unchecked syllables are classed together, and not counted separately.) The tones fall into two classes: one class only occurs with unaspirated stops, while the other only occurs with aspirated stops. As for nasals, laterals, and fricatives, these can appear with either class of tone. The relationship between syllable initials and tones in Zhānglǔ Dong is illustrated in (11).

Some material in this chapter has appeared in "The Sounds of Rongjiang Kam" in *Comparative Kadai: Linguistic Studies Beyond Tai*, edited by Jerold A. Edmondson and David B. Solnit, 1988.

(11) Tones   Stops   Other initials

Quán Yīn (全阴) and Yáng (阳) six of nine tones: 1, 2, 3, 4, 5, 6	*p* *t* *ţ* *k* *ʔ* *pj* *kw*	*m* *n* *ɲ* *ŋ* *mj* *ŋw*		
Cì Yīn (次阴) three of nine tones: 1', 3', 5'	*ph* *th* *ţh* *kh* *phj* *khw*	*l* *lj* *s* *ɕ* *h* *w* *j*		

It can be seen from (11) that the two sets of stops (aspirated and unaspirated) appear in different tone environments. Looking at Zhānglǔ Dong from the standpoint of phonemes, we can take the aspirated stops as allophones of their unaspirated counterparts, differentiated by tones; we do not need two separate sets of phonemes. When an orthography for Dong was being developed, however, it had to take other issues into account: Chinese loan words in modern Dong, vernaculars of Dong different from Zhānglǔ Dong, and a correspondence with Chinese pīnyīn. Thus aspirated and unaspirated stops were treated as distinct phonemes.

Pronunciations of syllable initials of Modern Chinese loan words. Certain syllable initials used in Chinese do not occur in Dong. The pronunciation of such syllable initials, when they are borrowed into Chējiāng Dong, typically varies from person to person. Older people and those who rarely come into contact with Hàn Chinese tend to make the borrowed words fall into line with Dong's own phonology. However, younger people and those who are in frequent contact with Hàn Chinese tend to adopt the Chinese pronunciations. The result is that seven new borrowed syllable initials are introduced into Dong: *tj, thj, f, z, wj, ts*, and *tsh*.

In addition, the rule that aspirated stops do not occur together with Yáng (even) tones is broken by Chinese loan words. Thus six aspirated phones which were formerly allophones of their unaspirated counterparts become phonemes in their own right: *ph, th, ţh, kh, phj*, and *khw*. Adding these new phonemes is equivalent to introducing six new syllable initials.

The pronunciations of syllable initials of Chinese loan words, however, are still not completely fixed. Differences in pronunciation are presented in (12).

Phonology

(12) Different ways of pronouncing sounds introduced to Dong from Chinese: Pīnyīn is the symbol for the sound in Chinese pīnyīn, Old is the IPA pronunciation of that sound in Dong which is inherently Dong, and New is the IPA pronunciation of the sound in Dong which is adopted from local Chinese

Pīnyīn	Old	New	
p	p, pj	ph, phj	判 pàn, 硼 péng, 贫 pín
f	w (~hw)	f	风 fēng, 匪 fěi, 范 fàn
d	t, ƚ	t, tj	道 dào, 点 diǎn, 调 diào
t	t, ƚ	th, thj	头 tóu, 亭 tíng, 天 tiān
k	k, kw	kh, khw	开 kāi, 空 kōng, 况 kuàng
q	ƚ	ṭh	区 qū, 情 qíng
zh	ƚ	ts	志 zhì, 长 zhǎng, 中 zhōng
ch	ƚ (~s)	tsh	唱 chàng, 产 chǎn
r	l (~j)	z	人 rén, 容 róng
z	s	ts	资 zī, 族 zú
c	s	tsh	操 cāo, 从 cóng
y	j	wj (~j)	员 yuán, 约 yuē

In keeping with the scheme used for developing the Dong orthography, this book accepts the new widely assimilated syllable initials into the system of syllable initials of the Dong language.

Syllable initial phonemes

(13) Syllable initial phonemes: Lab–labial, Alv–alveolar, Cor–coronal, Vel–velar, Glot–glottal, Palz–palatalized, and Labz–labialized

	Lab	Alv	Cor	Vel	Glot	Palz	Labz
stop, unaspirated	p	t	ṭ	k	ʔ	pj, tj	kw
stop, aspirated	ph	th	ṭh	kh		phj, thj	khw
nasal	m	n	ṇ	ŋ		mj	ŋw
fricative, voiceless	f	s	ɕ		h		
fricative, voiced	w	z	j			wj	
lateral		l				lj	
affricate, unaspirated		ts					
affricate, aspirated		tsh					

Notes
1. When *w* occurs before unrounded vowels, the lips are not entirely closed, the rear of the tongue is not much raised, and friction is very slight.
2. With the sounds *t*, *n*, and *l*, the tongue tip touches the alveolar ridge; with *s*, the tongue tip touches the back of the teeth.
3. The sound ȶ occurs in Dong, as opposed to the Chinese *tɕ*. The tongue position for *j* is the same as that for *ɕ*, slightly more advanced than the IPA [j], with only very slight friction.
4. When *k* occurs before the close front vowel *i*, it becomes slightly palatalized.
5. The tongue position for *h* is somewhere between velar and glottal, close to the uvular sound.

(14) Vocabulary exemplifying different syllable initial phonemes[12]

Initial	Dong	Chinese	
p	pa^{55}	鱼 yú	fish
	pui^{55}	火 huǒ	fire
ph	pha^{35}	灰色 huī sè	gray
	$phui^{35}$	痣 zhì	mole, nevus
t	ta^{55}	眼睛 yǎn jīng	eye
	to^{55}	门 mén	door
th	tha^{35}	出奔 chū bēn	flee
	tha^{35}	拖 tuō	drag, haul
ȶ	$ȶa^{55}$	茅草 máo cǎo	cogongrass
	$ȶak^{323}$	草鞋 cǎo xié	straw sandals
ȶh	$ȶha^{453}$	上 shàng	go up
	$ȶhak^{13}$	三脚架 sān jiǎo jià	tripod
k	ka^{55}	剩 shèng	surplus
	kai^{53}	讨 tǎo	discuss
kh	kha^{35}	耳朵 ěr duō	ear
	$khai^{453}$	耙 pá	rake (n, v)
ʔ	$ʔau^{55}$	拿 ná	take
	$ʔe^{55}$	家 jiā	home
pj	pja^{55}	石头 shí tou	stone
	pji^{55}	修理 xiū lǐ	repair
phj	$phja^{35}$	喂 wèi	feed (v)
	$phji^{35}$	削 xuē	peel (v), cut

---

[12]Initials marked with an asterisk have been introduced to Dong through Chinese loan words.

Phonology

tj*	tjen⁵³	电 diàn	electricity
thj*	thje¹³	铁 tiě	iron
kw	kwa⁵⁵	挂柱 guà zhù	roof beam
	kwaŋ³²³	碗 wǎn	bowl
khw	khwa³⁵	抓 zhuā, 摸 mō	grope for
	khwaŋ¹³	宽 kuān	wide
m	ma⁵⁵	菜 cài	vegetable
	ma³⁵	来 lái	come
n	na⁵⁵	厚 hòu	thick
	na¹³	弓 gōng	bow (n)
ɲ	ɲa⁵⁵	河 hé	river
	ɲa³⁵	啄木鸟 zhuó mù niǎo	woodpecker
ŋ	ŋa⁵⁵	芝麻 zhī ma	sesame
	ŋu⁴⁵³	猪 zhū	pig
mj	mja⁵³	烦闷 fán mèn	be unhappy
	mja⁴⁵³	脾脏 pí zàng	spleen
ŋw	ŋwe²¹²	口水 kǒu shuǐ	saliva
	ŋwa³⁵	狗 gǒu	dog
f*	fa¹³	发 fā	send out
s	sa³³	急水滩 jī shuǐ tān	rapids
	sa³⁵	肩膀 jiān bǎng	shoulder (n)
ɕ	ɕa⁵⁵	盖 gài	cover (v)
	ɕa³⁵	水车 shuǐ chē	water wheel
h	ha³³	才 cái	just now
	ha³⁵	吓唬 xià hu	frighten
w	wa⁵⁵	山窝 shān wō	remote mountain area
	wa³⁵	右 yòu	right (side)
z*	zen²¹²	人 rén	person
j	ja⁵³	田 tián	field
	ja⁴⁵³	红 hóng	red
wj*	wjen²¹²	员 yuán	member
l	la³³	讨 tǎo	beg
	la³⁵	树结子 shù jié zi	tree knot
lj	lja¹³	儿媳 ér xí	daughter-in-law
	ljai¹³	麻雀 má què	sparrow
ts*	tsau³¹	早 zǎo	early
tsh*	tshau³³	操 cāo	exercise (v)

2.2 Syllable rhymes

Codas. Zhānglǔ Dong has two vowel codas *i* and *u*, three nasal codas *m*, *n*, and *ŋ*, and three stop codas *p*, *t*, and *k*.

Vowels. Zhānglǔ Dong has seven vowel phonemes: *a, e, i, o, u, ɐ*, and *ə*. Each phoneme has up to four allophones. The phonetic values of the vowels are related to the adjacent phones (syllable initials and syllable codas). Usually, after coronal or palatalized syllable initials, or before syllable codas *i, n,* or *t,* the tongue position is more advanced or higher than in other environments. Differences are illustrated below.

/a/, with three allophones: [ɑ], [A], and [a]

[ɑ] In monophthong rhymes, or before syllable codas *u, m, ŋ, p,* or *k*, if the syllable initial is not palatalized or coronal, the phoneme /a/ is realized as the open back vowel [ɑ]. For example: *la^{53}* 'break (v)' (破), *ka^{323}* 'rice seedling' (秧), *pau^{55}* 'horn' (角), *sam^{35}* 'three' (三), *paŋ^{55}* 'rice straw' (稻草), *kwaŋ^{323}* 'bowl' (碗), *tap^{323}* 'carry with pole' (挑), and a measure word *pak^{323}* (口).

If the /a/ in [au] follows the coronal *t̪*, it is also a very slightly advanced version of [ɑ]. For example: *t̪au^{55}* 'vine' (藤).

[A] If the syllable initial is coronal or palatalized, either in monophthong rhymes or before syllable codas *m, ŋ, p,* or *k*, the phoneme /a/ is realized as the open central vowel [A]. For example: *ɕa^{35}* 'fall short of' (差), *ja^{53}* 'field' (田), *mja^{212}* 'hand' (手), *lam^{33}* 'rope' (绳子), *n̪aŋ^{13}* 'grass' (草), *t̪ap^{31}* 'link up' (衔接), and *pjak^{323}* 'forehead' (额头).

Before syllable codas *n* and *t*, if the vowel doesn't follow a coronal or palatalized initial, it is also realized as [A]. For example: *man^{13}* 'yellow' (黄色), *kwan^{53}* 'smooth' (光滑), *ŋat^{31}* 'alkali' (碱), and *pat^{323}* 'tart (adj)' (涩味).

[a] Preceding the syllable coda *i*, /a/ is realized as the open front vowel [a]. When the corresponding syllable initial is neither coronal nor palatalized, the tongue position moves slightly towards the central vowel [A]. For example: *t̪ai^{31}* 'older brother' (兄), *ɕai^{323}* 'ask' (问), *mjai^{53}* 'gourd ladle' (瓢), *pai^{55}* 'go' (去), *kai^{212}* 'pull' (拉扯), and *ʔai^{53}* 'chicken' (鸡).

Realizations of /a/ occurring between coronal or palatalized syllable initials and syllable codas *n* or *t* are also the front [a].

Phonology 25

For example: ȶan³³ 'bump' (碰), ȵan⁵⁵ 'moon' (月), and pjat³²³ 'cluster' (串).

/e/, realized as [E], the front vowel between [e] and [ɛ]

For example: pe⁵⁵ 'sell' (卖), meu²¹² 'pheasant' (雉), lem⁵⁵ 'hit' (打), ʔeŋ⁵⁵ 'porridge' (粥), pep³²³ 'pierce' (刺入), kwet³¹ 'scrape (v)' (刮), and ʔek¹³ 'guest' (客人).

Before the coda n, or after coronal or palatalized initials, the tongue position moves slightly higher than for [E]. For example: wen³³ 'ten thousand' (万), ȵe⁵⁵ 'vomit' (吐), and mjek³²³ 'girl' (姑娘).

/i/, with two allophones: [i] and [ɪ]

[i] After coronals or palatalization, irrespective of whether there is a syllable coda or what the coda is, the tongue position is always high, and the close front vowel [i] is realized. For example: ɕi³²³ 'paper' (纸), ɕiŋ²¹² 'wall' (墙), mjiu²¹² 'gourd vine' (瓜藤), ljim²¹² 'sickle' (镰刀), pjin³²³ 'soft-shelled turtle' (团鱼), ljip³²³ 'lunch box' (饭盒), phjit¹³ 'scold' (骂), and pjik³²³ 'reduce' (减).

[ɪ] After consonants other than coronals and palatalized ones, irrespective of whether there is a syllable coda or what the coda is, the phoneme becomes slightly more open. The pronunciation tends to move from a slightly back and open [ɪ] to the front and closed [i]. If there is a coda, it also moves towards the coda. For example: miu²¹² 'scissors' (剪刀), lim²¹² 'straight and flat' (直而平), pin³²³ 'rice-wine yeast' (酒药), tiŋ⁵³ 'deceive' (欺骗), sip³²³ 'meet' (接), pit³²³ 'bounce (v)' (弹跳), and pik³¹ 'crucian carp' (鲫鱼).

Monophthong rhymes seem as though they are preceded by a short e glide. For example: pi²¹² 'skin' (皮) and si³⁵ 'rain cape' (蓑衣).

When /i/ appears as a syllable coda, it also tends to be relatively open, close to [ɪ]. For example: sai³²³ 'intestines' (肠子), soi³¹ 'crime' (罪), pui⁵⁵ 'fire' (火), and tɐi²¹² 'take' (拿).

/o/, with two allophones: the phone [o̞] (slightly more open than [o]) and the phone [oᵁ] [ɷ] The monophthong rhyme and that before syllable codas *m*, *ŋ*, *p*, and *k* are realizations of the non-glide-carrying phone [ɷ]. For example: *so³¹* 'barn' (仓房), *pom⁵⁵* 'bubble' (水泡), *poŋ²¹²* 'float (v)' (浮), *ɲop³²³* 'tuft' (撮), and *mok²¹* 'bird' (鸟).

[oᵉ] Before syllable codas *i*, *n*, or *t*, an ɐ glide appears between the main vowel and the syllable coda. For example: *ʨoi²¹²* 'seize' (抓), *ton⁵³* 'guess (v)' (猜), and *thot¹³* 'take off' (脱).

/u/, with three allophones: [ʊ], [ᵊu], and [uᵊ]

[ʊ] The monophthong rhyme occurring after labialization, and the vowel occurring before codas *i*, *m*, *n*, *ŋ*, *p*, and *k*, is realized as [ʊ], the slightly more open version of [u]. Except for when following the syllable initial *w*, the lips are never very rounded. For example: *pu⁵⁵* 'swell (v)' (肿), *nui²¹²* 'insect' (虫), *tum⁵⁵* 'blister' (水疱), *pun⁵⁵* 'pillow' (枕头), *tuŋ³²³* 'meet unexpectedly' (遇见), *pup³²³* 'lung' (肺), and *nuk³²³* 'outside' (外).

/u/ in the syllable coda position is also realized as the more open [ʊ]. For example: *ʨiu⁵⁵* 'we, us (exc)' (我们), *lau³¹* 'big' (大), *tɐu⁵⁵* 'moss' (青苔), and *ɲeu⁵³* 'urine' (尿).

[ᵊu] The monophthong rhyme occurring after non-labialized syllable initials always carries an ə on-glide. For example: a classifier *tu²¹²* (只), *ʨu³²³* 'nine' (九), *ɕu⁵⁵* 'pearl' (珠), *ju⁵⁵* 'squat (v)' (蹲), and *ʔu²¹²* 'throat' (喉).

[uᵊ] When occurring before the syllable coda *t*, /u/ is relatively short and carries a short off-glide ə. For example: *mut³¹* 'beard' (胡须) and *sut³¹* 'water chestnut' (荸荠).

The above five vowels *a*, *e*, *i*, *o*, and *u* are usually long in quality.

/ɐ/, with three allophones: the central open vowel [ɐ], the mid-high short front vowel [ĕ], and the central vowel [ə]

[ɐ] When [ɐi] occurs after initials other than coronal, velar, or palatalized initials, when the phone [ɐu] occurs after initials other than labialized, coronal, velar, or palatalized initials, and with all rhymes which have consonants as syllable codas, the main vowel

Phonology

is pronounced [ɐ]. For example: *pɐi³¹* 'girl' (女孩), *ʔɐi³⁵* 'open (v)' (开), *nɐu²¹²* 'who' (谁), *ʔɐu³¹* 'rice' (米), *tɐm⁵⁵* 'pond' (池塘), *pɐn⁵⁵* 'bamboo' (竹子), *sɐŋ²¹²* 'straight' (直), *tɐp⁵⁵* 'liver' (肝), *tɐt⁵⁵* 'chop' (砍), and *nɐk³⁵* 'sleep' (睡).

[ĕ] When [ɐi] occurs after coronal, velar, or palatalized initials, the main vowel is pronounced [ĕ]. Its tongue position is higher than that of the vowel [e], and it is shorter. For example: *tɐi³²³* 'buy' (买), *kɐi⁵³* 'egg' (蛋), and *mjɐi³¹* 'carp' (鲤鱼).

[ǝ̙] The rhyme [ɐu], when it occurs after coronal, velar, or palatalized initials, has a main vowel which is a slightly back version of [ǝ]. For example: *tɐu³³* 'pair' (双), *kɐu⁴⁵³* 'bark (v)' (吠), and *ljɐu¹³* 'urge (v)' (催促).

When [ɐu] appears after labialization, the main vowel is similar to [o], but shorter and higher than [o], and more central. It is actually a labialized central vowel [ǝ]. For example: *pɐu²¹²* 'pigeon' (鸽子), *mɐu⁵³* 'tadpole' (蝌蚪), and *wɐu²¹²* 'bird cage' (鸟笼).

/ǝ/, with four allophones: [ɤ], [ĭ], [ŭ], and [ǝ]

[ɤ] In [ǝp] and [ǝk] rhymes occurring after coronal or palatalized initials, the main vowel is the close-mid back vowel [ɤ], approaching [ɯ]. For example: *tǝp⁵⁵* 'pick up' (拾捡), *tǝk²¹* 'deserve' (值得), *nǝp⁵⁵* 'fingernail' (指甲), *nǝk²¹* 'chide' (教训), and *ljǝp³⁵* 'talk nonsense' (乱说).

[ĭ] In [ǝn] and [ǝt] rhymes occurring after coronal or palatalized initials, the vowel is pronounced [ĭ]. The vowel is shorter than the vowel [i] allophone of the phoneme /i/, which is realized after coronal and palatalized initials, and also shorter than the [ɪ] allophone of /i/, which is realized after initials which are non-coronal and nonpalatalized. For example, comparing *tin²¹²* 'fill (v)' (填) and *tǝn²¹²* 'mountain' (山), or *ɲin²¹²* 'year' (年) and *ɲǝn²¹²* 'person' (人), the former vowel in each pair—the [i] allophone of /i/—is longer with tongue position higher. Likewise, in comparing *pit³²³* 'bounce (v)' (弹跳) and *pjǝt⁵⁵* 'pen' (笔), or *mit³¹* 'knife' (刀) and *mjǝt²¹* 'lame' (跛), the former vowel in each pair—the [ɪ] allophone of /i/—is longer with tongue position higher. Thus the ə pronounced as [ĭ] is not a realization of the phoneme /i/.

[ŭ] The [ŭ] allophone only occurs with the rhyme [ət] after labialized initials. It is a short vowel somewhere between [ɯ] and [ɤ]. Under the influence of the preceding labialized initial, it sounds very like a short [u]. For example: *pət*[55] 'duck' (鸭), *kwət*[55] 'hawk' (鹰), *khwət*[35] 'iron' (铁), and *ŋwət*[21] 'loach' (泥鳅).

[ə] When the *ən* rhyme occurs after noncoronal and nonpalatalized initials, and when *əm* occurs, the vowel is pronounced [ə]. The default pronunciation for other rhymes, when not complying with conditions for the above three allophones, is also [ə]. For example: *mən*[55] 'sky' (天空), *sən*[212] 'cow' (黄牛), *məm*[31] 'tiger' (老虎), *təm*[55] 'bamboo hat' (斗笠), *thəm*[35] 'needle' (针), *jəm*[53] 'flood (v)' (淹), *pəp*[21] 'bend over' (伏), *lək*[21] 'strength' (力气), and *təŋ*[53] 'dark' (黑).

The vowels /ɐ/ and /ə/ are realized as short vowels, never occurring syllable-final.

Rhymes. Eight syllable codas and seven vowels combine to give fifty-five rhymes. Adding the apical vowel [ɿ] which comes from pronunciations of Modern Chinese loan words, we end up with fifty-six rhymes altogether, as in (15).

(15)	Vowel Syllable coda	a	e	i	o	u	ɐ	ə
		a	e	i	o	u	—	ɿ
i		ai	—	—	oi	ui	ɐi	—
u		au	eu	iu	—	—	ɐu	—
m		am	em	im	om	um	ɐm	əm
n		an	en	in	on	un	ɐn	ən
ŋ		aŋ	eŋ	iŋ	oŋ	uŋ	ɐŋ	əŋ
p		ap	ep	ip	op	up	ɐp	əp
t		at	et	it	ot	ut	ɐt	ət
k		ak	ek	ik	ok	uk	ɐk	ək

(16) Vocabulary exemplifying different rhymes

Rhyme	Dong	Chinese	
a	sa^{35}	肩膀 jiān bǎng	shoulder (n)
ai	sai^{35}	给 gěi	give
au	sau^{35}	芭芒草 bā máng cǎo	straw
am	sam^{35}	三 sān	three
an	san^{35}	编织 biān zhī	knit
aŋ	$saŋ^{35}$	树根 shù gēn	root of tree
ap	sap^{323}	连接 lián jiē	connect
at	sat^{13}	踏 tà	step on
ak	sak^{13}	舂 chōng	pound (v)
e	se^{55}	带子 dài zi	belt (n)
eu	seu^{35}	喇叭 lǎ ba	loudspeaker
em	sem^{55}	陡而尖 dǒu ér jiān	steep and sharp
en	$ɕen^{212}$	痰 tán	phlegm
eŋ	$ɕeŋ^{55}$	争 zhēng	contend
ep	sep^{13}	耳语 ěr yǔ	whisper (v)
et	$ɕet^{13}$	都 dōu	all
ek	sek^{13}	饭豆 fàn dòu	cereal grain
i	si^{55}	浸入 jìn rù	soak into
iu	siu^{55}	焦 jiāo	burnt
im	sim^{55}	引线 yǐn xiàn	fuse (n)
in	sin^{55}	煎熬 jiān áo	suffer (v)
iŋ	$siŋ^{55}$	楼门 lóu mén	entrance (n)
ip	sip^{323}	接 jiē	meet (v)
it	sit^{13}	剪 jiǎn	cut (with scissors)
ik	sik^{13}	谈 tán	talk (v)
o	so^{35}	粗 cū	coarse
oi	soi^{212}	懒惰 lǎn duò	lazy
om	som^{33}	群 qún, 堆 duī	group, pile
on	son^{55}	鼻鼾 bí hān	snore
oŋ	$soŋ^{55}$	马鬃 mǎ zōng	horse's mane
op	kop^{323}	刚才 gāng cái	just now
ot	sot^{323}	吸 xī	breathe in
ok	sok^{35}	窄 zhǎi	narrow (adj)
u	su^{35}	青 qīng	green
ui	sui^{212}	蛇 shé	snake
um	sum^{31}	房间 fáng jiān	room
un	sun^{55}	刺 cì	thorn
uŋ	$suŋ^{35}$	话 huà	word
up	sup^{323}	逢 féng	come upon

ut	sut^{31}	荸荠 bí qí	water chestnut
uk	suk^{323}	梧桐 wú tóng	phoenix tree
ɐi	$sɐi^{13}$	雄性 xióng xìng	male (birds)
ɐu	$sɐu^{323}$	醋 cù	vinegar
ɐm	$sɐm^{35}$	早 zǎo	early
ɐn	$sɐn^{55}$	秧鸡 yāng jī	water rail
ɐŋ	$sɐŋ^{55}$	恨 hèn	hate (v)
ɐp	$sɐp^{55}$	捉 zhuō	arrest (v)
ɐt	$sɐt^{55}$	不滑 bù huá	not slippery
ɐk	$sɐk^{55}$	洗 xǐ	wash (clothes)
ʔ	$tsʅ^{33}sʅ^{212}$	知识 zhī shi	knowledge
əm	$səm^{35}$	心 xīn	heart
ən	$sən^{35}$	亲戚 qīn qī	relatives
əŋ	$təŋ^{53}$	黑 hēi	black
əp	$səp^{21}$	吹 chuī	blow (v)
ət	$sət^{55}$	尾巴 wěi ba	tail (n)
ək	$çək^{55}$	歪斜 wāi xié	crooked

2.3 Tones

Number and naming of tones. Zhānglǔ Dong has nine tones in unchecked syllables and six in checked syllables. Tone values for the checked syllables are equivalent to or very close to those for corresponding unchecked syllables. Combining ideas from Chinese tone history with knowledge of Dong, we can divide the tones into eight categories: six unchecked syllable categories and two checked syllable categories. These closely parallel the tone system for Ancient Chinese, in which four tones were each divided into Yīn (阴) and Yáng (阳) components. Odd-numbered Dong tones are equivalent to the Chinese Yīn tones, and even-numbered tones are equivalent to the Chinese Yáng tones. The odd-numbered tones each divide into two categories according to whether or not the corresponding syllable initial is aspirated. Tones occurring with unaspirated syllable initials are known as Quán (全, first) Yīn tones, while those occurring with aspirated initials are known as Cì (次, second) Yīn tones. Similarly, tones among the checked syllables each divide into two categories according to the length of the accompanying vowel; they are known as Duǎn (短 'short') Rù (入) and Cháng (长 'long') Rù tones, respectively.

The nine Dong tones in unchecked syllables are named in (17) and the six tones in checked syllables are named in (19). Their correspondence with the eight Ancient Chinese tone categories is presented in (35). Tonal values corresponding to the fifteen tonal categories are presented in (357) for the Dong spoken in eleven different areas in Guìzhōu.

Phonology   31

(17) Zhānglǔ's tone categories and values in unchecked syllables

Tone categories	Chinese names	Chinese pīnyīn	Tone values
1	全阴平	Quán Yīn Píng	55
1'	次阴平	Cì Yīn Píng	35
2	阳平	Yáng Píng	11/212
3	全阴上	Quán Yīn Shàng	24/323
3'	次阴上	Cì Yīn Shàng	13
4	阳上	Yáng Shàng	31
5	全阴去	Quán Yīn Qù	53
5'	次阴去	Cì Yīn Qù	453
6	阳去	Yáng Qù	33

(18) Examples of unchecked syllables

Tone		English, Chinese		English, Chinese
1	pa^{55}	fish, 鱼	sau^{55}	twist, 绞
1'	pha^{35}	gray, 灰色	sau^{35}	straw, 芭芒草
2	pa^{212}	rake (n), 耙	sau^{212}	rear (v), 饲养
3	pja^{323}	thunder (n), 雷	sau^{323}	steam (v), 蒸
3'	$phja^{13}$	turn over, 翻	sau^{13}	grass carp, 草鱼
4	pa^{31}	locust, 蝗虫	sau^{31}	husband, 丈夫
5	pa^{53}	leaf, 树叶	sau^{53}	soup, 汤
5'	pha^{453}	break (v), 破	sau^{453}	egret, 鹭鸶
6	pa^{33}	chaff, 糠	sau^{33}	create, 造

(19) Zhānglǔ's tone categories and values in checked syllables

Tone categories	Chinese names	Chinese pīnyīn	Tone values
7	全阴短入	Quán Yīn Duǎn Rù	55
7'	次阴短入	Cì Yīn Duǎn Rù	35
8	阳短入	Yáng Duǎn Rù	21
9	全阴长入	Quán Yīn Cháng Rù	24/323
9'	次阴长入	Cì Yīn Cháng Rù	13
10	阳长入	Yáng Cháng Rù	31

(20)   Examples of checked syllables

Tone		English, Chinese		English, Chinese
7	$jɐk^{55}$	wet, 湿	tok^{55}	river bend, 河湾
7'	$jɐk^{35}$	hard-working, 勤快	$thok^{35}$	bend (v), 弯腰
8	$jɐk^{21}$	pitiful, 可怜	tok^{21}	kneel, 跪
9	jak^{323}	hungry, 饿	tot^{323}	hair in bun, 发髻
9'	jak^{13}	fish pond, 鱼栏	$thok^{13}$	capture, 夺取
10	jak^{31}	rust (n), 锈	tok^{31}	bracelet, 手镯

Notes
1. Tone 2 is a low circumflex tone with a fall and a rise. It is sometimes realized as a flat low tone.
2. At first tone 3 falls very slightly, then it rises; or it may be rising from start to finish. The end point of tone 3 is slightly higher than that of tone 6, while the end point of 3' is slightly lower than that of tone 6.
3. The starting point of tone 4 is slightly higher than that of tone 6, but similar to that of the end point of tone 3.
4. The starting point for tone 7' is slightly higher than that for tone 1'. Its actual tone value could be written as 45.
5. The tone values of tones 8 and 10 are extremely close. With tone 8 the starting point is slightly lower, and it occurs with shorter vowels.

Relationship between checked syllable tones and vowel length. Tone categories of checked syllable tones are closely related to vowel length, as illustrated in (21), showing syllable rhymes in checked syllables.

(21)   Tone: Short—7, 7', 8   Long—9, 9', 10

ɐp	ɐt	ɐk	ap	at	ak
əp	ət	ək	ep	et	ek
		ok	ip	it	ik
			op	ot	ok
			up	ut	uk

In the system of vowels, *a*, *e*, *i*, and *u* are long vowels, and these only occur as main vowels for checked rhymes with tones 9, 9', and 10. The vowels *ɐ* and *ə* are short, and they only occur as main vowels for checked rhymes with tones 7, 7', and 8. Only the long vowel *o* differs from the usual pattern for long vowels: in keeping with the usual pattern, when *o* occurs in syllable rhymes as [op] or [ot], it only occurs with tones 9, 9', and 10; the

[ok] rhyme, however, occurs with all the checked syllable tones, including 7, 7', and 8. The southern dialect of Dong differentiates between long and short realizations of the rhyme oŋ, and this may explain why Zhānglǔ Dong's rhyme [ok] has two distinct realizations according to length—the short [ŏk] may have originated as a short [ŏŋ].

If the difference between the 7, 7', and 8 tones and the 9, 9', and 10 tones were consistently reflected in corresponding differences in vowels, then we could choose either to combine tones or to combine vowel phonemes. In the given case, however, if tones are combined and are taken to be conditioned by rhymes, the [ok] rhyme remains a problem: it can occur with any of the checked syllable tones. We instead retain the differences in tones and take rhymes to be conditioned by tones, merging the main vowels of long and short syllable rhymes into one, thus taking [a] and [ɐ], and [e] and [ə], respectively, each to be represented by one vowel phoneme. This is just how the Dong orthography treats the problem.

2.4 Differences within standard Dong

One lect of Dong was selected as standard from all the different lects of Dong. The place where the standard is spoken is Róngjiāng's Chējiāng. As soon as you leave the town gate of Róngjiāng county town and cross the big bridge, you have arrived in Chējiāng. It encompasses several Dong villages. First there is Chēzhài (车寨, ɕai³³ɕa³⁵), then Mèizhài (妹寨, ɕai³³mɐi⁴⁵³), followed by Zhānglǔ (章鲁, saŋ⁵⁵lu³³), Zhàitóu (寨头, ɕai³³tɐu²¹²), Màizhài (麦寨, ɕai³³mek³¹), Yuèzhài (月寨, ɕai³³jot³¹), and Kǒuzhài (口寨, ɕai³³khɐu¹³). The Dong language in these various villages is nearly the same, except for some slight differences between Chēzhài Dong and Dong in the other villages, as illustrated below.

Syllable initials. Chēzhài Dong has the voiceless uvular stop [q] and the voiced velar fricative [ɣ], while the other villages pronounce these as [ʔ] and [j], respectively.

(22)	Chēzhài	Zhānglǔ	Chinese	
	qa⁵⁵	ʔa⁵⁵	歌	song
	qɐu³¹	ʔɐu³¹	米	rice
	qhek¹³	ʔek¹³	客	visitor
	ɣa⁵³	ja⁵³	田	field
	ɣa⁴⁵³	ja⁴⁵³	红	red
	ɣai³²³	jai³²³	长	long (adj)

Syllable rhymes. In Chēzhài, the sound *i* consistently replaces *ɐi* in the other villages when *ɐi* follows a coronal initial; and the sound *u* replaces *ɐu* when *ɐu* follows *p*, *m*, or *k*.

(23)   Chēzhài   Zhānglǔ   Chinese

   ti^{323} $tɐi^{323}$ 买   buy
   ti^{33} $tɐi^{33}$ 螃蟹   crab
   $ɕi^{35}$ $ɕɐi^{35}$ 灵巧   dextrous
   $ɕi^{323}$ $ɕɐi^{323}$ 黄豆雀   siskin (kind of sparrow)
   yi^{212} $jɐi^{212}$ 梨   pear
   yi^{33} $jɐi^{33}$ 计算   count (v)
   pu^{55} $pɐu^{55}$ 坡   hill
   pu^{212} $pɐu^{212}$ 鸽子   pigeon
   mu^{31} $mɐu^{31}$ 关节   joint
   mu^{53} $mɐu^{53}$ 蝌蚪   tadpole
   ku^{53} $kɐu^{53}$ 对, 双   pair
   khu^{453} $khɐu^{453}$ 抖   tremble

Miscellaneous irregular. Examples are presented in (24).

(24)   Chēzhài   Zhānglǔ   Chinese

   khe^{13} ke^{323} 窗格   window lattice
   the^{13} te^{323} 没有   not have
   $ɕem^{53}$ $ɕem^{453}$ 匀菜   to thin vegetables
   wan^{35} $khwan^{35}$ 甜   sweet (adj)
   $khwau^{35}$ $khau^{35}$ 搜   search (v)
   $quŋ^{323}$ $ʔuŋ^{13}$ 响   sound (n, v)

2.5 Pronunciation of Chinese loan words

Dong has borrowed a large number of words from Chinese. From the point of view of pronunciation, these loan words basically fall into two classes: Ancient and Modern loans. It is possible to differentiate individual periods within each class, but the differences are not that marked. On the other hand, differences in pronunciation between Ancient and Modern loan words are very clear, especially in regard to the tones. Early loan words from Chinese have tones corresponding to Ancient Chinese, in which four tones were each divided into Yīn and Yáng components. Modern loan words from Chinese carry tones corresponding to the local Southwestern Mandarin system of Yīn, Yáng, Shàng, and Qù.

Phonology

At present, it is still difficult to differentiate Ancient Chinese loan words from words which had a common origin for both Chinese and Dong. Words in Dong and related words in Ancient Chinese both follow the rules of the Qiè Yùn (切韵) system of Ancient Chinese. Changes in Chinese pronunciation basically parallel changes in Dong. It is impossible to locate boundaries for establishing differences in word origin. Irregular correspondences in a small number of words should not be used as a basis for differentiating common-origin words from early loan words. Thus, in talking about pronunciations of Ancient Chinese loan words, we are actually talking about pronunciations of words in Dong which are related to Chinese and are not Modern loan words.

2.5.1 Pronunciation of Ancient Chinese loans

Syllable initials

Voiced versus voiceless initials. Ancient Chinese Quán (全) voiced initials are all pronounced in modern Dong as the corresponding voiceless initials, but modern tones differentiate ancient voiced and voiceless initials. Voiced initials are pronounced with even tones, voiceless initials with odd tones. Examples are presented in (25) (tone categories are given).

(25)	Ancient Chinese voiced/voiceless initial	Dong initial		Chinese	
	b (并 bìng)	p	pi^2	皮 pí	skin
			pan^4	伴 bàn	companion
			pen^6	办 bàn	do
	p (帮 bāng)	p	pi^1	杯 bēi	cup
			pen^3	板 bǎn	board, plank
			pan^5	半 bàn	half
	d (定 dìng)	t	$toŋ^2$	铜 tóng	copper
			tu^4	肚 dù	belly
			$tɐi^6$	袋 dài	pocket
	t (端 duān)	t	$toŋ^1$	冬 dōng	winter
			$tɐu^3$	斗 dǒu	fight (v)
			toi^5	对 duì	right, correct
	g (群 qún)	ʈ	$ʈa^2$	茄 jiā	eggplant
			$ʈɐn^4$	近 jìn	near
			$ʈui^6$	柜 jù	wardrobe
	k (见 jiàn)	ʔ	$ʔe^1$	家 jiā	family
			$ʔaŋ^3$	讲 jiǎng	talk (v)
			$ʔɐu^5$	够 gòu	enough

Voiceless initials. Ancient Chinese Cì (次) voiceless initials are pronounced in modern Dong with aspiration and with Cì Yīn tones (1', 3', 5', 7', and 9').

(26)   Ancient Chinese   Dong   Chinese
         voiceless initial   initial

Ancient Chinese voiceless initial	Dong initial		Chinese	
ph (滂 *páng*)	ph	*phjin*$^{1'}$	偏 *piān*	willfully
		pha$^{5'}$	破 *pò*	break (v)
		phi$^{5'}$	配 *pèi*	mix (v)
th (透 *tòu*)	th	*tho*$^{1'}$	拖 *tuō*	drag, haul
		thu$^{3'}$	土 *tǔ*	soil
		than$^{5'}$	炭 *tàn*	charcoal
kh (溪 *xī*)	ʔ	*ʔei*$^{1'}$	开 *kāi*	open (v)
		ʔeu$^{3'}$	口 *kǒu*	opening (n)
		ʔu$^{5'}$	裤 *kù*	trousers

Coronal initials. Words in Zhānglǔ Dong which have been borrowed from Ancient Chinese words with unvoiced, voiced, and aspirated coronal initials do not differentiate these initials. Most are pronounced ç and a few are pronounced *ṭ*. Tones, however, do differentiate: words borrowed from *ṭ* (知 *zhī*) and *tç* (照 *zhào*) initials appear with Quán Yīn tones (1, 3, 5, 7, and 9); *ḍ* (澄 *chéng*), *dẓ* (床 *chuáng*), and *ẓ* (禅 *chán*) initials appear with Yáng tones (2, 4, 6, 8, and 10); *ṭh* (彻 *chè*), *tçh* (穿 *chuān*), and ç (审 *shěn*) initials appear with Cì Yīn tones (1', 3', 5', 7', and 9').

Ancient Chinese coronal initial	Dong initial		Chinese	
ṭ (知 *zhī*)	ç	*çu*^{1}	珠 *zhū*	pearl
		çon^{5}	转 *zhuǎn*	turn (v)
tç (照 *zhào*)	ç	*çe*^{1}	渣 *zhā*	dregs
		çu^{3}	主 *zhǔ*	master (n)
ḍ (澄 *chéng*)	ç	*çe*^{2}	茶 *chá*	tea
		ço^{6}	箸 *zhù*	chopsticks
dẓ (床 *chuáng*)	ç	*çai*^{6}	寨 *zhài*	village
		çu^{2}	锄 *chú*	hoe (n)
ẓ (禅 *chán*)	ç	*çi*^{2}	时 *shí*	time (n)
		çok^{8}	熟 *shú*	cooked
ṭh (彻 *chè*)	ç	*çu*$^{3'}$	丑 *chǒu*	second of twelve Earthly Branches
		çeŋ$^{1'}$	撑 *chēng*	prop up
tçh (穿 *chuān*)	ç	*çən*$^{1'}$	春 *chūn*	Spring

Phonology 37

ɕ (审 shěn)	ɕ	ɕen³'	铲 chǎn	shovel (n, v)
		ɕe¹'	沙 shā	sand (n)
		ɕi⁵'	试 shì	try (v)

Among the small number of words which originate from Ancient Chinese words with coronal initials and which have the borrowed pronunciation ṭ in Dong are the following: zhú (竹) and zhì (置) from the ṭ (知 zhī) initial, pronounced ṭok¹ and ṭi⁵, respectively; zhāi (斋), zhǐ (只), and zhōng (钟) from the ṭɕ (照 zhào) initial, pronounced ṭai¹, ṭik⁹, and ṭoŋ¹, respectively; zhí (值) from the ḍ (澄 chéng) initial, pronounced ṭək⁸; and zhuó (镯) from the ḍʐ (床 chuáng) initial, pronounced ṭok⁴.

Alveolar initials. Alveolar and coronal initials in Ancient Chinese are sometimes pronounced differently from each other when borrowed into Dong. Coronal sounds are borrowed as coronal initials (see examples in (27)). Alveolar sounds are usually borrowed with the pronunciation s, though some are pronounced like the coronal sounds. Tones are all borrowed as Quán Yīn, Yáng, or Cì Yīn, according to the voicing and aspiration status of the syllable initial.

(28)	Ancient Chinese alveolar initial	Dong initial		Chinese	
	ts (精 jīng)	s/ɕ	səm⁵	浸 jìn	soak
			ɕaŋ¹	浆 jiāng	thick liquid
	dz (从 cóng)	s/ɕ	sin²	钱 qián	money
			ɕot⁴	绝 jué	cut off
	z (邪 xié)	s/ɕ	səm⁶	寻 xún	look for
			ɕon⁶	旋 xuán	revolve
	tsh (清 qīng)	s/ɕ	sin¹'	千 qiān	thousand
			ɕai³'	踩 cǎi	step on
	s (心 xīn)	s/ɕ	sam¹'	三 sān	three
			ɕoi⁵'	岁 suì	year (of age)

Labial initials. Words from the [p] (帮 bāng) series of Ancient Chinese are usually differentiated according to complete or incomplete closure. Examples are presented in (29) (where the first four initials are initials with complete closure, the last four with incomplete closure).

(29) | Ancient Chinese bilabial initial | Dong initial | | Chinese | |
|---|---|---|---|---|
| p (帮 bāng) | p | peu¹ | 包 bāo | bag (n) |
| | | pa³ | 坝 bà | dam (n) |
| | | pai⁵ | 拜 bài | do obeisance |
| ph (滂 páng) | ph | pheu⁵ | 炮 pào | canon |
| | | phek³' | 拍 pāi | clap, pat |
| | | phai⁵ | 派 pài | dispatch (v) |
| b (并 bìng) | p | pən² | 盆 pén | basin |
| | | poŋ² | 篷 péng | awning |
| | | pu⁶ | 步 bù | step (n) |
| m (明 míng) | m | ma⁴ | 马 mǎ | horse |
| | | mui⁶ | 妹 mèi | younger sister |
| | | mɐk⁸ | 墨 mò | ink |
| f (非 fēi) | w | wən¹' | 分 fēn | 0.01 Rénmínbì |
| | | wen⁵ | 贩 fàn | buy to resell |
| | | wet³' | 发 fā | send out |
| fh (敷 fū) | w | wen¹' | 翻 fān | turn over |
| v (奉 fèng) | w | wən² | 坟 fén | grave (n) |
| | | wen⁶ | 饭 fàn | cooked rice |
| | | wet⁴ | 罚 fá | punish |
| ɱ (微 wéi) | w | wən² | 文 wén | writing |
| | | wen⁶ | 万 wàn | ten thousand |

There are also some incomplete closure sounds in Ancient Chinese which are pronounced as complete closure sounds in Dong. For example: *fěn mò* (粉末) from the *f* (非 *fēi*) initial is pronounced *pən⁵*, *fù* (父), *féi* (肥), and *fèn* (份) from the *v* (奉 *fèng*) initial are pronounced *pu⁴*, *pui²*, and *pən⁶*, respectively; and *wèi* (未) and *wú* (无) from the *ɱ* (微 *wēi*) initial are pronounced *mi⁴* and *mu²*, respectively.

Velar fricative initials. The voiced velar initial *ɣ* (匣 *xiá*) of Ancient Chinese is pronounced in Dong like its voiceless counterpart *x* (晓 *xiǎo*): both are borrowed into Dong as *h*, as illustrated in (30).

(30) | Ancient Chinese velar initial | Dong initial | | Chinese | |
|---|---|---|---|---|
| x (晓 xiǎo) | h | hoi¹' | 灰 huī | dust (n) |
| | | hɐi³' | 海 hǎi | sea |
| | | heu⁵ | 孝 xiào | filial |

Phonology

ɣ (匣 *xiá*)	h	*hai²*	鞋 *xié*	shoe
		hai⁵	害 *hài*	evil, harm
		hak³'	学 *xué*	study (v)

Nasal initials. Ancient Chinese words from the ɳ (娘 *niáng*) initial, the nʑ (日 *rì*) initial, and the ŋ (疑 *yí*) initial third division are all pronounced ɳ, as shown in (31). Tone values, as opposed to categories, are given in (31).

(31)

Ancient Chinese initial	Dong initial			Chinese	
ɳ (娘 *niáng*)	ɳ	*ɳin²¹²*	年 *nián*	year
		ɳen³¹	碾 *niǎn*	stone roller
		ɳip³¹	镊 *niè*	tweezers
nʑ (日 *rì*)	ɳ	*ɳi³³*	二 *èr*	two
		ɳən²¹²	人 *rén*	person
		ɳət²¹	日 *rì*	day
ŋ (疑 *yí*)	ɳ	*ɳɐn²¹²*	银 *yín*	silver
		ɳi²¹²	疑 *yí*	doubt (v)
		ɳon³³	愿 *yuàn*	hope (v)

Divisions in Ancient Chinese loan words. According to scholars of Chinese Děng Yùn (等韵)—that is, Chinese philologists—the idea of Děng (division) in pronunciation of Chinese is reflected in the syllable initials of Chinese loan words in Dong. Words borrowed from the third and fourth divisions typically have coronal, velar, or palatalized initials. Words from the first and second divisions typically have initials which are neither coronal, nor velar, nor palatalized. Classification of divisions as open or closed, except with ancient glottal and dental initials, is usually reflected in the vowel sound of the borrowed syllable rhyme.

With ancient glottal and dental initials, open or closed division is reflected both in the syllable initial and in the vowel sound of the borrowed syllable rhyme; ancient words from the closed divisions are borrowed with labialized initials or rounded vowels. See the examples in (32) and (33) from the ancient glottal initials *k* (见 *jiàn*) and ʔ (影 *yǐng*), respectively.

(32) Words borrowed from Ancient Chinese with the *k* (见 *jiàn*) initial

Division	Dong	Chinese	
first open	*ʔa⁵⁵*	歌 *gē*	song
	ʔam³²³	敢 *gǎn*	dare
	ʔɐu⁵³	够 *gòu*	enough

second open	ʔai⁵⁵	街 jiē	street
	ʔeu³²³	教 jiào	teach
	ʔe⁵³	嫁 jià	(of a woman) marry
third open	ȶen⁵⁵	斤 jīn	0.5 kilogram
	ȶəm⁵⁵	金 jīn	gold
	ȶi³²³	纪 jì	record (v)
fourth open	ȶi⁵⁵	金鸡 jīn jī	golden pheasant
	ȶin⁵³	见 jiàn	see
	ȶit³²³	结 jié	tie (v)
first closed	kwaŋ⁵⁵	光 guāng	light (n)
	ʔu⁵⁵	姑 gū	father's sister
	ʔoŋ⁵⁵	工 gōng	work (n)
second closed	kwe⁵⁵	黄瓜 huáng guā	cucumber
	kwai⁵³	怪 guài	strange
	kwen⁵³	惯 guàn	be used to
third closed	ȶo⁵³	锯 jù	saw (n)
	ȶu³²³	九 jiǔ	nine
	ȶui³²³	鬼 guǐ	ghost

(33)   Words borrowed from Ancient Chinese with the ʔ (影 yǐng) initial

Division	Dong	Chinese	
first open	ʔan⁵⁵	鞍 ān	saddle (n)
	ʔɐn⁵⁵	恩 ēn	kindness
	ʔɐi⁵³	爱 ài	love (v)
second open	ʔeu³²³	拗 niù	stubborn
	ʔa⁵⁵	乌鸦 wū yā	crow (n)
	ʔek³²³	轭 è	yoke (n)
third open	jim⁵⁵	阉 yān	castrate or spay
	jəm⁵⁵	阴 yīn	overcast
	jiŋ³²³	影 yǐng	shadow
	ʔi⁵⁵	依 yī	depend on
	ʔət⁵⁵	一 yī	one
	ʔən⁵³	印 yìn	seal (n)
fourth open	jin⁵⁵	烟 yān	smoke (n)
	ʔin⁵³	燕 yàn	swallow (n)
first closed	wən³²³	稳 wěn	steady
	ʔoŋ⁵³	翁 wèng	urn
second closed	wet³²³	挖 wā	dig
third closed	ʔoŋ⁵⁵	雍 yōng	stop up

Syllable rhymes. The rhyme group system used by Děng Yùn scholars when researching the rhymes in Chinese is used here as the main vehicle for presenting pronunciation of syllable rhymes of Ancient Chinese loan words in Dong.

Main vowels. Loan words in Dong borrowed from words belonging to the five rhyme groups [uŋ/k], [ən/t], [əŋ/k], [əu], and [əm/p] of Ancient Chinese (corresponding to the five rhyme group words *tōng* (通), *zhēn* (臻), *zēng* (曾), *liú* (流), and *shēn* (深), respectively) are pronounced with short vowels. Loans from the [uŋ/k] group have *o* as their main vowel (short *o*). Loans from the other four groups [ən/t], [əŋ/k], [əu], and [əm/p] have either *ə* or *ɐ* as the main vowel.

Words in Dong borrowed from any of the following six rhyme groups of Ancient Chinese—[aŋ/k], [an/t], [au], [ɑŋ/k], [am/p], and [ɐŋ/k] (corresponding to the six rhyme group words *jiāng* (江), *shān* (山), *xiào* (效), *dàng* (宕), *xián* (咸), and *gěng* (梗), respectively)—all have long vowels. Usually, the first division has *a* as the main vowel, the second division has *e* as the main vowel, and the third and fourth divisions have *i* as their main vowel. For words borrowed from the [ai] group (corresponding to the rhyme group word *xiè* (蟹)), long vowels are more common than short ones.

Syllable codas. Loan words in Dong borrowed from words belonging to the four rhyme groups [ɑ], [a], [u], and [i] of Ancient Chinese (corresponding to the four rhyme group words *guǒ* (果), *jiǎ* (假), *yù* (遇), and *zhǐ* (止)) are pronounced with monophthong rhymes. The rest all have syllable codas—apart from words of the [ai] group (corresponding to the rhyme group word *xiè* (蟹)) which may or may not have codas.

The coda corresponding to the rhyme group [ai] is *i*, the coda for the two groups [əu] and [au] is *u*, for [am/p] and [əm/p] it is either *m* or *p*, for [an/t] and [ən/t] it is either *n* or *t*, and for [ɑŋ/k], [aŋ/k], [əŋ/k], [ɐŋ/k], and [uŋ/k] the coda is either *ŋ* or *k*.

Pronunciations of words in Zhānglǔ Dong borrowed from Ancient Chinese, classified according to rhyme groups of Ancient Chinese, are presented in (34).

(34)

Rhyme group	Division	Dong rhyme		Chinese	
[uŋ/k] (通 tōng)	first closed	oŋ	ʔoŋ⁵⁵	工	gōng
			toŋ²¹²	铜	tóng
		ok	mok²¹	木	mù
			tok²¹	读	dú
	third closed	oŋ	ljoŋ²¹²	龙	lóng
			joŋ³³	用	yòng
		ok	ljok²¹	六	liù
			ɕok²¹	熟	shú
[ən/t] (臻 zhēn)	first open	ɐn	ʔɐn⁵⁵	恩	ēn
			hɐn³¹	恨	hèn
	third open	ɐn	ȶɐn⁵⁵	斤	jīn
			nɐn²¹²	银	yín
		ən	ɕən³⁵	身	shēn
			sən⁴⁵³	信	xìn
		ət	pjət⁵⁵	笔	bǐ
			lət²¹	栗子	lì zi
	first closed	ən	pən²¹²	盆	pén
			sən⁴⁵³	寸	cùn
	third closed	ən	wən³⁵	分	fēn
			wən³¹	运	yùn
		ət	ɕət³⁵	戌	xū
[əŋ/k] (曾 zēng)	first open	ɐŋ	pɐŋ⁵⁵	崩	bēng
			tɐŋ⁵³	凳	dèng
		ɐk	pɐk⁵⁵	北	běi
			mɐk²¹	墨	mò
		əŋ	ɕəŋ³⁵	升	shēng
		ək	lək²¹	力	lì
[əu] (流 liú)	first open	ɐu	tɐu²¹²	头	tóu
			lɐu³³	漏	lòu
[əm/p] (深 shēn)	third open	əm	səm³⁵	心	xīn
			səm³³	寻	xún
		əp	ɕəp²¹	十	shí
		ip	ȶip³¹	及	jí
[aŋ/k] (江 jiāng)	second open	aŋ	ʔaŋ⁵⁵	江	jiāng
			haŋ⁴⁵³	巷	hàng

Phonology

		oŋ	ɕoŋ⁵⁵	双 shuāng
		ak	hak¹³	学 xué
		ok	pok³²³	剥 bō
			ȶok³¹	镯 zhuó
[an/t] (山 shān)	first open	an	ʔan⁵⁵	鞍 ān
			than⁴⁵³	炭 tàn
		at	ʔat³²³	割 gē
			sat¹³	擦 cā
	second open	en	ɕen¹³	铲 chǎn
			pen³³	办 bàn
		et	pet³²³	八 bā
	third open	in	mjin²¹²	棉 mián
			sin²¹²	钱 qián
		en	ȵen³¹	碾 niǎn
			ȶen⁵³	毽 jiàn
	fourth open	in	sin³⁵	千 qiān
			ȵin²¹²	年 nián
		it	ȶit³²³	结 jié
			sit¹³	切 qiē
	first closed	on	lon³³	乱 luàn
			son⁴⁵³	算 suàn
		an	kwan³²³	管 guǎn
			pan⁵³	半 bàn
		ot	thot¹³	脱 tuō
			sot¹³	撮 cuō
	second closed	en	kwen⁵³	惯 guàn
		et	wet³²³	挖 wā
	third closed	on	ɕon⁵⁵	砖 zhuān
			ɕon⁵³	转 zhuǎn
		en	wen³⁵	翻 fān
			wen³³	万 wàn
		ot	ɕot³¹	绝 jué
			ɕot¹³	说 shuō
		et	wet³¹	罚 fá
			ŋwet³¹	月 yuè
	fourth closed	in	jin³³	县 xiàn
[au] (效 xiào)	first open	au	pau⁵³	告 gào
			sau³³	造 zào
	second open	eu	peu⁵⁵	包 bāo
			ɕeu³²³	爪 zhuǎ
	third open	iu	ȶiu²¹²	桥 qiáo

	fourth open	iu	mjiu³³	庙 miào
			ȶiu²¹²	条 tiáo
			jiu³³	鹞 yáo
[aŋ/k] (宕 dǎng)	first open	aŋ	paŋ⁵⁵	帮 bāng
			taŋ²¹²	糖 táng
		ak	ʔak³²³	各 gè
	third open	aŋ	ɕaŋ²¹²	床 chuáng
			saŋ³³	匠 jiàng
		oŋ	ɕoŋ⁵⁵	装 zhuāng
	first closed	aŋ	kwaŋ⁵⁵	光 guāng
			waŋ²¹²	皇 huáng
	third closed	aŋ	waŋ³⁵	方 fāng
			waŋ⁴⁵³	放 fàng
		ak	ɕak¹³	鹊 què
[am/p] (咸 xián)	first open	am	nam²¹²	南 nán
			ʔam³²³	敢 gǎn
		ap	lap³¹	腊 là
			ʔap³²³	合拢 hé lǒng
	second open	em	ʔem³²³	减 jiǎn
		ep	ɕep¹³	插 chā
			ʔep³²³	甲 jiǎ
	third open	im	ljim²¹²	镰 lián
			jim⁵⁵	阉 yān
		ip	sip³²³	接 jiē
			ɲip³¹	镊 niè
	fourth open	im	ȶhim³⁵	添 tiān
			jim²¹²	嫌 xián
		ip	ȶip³¹	碟 dié
			ȶip³²³	叠 dié
[ɐŋ/k] (梗 gěng)	second open	eŋ	ʔeŋ⁵⁵	羹 gēng
			ɕeŋ³⁵	撑 chēng
		ek	pek³²³	百 bǎi
			ʔek³²³	隔 gé
	third open	iŋ	ɕiŋ⁵⁵	正 zhēng
			pjiŋ³³	病 bìng
		ik	ɕik³²³	只 zhǐ
			ɕik¹³	尺 chǐ
	fourth open	iŋ	ȶiŋ⁵⁵	钉 dīng
			ȶhiŋ⁴⁵³	听 tīng
		ik	sik¹³	锡 xī

Phonology

	second closed	eŋ	ljik³¹	历 lì
		ek	weŋ²¹²	横 héng
			wek¹³	划 huà
[ai] (蟹 xiè)	first open	ai	tai⁵³	带 dài
			ɕai¹³	踩 căi
		ɐi	tɐi³³	袋 dài
			ʔɐi³⁵	开 kāi
	second open	ai	pai⁵³	拜 bài
			ɕai³³	寨 zhài
	fourth open	i	t̺hi⁴⁵³	替 tì
			si³⁵	西 xī
	first closed	oi	toi⁵³	对 duì
			soi³¹	罪 zuì
		i	pi⁵⁵	杯 bēi
			phi⁴⁵³	配 pèi
	second closed	ai	kwai⁵³	怪 guài
			wai³³	坏 huài
	third closed	oi	ɕoi⁴⁵³	岁 suì
			t̺oi⁵³	鳜 guì
[ɑ] (果 guǒ)	first open	a	tha³⁵	拖 tuō
			la²¹²	锣 luó
	second open	a	t̺a²¹²	茄 qié
	first closed	a	sa⁴⁵³	锉 cuò
			wa²¹²	禾 hé
		o	so¹³	锁 suǒ
			mo³³	磨 mò
[a] (假 jià)	second open	a	ɕa⁵⁵	遮 zhé
			ʔa³²³	假 jià
		e	ɕe²¹²	茶 chá
			ŋe²¹²	牙 yá
	third open	a	ɕa³⁵	差 chà
			ɕa³²³	写 xiě
	second closed	a	wa³⁵	花 huā
			wa⁴⁵³	画 huà
		e	kwe⁵⁵	瓜 guā
			ŋwe³¹	瓦 wǎ
[u] (遇 yù)	first closed	u	thu¹³	土 tǔ
			tu³³	渡 dù
		o	so³⁵	粗 cū

	third closed	u	ŋo³¹	五 wǔ
			pu³¹	父 fù
			ɕu³²³	主 zhǔ
		o	ɕo³³	箸 zhù
			ʈo⁵³	锯 jù
[i]	third open	i	pi²¹²	皮 pí
(止 zhǐ)			ɕi²¹²	时 shí
	third closed	i	mi³¹	未 wèi
			khwi³⁵	亏 kuī

Tones. Pronunciation of tones accords with Ancient Chinese, which divided each of the Píng, Shàng, Qù, and Rù tones into Yīn and Yáng. Zhānglǔ Dong (and the Dong of most other areas) divides the Yīn tones into two categories: Quán and Cì. The Rù tones are also divided into two categories: Duǎn (short) and Cháng (long). The relationship between tone categories of Ancient Chinese and Dong loan words from Ancient Chinese is presented in (35), with example words given in (36). Note that Quán Yīn tones in Dong (tones 1, 3, 5, 7, and 9) are associated with voiceless unaspirated initials, Cì Yīn tones (1', 3', 5', 7', and 9') are associated with voiceless aspirated initials, and Yáng tones (2, 4, 6, 8, and 10) are associated with voiced initials.

(35)

Dong tones	Dong tones (Chinese pīnyīn)[13]	Ancient Chinese tone categories	Ancient Chinese syllable initials
1	Quán Yīn Píng	Yīn Píng	Quán voiceless
1'	Cì Yīn Píng	Yīn Píng	Cì voiceless
2	Yáng Píng	Yáng Píng	voiced
3	Quán Yīn Shàng	Yīn Shàng	Quán voiceless
3'	Cì Yīn Shàng	Yīn Shàng	Cì voiceless
4	Yáng Shàng	Yáng Shàng	voiced
5	Quán Yīn Qù	Yīn Qù	Quán voiceless
5'	Cì Yīn Qù	Yīn Qù	Cì voiceless
6	Yáng Qù	Yáng Qù	voiced
7	Quán Yīn Duǎn Rù	Yīn Rù	Quán voiceless short
7'	Cì Yīn Duǎn Rù	Yīn Rù	Cì voiceless short
8	Yáng Duǎn Rù	Yáng Rù	voiced short
9	Quán Yīn Cháng Rù	Yīn Rù	Quán voiceless long
9'	Cì Yīn Cháng Rù	Yīn Rù	Cì voiceless long
10	Yáng Cháng Rù	Yáng Rù	voiced long

---

[13] cf. (17) and (19).

Phonology

(36)

Dong tones		Chinese	
1	toŋ⁵⁵	冬 dōng	winter (n)
1'	thoŋ³⁵	通 tōng	open, through
2	mjin²¹²	棉 mián	cotton
3	tui³²³	鬼 guǐ	ghost
3'	thoŋ¹³	桶 tǒng	bucket
4	ma³¹	马 mǎ	horse
5	tui⁵³	贵 guì	expensive
5'	thi⁴⁵³	气 qì	gas
6	mjiu³³	庙 miào	temple
7	ʔət⁵⁵	一 yī	one
7'	sət³⁵	七 qī	seven
8	ɕəp²¹	十 shí	ten
9	pet³²³	八 bā	eight
9'	ʔek¹³	客 kè	guest
10	pak³¹	白 bái	white

2.5.2 Pronunciation of Modern Chinese loans

The variety of Chinese spoken in the areas around where Dong people live is Southwestern Chinese. Thus Modern Chinese loan words are borrowed from Southwestern Chinese. The syllable initials, syllable rhymes, and tones of Chinese are all usually simpler than those of Dong, but there are a few sounds in Chinese that are not native to Dong. When sounds are borrowed, those which are identical to Dong sounds are easily absorbed. Those which are not identical are adapted to the Dong sound system, either by pronouncing them with sounds which are as close as possible to Dong sounds, or by simply using the Chinese pronunciation, thereby increasing the number of phonemes in the Dong sound system (cf. §2.1).

Syllable initials

1. Standard Chinese distinguishes the alveolar sounds *ts*, *tsh*, and *s* from the retroflex sounds *tʂ*, *tʂh*, *ʂ*, and *ʐ*, but Dong pronounces these sounds as a single set, in keeping with local pronunciations of Chinese: *ts*, *tsh*, *s*, and *z*. For example: 中 zhōng in Chinese becomes *tsoŋ³³* in Dong, 产 chǎn becomes *tshan³¹*, 社 shè becomes *se³⁵*, 人 rén becomes *zən²¹²*, 遵 zūn becomes *tsən³³*, 错 cuò becomes *tsho³⁵*, and 岁 suì becomes *sʋi³⁵*.

2. The coronal sounds *tɕ*, *tɕh*, and *ɕ* of Standard Chinese are borrowed into Dong as *t*, *th*, and *ɕ*, respectively. For example: 缺 quē becomes *the²¹²* and 训 xùn becomes *ɕən³⁵*.

In some instances, however, Southwestern Chinese pronounces these coronal sounds as velar sounds and Dong follows suit. For example: 解决 *jiě jué* becomes *kai³¹ țe²¹²* and 敲 *qiāo* becomes *khau³³*.

3. Chinese initials occurring before the close front vowel *i* usually occur as palatalized or coronal initials in Dong. For example: 兵 *bīng* becomes *pjən³³*, 贫 *pín* becomes *phjən²¹²*, 民 *mín* becomes *mjən²¹²*, 铁 *tiě* becomes *thje¹³*, 粮 *liáng* becomes *ljaŋ²¹²*, and 电 *diàn* becomes *țen⁵⁵* or *tjen⁵⁵*.

4. The initials *k* and *kh* in Chinese, when they precede the on-glide *u*, are usually pronounced as the labialized initials *kw* and *khw* in Dong. For example: 国 *guó* becomes *kwe²¹²* and 困 *kùn* becomes *khwən³⁵*.

5. When Chinese pīnyīn writes a word starting in a vowel, Dong borrows the word, in line with Southwestern Chinese, by inserting the nasal initial *ŋ*. For example: 额 *é* becomes *ŋe²¹²*, 爱 *ài* becomes *ŋai⁵⁵*, 袄 *ǎo* becomes *ŋau³¹*, 藕 *ǒu* becomes *ŋɐu³¹*, 安 *ān* becomes *ŋan³³*, 昂 *áng* becomes *ŋaŋ²¹²*, and 恩 *ēn* becomes *ŋən³³*.

6. When a Chinese word starts with *w* using pīnyīn, Dong pronounces it *w*, or in some cases *ŋ*; words in Chinese beginning in *y* [j], are pronounced as *j* in Dong, or in some cases *ŋ* or *n*; Chinese words beginning in *y* [ü] are pronounced *wj*. For example: 文 *wén* becomes *wən²¹²*, 我 *wǒ* becomes *ŋo³¹*, 药 *yào* becomes *jo²¹²*, 硬 *yìng* becomes *ŋən⁵⁵*, 验 *yàn* becomes *nen⁵⁵*, and 月 *yuè* becomes *wje²¹²*.

Syllable rhymes

1. Syllable rhymes in the Dong language do not carry on-glides. When Chinese syllables with on-glides *i*, *u*, or *y* (the sound *ü*) are borrowed into Dong, the glides are either expressed in coronal, velar, palatalized, or labialized initials, or expressed via a different main vowel, or simply omitted. For example:

   (a) palatalized rhymes in Chinese (corresponding to *i* on-glide): 调 *diào* in Chinese becomes *țau⁵⁵* or *tjau⁵⁵* in Dong, 江 *jiāng* becomes *țaŋ³³*, 仙 *xiān* becomes *ɕen³³*, 野 *yě* becomes *je³¹*, 药 *yào* becomes *jo²¹²*, 勇 *yǒng* becomes *joŋ³¹*, 油 *yóu* becomes *ju²¹²*, 永 *yǒng* becomes *wjən³¹*, and 六 *liù* becomes *lu²¹²*;

   (b) labialized rhymes in Chinese (corresponding to *u* on-glide): 外 *wài* becomes *wai⁵⁵*, 王 *wáng* becomes *waŋ²¹²*, 文 *wén* becomes *wən²¹²*, 瓜 *guā* becomes *kwa³³*, 还 *huán* becomes *fan²¹²*, 会 *huì* becomes *fəi³⁵*, 追 *zhuī* becomes *tsui³³*, 团 *tuán* becomes *thon²¹²*, and 双 *shuāng* becomes *soŋ³³*; and

   (c) rhymes in Chinese corresponding to *ü* on-glide: 圈 *quān* becomes *țhen³³*, 元 *yuán* becomes *wjən²¹²*, and 学 *xué* becomes *ɕo²¹²*.

Phonology

2. The Dong language has three pronunciations for each of the Standard Chinese vowels ə and o. In olden times these vowels split into many different categories, but Standard Chinese has merged each of them into one. Dong borrows them according to pronunciations that prevail in Southwestern Chinese. For example: 歌 gē becomes ko^{33}, 社 shè becomes se^{35}, 德 dé becomes $tə^{212}$, 玻 bō becomes po^{33}, 迫 pò becomes phe^{13}, and 佛 fó becomes fu^{212}.

3. The two apical vowels of Standard Chinese, ɿ and ʅ, are borrowed by Dong as ɿ, again following local Southwestern Chinese. For example: 自 zì becomes $tsɿ^{55}$.

Because some people pronounce the Chinese nonretroflex and retroflex sounds as the coronals ʈ, ʈh, and ɕ, back vowels ɿ and ʅ are sometimes transformed to the front vowel i. For example: 吃 chī becomes $ʈi^{55}$.

4. The rhyme ie in Standard Chinese, for words which derive from the second division of the rhyme group xiè (蟹), is pronounced ai. For example: 解 jiě becomes kai^{31}, 街 jiē becomes kai^{55}, and 界 jiè becomes kai^{55}.

5. The sounds ai and ei in rhymes of Standard Chinese which formerly had Rù Shēng codas p, t, or k are pronounced e when borrowed into Dong. For example: 拍 pāi becomes phe^{13}, 色 shǎi becomes se^{212}, 北 běi becomes pe^{212}, and 贼 zéi becomes tse^{212}.

6. The sounds iao and iou in rhymes of Standard Chinese which formerly had Rù Shēng codas are borrowed into Dong as o and u, respectively. For example: 角 jiǎo becomes ko^{212}, 削 xiāo becomes $ɕo^{212}$, and 六 liù becomes lu^{212}.

7. Standard Chinese differentiates in from iŋ and ən from əŋ. Although Dong also differentiates these sounds, when it comes to loan words, it follows Southwestern Chinese and merges them. For example: 音 yīn and 英 yīng are both pronounced $jən^{33}$, 禁 jìn and 竞 jìng are both $ʈən^{55}$, 宾 bīn and 兵 bīng are both $pjən^{33}$, and 根 gēn and 更 gèng are both $kən^{33}$.

8. The sound üe in Standard Chinese formerly only occurred with words which had Rù Shēng codas. Dong, in parallel with Southwestern Chinese, pronounces the sound in two ways: for words originally from the [an/t] (山 shān) series, it is pronounced e, while for words originally from the [aŋ/k] (宕 dǎng) and [aŋ/k] (江 jiāng) series, it is pronounced o. For example: 越 yuè becomes wje^{212}, 决 jué becomes $ʈe^{212}$, 缺 quē becomes $ʈhe^{13}$, 略 lüè becomes ljo^{212}, 约 yuē becomes jo^{212}, and 觉 jué becomes $ʈo^{212}$.

Tones

1. Tones of Modern Chinese loan words in Dong are generally pronounced according to tone categories of the local Chinese words.

Southwestern Chinese has four tones: Yīn, Yáng, Shàng, and Qù. Zhānglǔ Dong borrows these into five or six tones.

2. Zhānglǔ Dong divides odd numbered tones into two groups, Cì Yīn tones and Quán Yīn tones, according to whether the syllable initial is aspirated or not. When Qù tone words are borrowed from Chinese into Dong, they adapt to this rule associating tones and syllable initials. Syllables in Chinese with syllable initials which are unaspirated stops, unaspirated affricates, nasals, laterals, or voiced fricatives are borrowed with Quán Yīn Píng tone (tone 1), while syllables with initials which are aspirated stops, aspirated affricates, and voiceless fricatives are borrowed with Cì Yīn Píng tone (tone 1').

3. Words with Rù Shēng codas *p*, *t*, or *k* from Ancient Chinese take Yáng Píng tones 2 in southwestern Chinese. In Zhānglǔ Dong they are also borrowed with Yáng Píng tones 2. For example: *bī* (逼) in Chinese becomes *pji²* in Dong, *bù* (from *bù guò*, 不过) becomes *pu²*, *luò* (from *luò hòu*, 落后) becomes *lo²*, *gè* (from *gè mín zú*, 各民族) becomes *ko²*, and *jiǎ* (甲) becomes *ta²*.

However, such words borrowed from Ancient Chinese words with initials which are aspirated or are voiceless fricatives are often pronounced with Cì Yīn Shàng tone 3'. For example: *tǎ* (塔) becomes *tha³'*, *shā* (杀) becomes *sa³'*, and *sè* (色) becomes *se³'*. The Cì Yīn Shàng and Yáng Píng tones are very close, with tone values written as 13 and 212, respectively, and it is easy to mix them up.

4. A table showing tone categories, tone values, and examples from Modern Chinese loan words in Zhānglǔ Dong is presented in (37).

(37)	Southwestern Chinese tone	Dong tone category	Dong tone value	Chinese	Dong	
	Yīn Píng (阴平)	6	33	单 *dān*	*tan³³*	single
	Yáng Píng (阳平)	2	212	达 *dá*	*ta²¹²*	reach
	Yáng Píng (阳平)	3'	13	杀 *shā*	*sa¹³*	kill
	Shàng (上)	4	31	党 *dǎng*	*taŋ³¹*	the Party
	Qù (去)	1	55	旦 *dàn*	*tan⁵⁵*	daybreak
	Qù (去)	1'	35	探 *tàn*	*than³⁵*	explore

Appendix 2 presents tables showing co-occurrences of initials, rhymes, and tones in Dong.

3
Lexicon

3.1 Syllable structure

The basic unit in the Dong language is the syllable. Most syllables in Dong carry their own independent meaning. The syllable is composed of an initial, a rhyme, and a tone. Initials are consonants, while a rhyme may consist either of a monophthong, a diphthong, or a monophthong plus coda. There are three syllable patterns, according to the kind of rhyme, as in (38).

(38) 1. consonant + vowel + tone
       pa^{55} 'fish (n)', ma^{212} 'tongue', se^{55} 'belt (n)'

   2. consonant + vowel + vowel + tone
       pai^{55} 'go', tiu^{55} '1p'[14], $mɐi^{31}$ 'tree'

   3. consonant + vowel + consonant + tone
       tin^{55} 'foot', $saŋ^{35}$ 'root of tree', tap^{323} 'carry with pole'

3.2 Word structure

From the structural point of view, there are two classes of words in Dong: simple and compound words.

Simple words. The great majority of simple words are monosyllabic, but there are also some polysyllabic ones.

---

[14]Here, and throughout this book, '1p' represents 'first-person plural', '2s' represents 'second-person singular', and so on.

Monosyllabic simple words. The foundation of Dong vocabulary is the monosyllabic simple word. For example: kau^{323} 'head', mja^{212} 'hand', $ɳa^{55}$ 'river', $nɐm^{31}$ 'water', $mən^{55}$ 'sky', $tham^{13}$ 'walk', nu^{53} 'look', man^{13} 'yellow', ja^{453} 'red', tu^{212} a classifier for animals, jau^{212} '1s', and $ɳa^{212}$ '2s'.

Polysyllabic simple words. According to word origin, there are two basic classes of polysyllabic simple words: those which have been borrowed from Chinese (mainly Modern Chinese) and those which are native to Dong. Those few which are native to Dong can usually only be disyllabic.

According to pronunciation, polysyllabic simple words can be divided into several types: alliterative, vowel rhyming, reduplicated, and others, as in (39).

(39)

		Dong	Chinese	
Alliterative		$ləm^{212}leŋ^{33}$	蝉	cicada
		$ŋo^{53}ŋet^{323}$	天牛	long-horned beetle
		$ma^{323}mən^{323}$	蝴蝶	butterfly
		$pu^{55}pe^{53}$	顽皮	mischievous
Vowel rhyming		$ka^{31}ɳa^{31}$	杂乱	disorderly
		$pi^{323}si^{13}$	模仿	imitate
Reduplicated		$wan^{35}wan^{35}$	静静的	calm
		$moŋ^{55}moŋ^{212}$	辽阔	vast
Others		$waŋ^{212}ŋa^{212}$	高果	sorghum
		$ma^{31}ʈai^{31}$	螳螂	mantis

Some of the disyllabic words are such that the meaning of one of the component syllables is unknown. Some examples are given in (40) (syllables with independent meaning are bolded).

(40)

tau^{33}**li^{31}**	language	**li^{31}**	word
$suŋ^{35}$ $tuŋ^{55}$	language	**$suŋ^{35}$**	word
$pəm^{323}$**pau^{212}**	algae	**pau^{212}**	algae
$jɐk^{21}$ sa^{212}	pitiful	**$jɐk^{21}$**	pitiful
$ʔok^{55}$**$ɕaŋ^{453}$**	recollect	**$ɕaŋ^{453}$**	think
sin^{55}**wa^{33}**	fabricate	**wa^{33}**	speak

The disyllabic simple words in (40) were probably compound words originally, with each component having its own meaning (either lexical or

Lexicon

affix); but in the process of being handed down, the meaning of one of the components has been forgotten.

For example, none of the syllables in the words $ma^{31}tai^{31}$ 'mantis' and $ma^{323}mən^{323}$ 'butterfly', from among the words in (39), has its own meaning. However in the Bùyī (布依) language of the same language family, the word for 'mantis' is $tăk^{35}ma^{31}$. In Bùyī, $tăk^{35}$ is a generic term and ma^{31} is a specific term meaning 'mantis'; both have their own lexical meaning. The Dong word ma^{31} is cognate with the Bùyī ma^{31}. In Bùyī 'butterfly' is $bi^{35}ba^{31}$ or $tuə^{11}ba^{31}$, where ba^{31} is the syllable expressing the main meaning. The Dong word ma^{323} is cognate with the Bùyī word ba^{31}. It can be seen that the two Dong syllables ma^{31} (from 'mantis') and ma^{323} (from 'butterfly') probably originally also had their own meanings.

Most polysyllabic simple words are transliterations from Chinese. These transliterated words are compound in Chinese, but simple in Dong. Some examples are given in (41).

(41) kai^{31} $faŋ^{35}$ $tən^{33}$
      jiě   fàng   jūn, 解放军
      liberation army

      pe^{212} $tən^{33}$
      běi   jīng, 北京
      Běijīng

      kai^{31} ke^{212}
      gǎi   gé, 改革
      reform

      $ʔaŋ^{55}$ ha^{212}
      jiāng   hé, 江河
      river

      $ɕən^{35}$ $ɕaŋ^{33}$
      shēn   shang, 身上
      on one's body

There is another group of words for which one syllable is borrowed from Chinese (bolded in (42)) while another syllable has no independent meaning. Such words can also be viewed as polysyllabic simple.

(42) $ŋa^{212}$ **$ŋan^{33}$**
      hóng   yàn, 鸿雁
      swan

ȵi⁵³ tot³²³
jì   cè, 计策
stratagem

Compound words. Nearly all the morphemes which combine to create compound words, apart from function morphemes, have their own independent meanings, and most constitute words in their own right. Compound words can be divided into two types: composite (content morpheme plus content morpheme) and affixational (content morpheme plus function morpheme). Each type can be further subdivided into a number of subtypes according to the way the morphemes combine.

Composite compounds. There are three kinds of composite compounds, as indicated below.

1. *Same-category.* Two content morphemes whose meanings are CLOSELY RELATED stand side by side to form a word, as in (43).

(43) tin⁵⁵   + mja²¹²   → tin⁵⁵mja²¹²
      foot   hand   craftsmanship

      kau³²³   + kha³⁵   → kau³²³kha³⁵
      head   ear   main argument

      na³²³   + nɐŋ⁵⁵   → na³²³nɐŋ⁵⁵
      face   nose   appearance

      phek¹³   + phɐu⁴⁵³   → phek¹³phɐu⁴⁵³
      pat (v)   beat lightly   comfort (v), coax

      ke⁵⁵   + pjen⁵⁵   → ke⁵⁵pjen⁵⁵
      border   border   border

      peŋ²¹²   + poŋ³²³   → peŋ²¹²poŋ³²³
      pile   pile   big pile

Usually morphemes which make up same-category compound words are words in their own right. After combining, however, the meanings of the words are somewhat extended, and their original meanings may partly or completely disappear. In addition, after combining, the new word structure is fixed: it is not possible to invert the order of the words or to insert other morphemes into the new word.

One group of same-category compound words is made up of pairs of component parts with NEARLY IDENTICAL meaning. The meaning of the

Lexicon

word after combining is equivalent to the original meanings of the individual component parts—there is no particular extension in meaning.

(44)   Group A

      tan^{212} + $çan^{35}$ → $tan^{212}çan^{35}$
      mountain   mountain   mountain

      mak^{31} + thu^{13} → $mak^{31}thu^{13}$
      soil   soil   soil

      $ʔɐu^{31}$ + wa^{212} → $ʔɐu^{31}wa^{212}$
      rice   standing rice grain   rice

      man^{13} + $waŋ^{212}$ → $man^{13}waŋ^{212}$
      yellow   yellow   yellow

      Group B

      $thau^{13}$ + wan^{33} → $thau^{13}wan^{33}$
      exchange   exchange   exchange

      lui^{212} + lan^{33} → $lui^{212}lan^{33}$
      rotten   rotten   rotten

      su^{33} + $lɐŋ^{31}$ → $su^{33}lɐŋ^{31}$
      just now   immediately   immediately

      tu^{55} + $lət^{35}$ → $tu^{55}lət^{35}$
      all   all   all

The words in (44) are generally made up of one part which is native to Dong and one part assimilated from Chinese. In group A, the morphemes which are native to Dong can stand on their own and have basically the same meaning and use as the combined words; while the components borrowed from Chinese generally cannot stand on their own as words. Group A combined words are compound words. The components of the combined words in group B can all stand on their own, with meaning and use basically equivalent to the combined words. Group B combined words are phrases.

Another class of same-category combined words arises from two components with OPPOSITE meanings standing side by side. The meaning of the combined words is extrapolated from the meanings of the component parts, as in (45).

(45) jɐm⁵⁵ + lin⁵³ → jɐm⁵⁵lin⁵³
      deep   shallow   depth

      phaŋ³⁵ + thɐm⁴⁵³ → phaŋ³⁵thɐm⁴⁵³
      tall   short   height

      ʈhɐn³⁵ + ʈha¹³ → ʈhɐn³⁵ʈha¹³
      heavy   light   weight

Other morphemes can be inserted between the component parts of these combined words.

(46) tau⁵⁵   nən²¹²   ta³³   sən⁵⁵   ʔɐi³²³   wo³¹   jɐm⁵⁵   ɕi³³
      1p^inc   person   cross village not   know   deep   or

      lin⁵³
      shallow

We who are from another village do not know whether people here are good or bad (words from the Dong opera *Qín Niángméi* (秦娘梅)).

It is clear that the component parts in this group of combined words are not that closely bound together and that each part can stand on its own as a word. Thus, in Dong, these are phrases and not compound words.

2. *Modification.* One content morpheme carries the main meaning, while another modifies it. The great majority of modification-type compound words are nouns; there are very few verbs or adjectives. There are three kinds, as listed below.

(a) Head-modifier. In these words the head appears first and the modifier follows. Four types are presented in (47)–(50).

(47) noun + noun → noun; the head is part of the modifier

      sən³¹   + lɐu⁵³ → sən³¹lɐu⁵³
      buttocks   snail   fingerprint

      ta⁵⁵   + tin⁵⁵ → ta⁵⁵tin⁵⁵
      eye   foot   anklebone

Lexicon

(48) noun + noun → noun; the modifier illustrates the form or use of the head

| cik^{13} | + | pa^{53} | → | $cik^{13}pa^{53}$ |
| ruler | | wing | | carpenter's square |

| $toŋ^{212}$ | + | pui^{55} | → | $toŋ^{212}pui^{55}$ |
| tube-shaped utensil | | fire | | pipe for blowing fire |

(49) noun + adjective → noun; the modifier illustrates the form of the head

| $mən^{55}$ | + | $kwaŋ^{55}$ | → | $mən^{55}kwaŋ^{55}$ |
| sky | | light | | this world |

| $toŋ^{53}$ | + | pak^{31} | → | $toŋ^{53}pak^{31}$ |
| jelly | | white | | dysentery with white mucous stool |

(50) noun + verb → noun; the modifier illustrates the way in which the head is used

| $kwaŋ^{55}$ | + | $sət^{55}$ | → | $kwaŋ^{55}sət^{55}$ |
| rice straw | | sweep | | broom |

| $ŋwa^{35}$ | + | $tɐn^{55}$ | → | $ŋwa^{35}tɐn^{55}$ |
| dog | | look for | | hunting dog |

In Dong, there are many words composed of two nouns or a noun plus an adjective. Those which do not undergo any extension or change in meaning after combination are considered phrases, exemplified in (51).

(51)

| pa^{53} | + | ma^{55} | → | $pa^{53}ma^{55}$ |
| leaf | | vegetable | | cabbage leaves |

| $nɐm^{31}$ | + | $ɲa^{55}$ | → | $nɐm^{31}ɲa^{55}$ |
| water | | river | | river water |

| jan^{212} | + | $ŋwe^{31}$ | → | $jan^{212}ŋwe^{31}$ |
| house | | tile | | tile-roofed house |

| mak^{31} | + | man^{13} | → | $mak^{31}man^{13}$ |
| soil | | yellow | | loess |

In the noun + verb combination, if the modifier is illustrating how the head is used, if the adverbs mi^{31} 'have not' or kwe^{212} 'not' can be inserted in between the two, and if the auxiliary $jaŋ^{31}$ (corresponding to the Chinese 了 *le*) can be added after the second part, then the combination is a phrase, rather than a compound word, as in (52).

(52) pa^{55} + $ɕik^{323}$ → $pa^{55}ɕik^{323}$
fish   roast   roasted fish

nan^{31} + $ɕaŋ^{31}$ → $nan^{31}ɕaŋ^{31}$
meat   cure (v)   bacon

mok^{21} + $pən^{323}$ → $mok^{21}pən^{323}$
bird   fly   (flying) bird

(b) Modifier-head. The modification-type compound words listed above are all of the type in which the head appears first and the modifier follows. There are also some modification-type compound words with the reverse order. These words include at least one part which is borrowed from Chinese, and among the borrowed parts there is very often one part which is unable to stand as a word on its own in Dong. For example, the heads in the five disyllabic words in (53) are all Chinese loan words, and none of them can stand alone as a Dong word.

(53) $toŋ^{212}$ + $ljiŋ^{212}$ → $toŋ^{212}ljiŋ^{212}$
copper   bell   copper bell

$toŋ^{212}$ + la^{212} → $toŋ^{212}la^{212}$
copper   gong   copper gong

$ljoŋ^{212}$ + $waŋ^{212}$ → $ljoŋ^{212}waŋ^{212}$
dragon   king   Dragon King

$ʔɐŋ^{55}$ + $tɐu^{212}$ → $ʔɐŋ^{55}tɐu^{212}$
ape   leader   king of the apes

nam^{212} + $waŋ^{35}$ → $nam^{212}waŋ^{35}$
south   direction   the south

(c) Generic-specific. The great majority of Dong animal and plant names are expressed using the generic-specific form, as in (54), where the specific components do not have independent meanings.

Lexicon

(54) ma^{55} → $ma^{55}\text{ʔ}u^{33}$
vegetable   a kind of vegetable—苦麻菜 kǔ má cài

to^{33} → $to^{33}soŋ^{212}$
bean   soya bean

mok^{21} → $mok^{21}si^{212}$
bird   egret

no^{13} → $no^{13}nən^{13}$
mouse   squirrel

Generic-specific names, however, are not necessarily compound words. Some have specific name components which are free to combine independently with other words; for example, $phak^{13}$ 'China fir' and $mjɐi^{31}$ 'carp' in (55).

(55) $mɐi^{31}$ $phak^{13}$ mja^{212} $phak^{13}$
      tree   China^fir   plant (v)   China^fir
      China fir (tree)   plant China fir

      lak^{31} $phak^{13}$ ja^{212} $ʔoŋ^{55}$ $phak^{13}$
      child   China^fir   two   CLF   China^fir
      China fir seedling   two China fir trees

      pa^{55} $mjɐi^{31}$ $soŋ^{453}$ $mjɐi^{31}$
      fish   carp   put^out^to^breed   carp
      carp   breed carp

      $mjɐi^{31}$ ja^{453} lak^{31} $mjɐi^{31}$
      carp   red   child   carp
      red carp   carp fry

      ja^{212} tu^{212} $mjɐi^{31}$
      two   CLF   carp
      two carp

The examples in (55) show that the specific names $phak^{13}$ and $mjɐi^{31}$ possess independent meaning and are the smallest language units that can be freely put to use—words. They can combine with generic names to make phrases.

Many time words also take the generic-specific form, as in (56).

(56)   mɐn⁵⁵   mɐn⁵⁵ȵuŋ⁵⁵   mɐn⁵⁵mu³²³
        day   yesterday   tomorrow

        ȵin²¹²   ȵin²¹²pe⁵⁵   ȵin²¹²sa²¹²
        year   last^year   next^year

The specific parts for the time words usually cannot stand alone as words. A few from old poems and songs can be used alone, but these can only be viewed as exceptions to the rule. Moreover, when used in this way their meaning is not completely the same as that in the time words.

(57)   mɐn⁵⁵mu³²³   mu³²³   jau²¹²   sɐi⁴⁵³   ma³⁵   ləp²¹   na²¹²
        tomorrow   later   1s   again   come   tell   2s
        tomorrow   I'll tell you again later.

        mɐn⁵⁵ȵuŋ⁵⁵   li³¹   ȵuŋ⁵⁵
        yesterday   word   old
        yesterday   old words

3. *Predicate-complement.* Two content morphemes combine to form a word, with one morpheme as the main word and the other complementing it. The first and main morpheme expresses some kind of action. Each morpheme can stand on its own as a word, but the structure of the combined word is fixed, and nothing can be inserted between the components. We can view these combined words as compound words. In Dong, there are relatively few predicate-complement type compound words. Some examples are given in (58)–(61).

(58)   verb + verb → verb

        tɐm³²³   +   tak³²³   →   tɐm³²³tak³²³
        weave   hammer (v)   weave

        we³¹   +   mɐŋ³¹   →   we³¹mɐŋ³¹
        do   gladden   play

(59)   verb + adjective → verb

        ʨi⁵⁵   +   wo³⁵   →   ʨi⁵⁵wo³⁵
        eat   clean (adj)   abstain from eating meat

        we³¹   +   kwa³²³   →   we³¹kwa³²³
        do   hard   stand firm

Lexicon

(60) verb + noun → verb

ɕoŋ⁵⁵	+	kha³⁵	→	ɕoŋ⁵⁵kha³⁵
fill		ear		listen

pha⁴⁵³	+	loŋ²¹²	→	pha⁴⁵³loŋ²¹²
break		belly		have diarrhea

sa⁵³	+	jen⁵⁵	→	sa⁵³jen⁵⁵
rest		cigarette		rest with a cigarette

tɐi⁵⁵	+	khwau¹³	→	tɐi⁵⁵khwau¹³
die		alcohol		get drunk

tɐi⁵⁵	+	nɐm³¹	→	tɐi⁵⁵nɐm³¹
die		water		drown

tɐi⁵⁵	+	ɕaŋ³⁵	→	tɐi⁵⁵ɕaŋ³⁵
die		gun-wound		die an unseemly death

(61) adjective + noun → adjective

ma³²³	+	lak³²³	→	ma³²³lak³²³
soft		bone		weary, weak

ɕeŋ⁵³	+	wen⁵³	→	ɕeŋ⁵³wen⁵³
expanded		fish lungs		arrogant

Dong also has many phrases made up of verbs and complementary adjectives.

(62)

nu⁵³	+	tha¹³	→	nu⁵³tha¹³
look		light		underestimate

wa³³	+	ljok⁵⁵	→	wa³³ ljok⁵⁵
speak		opaque		talk too much

sət⁵⁵	+	sin³⁵	→	sət⁵⁵ sin³⁵
sweep		clean		sweep clean

we³¹	+	lai⁵⁵	→	we³¹ lai⁵⁵
do		good		do well

With the phrases in (62), we can always insert an object, or the auxiliary word li^{323}, between the two words leading, for example, to the phrases in (63).

(63) nu^{53} mau^{33} tha^{13}
look 3s light
underestimate him

wa^{33} $suŋ^{35}$ $ljok^{55}$
speak word opaque
talk too much

$sət^{55}$ li^{323} sin^{35}
sweep PTC clean
sweep clean

we^{31} li^{323} lai^{55}
do PTC good
do well

Affixational compounds. These are composed of a content morpheme which expresses the main meaning and a function morpheme expressing an additional meaning. There are two kinds: prefix and suffix.

1. *Prefix.* Three examples are given.

(a) The word lak^{31} in the words in (64) means 'young' or 'immature'. In these words, lak^{31} refers to a person. If lak^{31} is left out, the remaining content morpheme can stand on its own, without any change in meaning.

(64) **lak^{31}** **$mjek^{323}$**
young female
girl

lak^{31} **pei^{31}**
young girl
young lady

lak^{31} **pan^{55}**
young male
boy

lak^{31} **han^{453}**
young fellow
young fellow

In the words in (65), *lak³¹* means 'small'. It cannot be omitted.

(65) **lak³¹**　　**mui³³**
　　　small　　girl's^name
　　　silkworm

　　　lak³¹　　**lau⁵⁵**
　　　small　　bee
　　　bee pupa

　　　lak³¹　　**lin²¹²**
　　　small　　kind^of^fish
　　　small 'lin' fish

　　　lak³¹　　**pje²¹²**
　　　small　　loquat
　　　loquat (a fruit)

(b) The word *ʔeŋ⁵⁵* means 'earlier' or 'later'. It is used before time words and intensifies their meaning.

(66) hət³⁵　　　　　ʔeŋ⁵⁵hət³⁵
　　　morning　　　　early morning

　　　tan⁵⁵　　　　　ʔeŋ⁵⁵tan⁵⁵
　　　night　　　　　deep in the night

(c) The word *ʔi⁵⁵* is a prefix added before demonstrative pronouns to indicate the manner of some action; yet it is also frequently omitted.

(67) nai³³　　　　　ʔi⁵⁵nai³³
　　　this　　　　　 like this

　　　ta⁵³　　　　　 ʔi⁵⁵ta⁵³
　　　that　　　　　 like that

　　　nu³⁵　　　　　 ʔi⁵⁵nu³⁵
　　　which, what　　how?

2. *Suffix.* After adjectives, monosyllabic function morphemes or reduplicated function morphemes may be added to convey a different feeling. These function morphemes do not have independent meanings. Examples are given in (68).

(68)   *ma³²³*   *ma³²³ɕa³²³*   or   *ma³²³məp⁵⁵*
       soft   weak   lithe

         ja⁴⁵³   *ja⁴⁵³ljen¹³*   or   *ja⁴⁵³ɕe⁵³ɕe⁵³*
         red   light (ugly) red   bright red

         təŋ⁵³   *təŋ⁵³təp⁵⁵*   or   *təŋ⁵³tum⁵⁵*
         dark   pitch-dark   very dark (but can still see)

Post-adjective function morphemes cannot be preposed and cannot have objects between them and the adjectives.

(69)   *təŋ⁵³*   *təp⁵⁵təp⁵⁵*
        dark   completely
        pitch-dark

        jan²¹²   *təŋ⁵³*   *təp⁵⁵təp⁵⁵*
        house   dark   completely
        Inside the house is pitch-dark.

        *təŋ⁵³   *jan²¹²*   *təp⁵⁵təp⁵⁵*
        dark   house   completely

        *təp⁵⁵təp⁵⁵   *jan²¹²*   *təŋ⁵³*
        completely   house   dark

Post-adjective function words are different from sound descriptive words (cf. §4.1.8) occurring after verbs. Such sound descriptive words can also be preposed. When postposed, an object can be inserted between them and the verbs.

(70)   *ɕo⁴⁵³ɕo⁴⁵³*   *tok⁵⁵*   *pjən⁵⁵*
        continuously   fall   rain
        continuously raining

        tok⁵⁵   *ɕo⁴⁵³ɕo⁴⁵³*
        fall   continuously
        fall continuously

        tok⁵⁵   *pjən⁵⁵*   *ɕo⁴⁵³ɕo⁴⁵³*
        fall   rain   continuously
        raining continuously

Lexicon

3.3 Homophones, polysemic words, and synonyms

Homophones. In Dong there are very many homophones: words having the same sound but meanings which are not related. Some examples are given in (71).

(71)
ʔak³²³	rafter	competent	extremely	oneself
ʔau⁵⁵	want	machine-part for weaving	bird food	take (v)
paŋ⁵⁵	sew	rice straw	help (v)	
mɐi³¹	tree	classifier for clothes, etc.	female	each
ta⁵⁵	eye	maternal grandfather	stick in	

There are fewer than 3,000 syllables in Dong, taking tones into account, but the number of words greatly exceeds the number of syllables. Indeed, vocabulary is increasing without limits and the language cannot but use one syllable for many different meanings. Homophones have emerged for a variety of reasons, including merging of different pronunciations, disintegration of polysemic words, and assimilation of loan words.

In Zhānglǔ (章鲁) Dong, the words for 'a kind of reed pipe wind instrument' (芦笙 *lú shēng*) and 'a long bamboo pipe for channelling water' (水笕 *shuǐjiàn*) are homophones, pronounced *len²¹²*. In the Guàndòng (贯洞) lect, however, these two words are pronounced differently: *lun¹²* and *lin¹²*, respectively. In Zhānglǔ and in the great majority of other places, the Dong words for 'eye' and 'maternal grandfather' are homophones, pronounced *ta⁵⁵*. In the sister Shuǐ (水) language, however, 'eye' is pronounced *da¹³* and '(maternal) grandfather' is pronounced *ta¹³*. It is likely that many homophones in Dong originally had different pronunciations, but pronunciations have merged.

The word *ta⁵⁵* in *ta⁵⁵* 'eye' and *ta⁵⁵tin⁵⁵* 'anklebone' seems as though it is homophonic in these two words, as does *ʔiu³²³* in *ʔiu³²³* 'plant stem' and *ma⁵⁵ʔiu³²³* 'a kind of vegetable' (蕨菜 *jué cài*): it seems that the meanings of the two words in each case are not related. On careful reflection, however, it is evident that the appearance of the anklebone resembles an eye, and the shape of *jué cài* is like the stem of a plant. Thus, it is likely that the two words *ta⁵⁵tin⁵⁵* and *ma⁵⁵ʔiu³²³* are extensions by association of the words *ta⁵⁵* and *ʔiu³²³*, respectively. The word *ƚu³²³* means a kind of bird, and *ʔe⁵⁵ƚu³²³* means the family wealth is meager. As far as the surface meaning is concerned, it seems that these two words are unconnected. But originally, *ʔe⁵⁵ƚu³²³* was derived from *ƚu³²³*. The bird is a kind that likes to eat unhusked rice. It is only once a year, at autumn harvest time, that the *ƚu³²³* is able to eat its fill. After the unhusked rice is harvested, its food is exhausted. People used this special characteristic of the *ƚu³²³* to describe a family's wealth as being very slight, unable to endure the cost of living. These various words have become homophones as a result of the disintegration of polysemic words.

The number of homophones is all the larger because of the assimilation of loan words from Chinese. Meanings from loan words in (72) are bolded.

(72) la^{212} **gong** (锣 *luó*)   **basket** (箩 *luó*)   mushroom
     taŋ^{212} **sugar** (糖 *táng*)   **main room** (堂 *táng*)   mound
     ɕe^{35} handspan   **society** (社 *shè*)   sand
     tau^{55}ɕən^{35} body tingles   **chide** (教训 *jiào xùn*)

Correct communication and understanding is frequently compromised by the many homophones. The context often forms the basis for differentiating between homophones, as in (73).

(73) teŋ^{212}tɐu^{31} heu^{35} kuŋ^{55} heu^{35} **la^{212}**   sip^{323} ɕau^{35} teŋ^{55}
     everyone   beat   drum   beat   **gong**   welcome   2p   come
     Everyone is beating drums and gongs to welcome you.

     jau^{212} la^{53} pɐn^{55} ma^{35} ɕau^{453} **la^{212}**
     1s   chop   bamboo   come   repair   **basket**
     I am chopping bamboo to repair the basket.

     mɐn^{55}nai^{33} tiu^{55} tha^{453} tən^{212} pai^{55} tan^{55} **la^{212}**
     today   1p   go^up   mountain   go   gather   **mushroom**
     Today we are going up the mountain to gather mushrooms.

When measure words are inserted, they can also distinguish between homophones, as in (74).

(74) ja^{212} **tu^{212}**   ʔa^{55}
     two   CLF   crow (n)
     two crows

     ja^{212} **mɐi^{31}**   ʔa^{55}
     two   CLF   song
     two songs

For certain homophones, you can also add affixes to differentiate, as in (75).

(75) **pan^{55}**   lak^{31} **pan^{55}**
     call^loudly   young   boy
     call loudly   boy

pau²¹²   *pau²¹²* *nɐm³¹*
pomelo   algae   water
pomelo   algae

Polysemic words. The many polysemic words in Dong evolved gradually. The extension of meaning of most words arose from association of similar characteristics among different things. For example, *tin⁵⁵* means 'foot'. Owing to its low position on the body, it came to mean the lower part of many different things, as illustrated in (76).

(76)   *tin⁵⁵*   *ɲa⁵⁵*   *tin⁵⁵*   *ʈən²¹²*
      foot   river   foot   mountain
      lower reaches (of a river)   foot of a mountain

      tin⁵⁵   *mən⁵⁵*   *tin⁵⁵*   *tuŋ³³*
      foot   sky   foot   pillar
      horizon   base of a pillar

      tin⁵⁵   *ta³²³*   *tin⁵⁵*   *ʔəp⁵⁵*
      foot   forest   foot   mouth
      bottom of a forest (on a hill)   lip

      tin⁵⁵   *je³⁵*
      foot   net
      bottom of a net

The meanings of various words were extended because of association with certain movements. For example, there is a broad range of contexts for using *to³²³* 'put, place' in Dong, with many extended meanings. It can be used to mean various actions such as put, pull, link, go down, apply, and so on.

(77)   *to³²³*   *ma⁵⁵*   *to³²³*   *ʔəm³²³*
      put   vegetable   put   medicine
      plant vegetables   treat with medicine

      to³²³   *so³³*   *to³²³*   *sai³²³*
      put   strength   put   intestines
      use one's strength   hope for

      to³²³   *mau²¹²*   *to³²³*   *khwau¹³*
      put   manure   put   alcohol
      spread manure   pour wine

to³²³	sən⁵⁵		to³²³	sin²¹²
put	village		put	money
enter a village			give money	

to³²³	se⁵⁵		to³²³	je³⁵
put	bird^trap		put	net
fix a bird trap			cast a net (fishing)	

Another illustration is the use of *tɐi⁵⁵* 'die' in (78).

(78) **tɐi⁵⁵** pui⁵⁵
die light (n)
turn off the light

tɐi⁵⁵ khwau¹³
die alcohol
be intoxicated

Although dying, turning off the light, and getting intoxicated are different actions, it can be seen how the second and third are derived from the first.

Meanings of some words are extended according to particular features of the things they indicate, as illustrated in (79).

(79) ʔin³⁵ arm bracelet
ʔin³⁵ʔuk³²³ sleeve (arm of clothing)
mjin²¹² cotton cloth
min³²³ grass used for making mats mat
nit¹³ cold malaria
lau³¹ old big old and big

The meanings of some words are extended from the concrete to the abstract, as in (80).

(80) lim²¹² + loŋ²¹² → lim²¹²loŋ²¹²
flat and straight belly feel relieved

jim⁴⁵³ + sai³²³ → jim⁴⁵³sai³²³
nice and cool intestines cheerful

khwan³⁵ + na³²³ → khwan³⁵na³²³
sweet face be all smiles

səm³⁵	+	phaŋ³⁵	→ səm³⁵phaŋ³⁵
heart		tall	greed, avarice

There are also a few ordinary words that have been derived from proper names. For example, the word *win*⁵⁵ in Róngjiāng's Chēzhài (榕江车寨) was the name of one of the forefathers; he was also known as *waŋ*²¹² *win*⁵⁵. This man was harsh and unreasonable in dealing with people, and everybody hated him. Later, the word *win*⁵⁵ was used to describe domineering behavior, as in (81).

(81) ta³³ʔun⁵³ ti³³waŋ³⁵ nai³³ son⁴⁵³ mau³³ we³¹ **win**⁵⁵
formerly place this calculate 3s do domineering
In the past, people here thought him to be domineering.

Some words came from extrapolation of a certain meaning, but in the process of time, the original meaning has been lost, and only the extended meaning remains. For example, the word *pak*³²³ comes from the word 'mouth'. (In the Zhuàng (壮) and Shuǐ (水) languages, from the same language family, the word for 'mouth' is still *pak*³⁵.) In modern Dong, however, the word can only be used to indicate quantity or position, not the mouths of people or animals. Some examples of modern usage are given in (82).

(82) ʔi⁵⁵ **pak**³²³ ʔɐu³¹
one mouth rice
a mouthful of rice

ʔi⁵⁵ **pak**³²³ suŋ³⁵
one mouth word
a sentence

pak³²³ to⁵⁵
mouth door
entrance

pak³²³ ɳa⁵⁵
mouth river
river mouth

Synonyms. Synonyms—words with different sounds but identical or similar meanings—are divided here into two groups: those whose meanings and use are identical and those which are slightly different in meaning and use.

In Dong, different words with identical meanings are quite rare. Following are two examples: $pu^{31}\textipa{?}un^{323}$, $pu^{31}\textipa{?}o^{53}$, and $pu^{31}nɐk^{55}$ all mean 'father's younger brother, uncle'; and $suŋ^{35}$ and li^{31} both mean 'word, remark'. These synonyms originated from different dialects of Dong.

There is a comparatively rich family of synonyms with slightly different uses and meanings. Although the main meanings of these words are identical, there are slight differences in their particular nuances, the scopes of their application, their collocation relationships, and so on. For example, consider the different shades of meaning of the synonyms of the word 'hit', presented in (83).

(83) heu^{35} hit (v)
      $peŋ^{53}$ use a gun or a stone to strike (with the meaning 'attack')
      $ŋweŋ^{453}$ abruptly strike with a cudgel
      $pheŋ^{35}$ use something to hit another thing
      tet^{323} hit very lightly
      $miŋ^{13}$ hit each other (playfully, two people)
      $tiŋ^{55}$ use fist to hit
      $ljik^{31}$ use hand to hit
      $miŋ^{453}$ hit a person, until finished
      $ŋwek^{13}$ hit a little (with knuckles)
      mek^{13} hit a little (usually with a stick, worse than $ŋwek^{13}$)
      $phek^{13}$ pat
      $teŋ^{55}$ slap on the ear
      sau^{55} beat up
      pek^{31} thresh unhusked rice
      $meŋ^{35}$ hit (children's word)
      pe^{323} bring along someone else to fight for you, or hit someone who does not hit back

The words in (84) express differences in properties.

(84) mim^{13} close together (no cracks, usually refers to doors, windows, or lids being closed very tightly)

      nim^{13} close together (no cracks, usually refers to wooden planks or partitions being set very tightly)

      nin^{13} close together (as in 'press things close together')

      $ŋim^{212}$ closed tight (e.g., pots for fermenting wine; also used to describe stale rice or *mán tou*, 馒头)

Lexicon

nit³²³   close together (used for tightly woven cloth)

Dong has many synonyms that can only be used in works of literature, improving the works' language and rhyme. See, for example, the Dong poem in (85).

(85)   *sam³⁵ mɐn⁵⁵ wa³³ ʔɐi³²³ piŋ³²³*
       sam³⁵ tan⁵⁵ ɕot¹³ ʔɐi³²³ ljeu³¹
       sam³⁵ mɐn⁵⁵ ʔaŋ³²³ ʔɐi³²³ wən³⁵
       sam³⁵ ɲin²¹² ləp²¹ ʔɐi³²³ ljeu³¹

   three days is not long enough to finish **speaking**
   three days is not long enough to finish **explaining**
   three days cannot exhaust the **talking**
   three years cannot exhaust the **telling**

Many of the synonyms which are used only in poems and songs are absorbed from Chinese. Some examples are given in (86).

(86)   Native Dong   Loan word   Chinese

       nɐm³¹ta⁵⁵   *ŋen³¹ljui³³*   眼泪 yǎn lèi   tears
       mɐn⁵⁵   *thin³⁵*   天 tiān   day
       tɐm⁵⁵ja⁵³   *tin²¹²taŋ²¹²*   田塘 tián táng   pond in field
       lak³¹   *ɲi²¹²si³³*   儿子 ér zi   son

3.4 Cognate words

Cognate words among the Dong dialects and lects. The Dong language has two dialects, southern and northern, each with various lects, but embedded in each area's basic vocabulary is a large number of mutually common cognate words. These words are the everyday-life words of the Dong people, words representing the most important things, actions, qualities, and ideas in their lives. They could be called the core part of Dong vocabulary. In (87), some cognate vocabulary is listed from the language of three places in Guìzhōu province: Chējiāng (车江) in Róngjiāng (榕江) County (the first lect of the southern dialect), Shuǐkǒu (水口) in Lípíng (黎平) County (the second lect of the southern dialect), and Shídòng (石洞) in Tiānzhù (天柱) County (the first lect of the northern dialect). The words are selected from names of things commonly seen in the natural world, names of human body parts, animal and plant names, the most commonly encountered action words, and typical properties of things. A more extensive list is given in appendix 3.

(87) Chējiāng   Shuǐkǒu   Shídòng   Chinese
      southern, 1   southern, 2   northern, 1

      mən⁵⁵   mən⁴⁴   mən³⁵   天 tiān   sky
      kau³²³   kau³⁵   kau³³   头 tóu   head
      məm³¹   məm¹¹   məm³¹   虎 hǔ   tiger
      ṭham¹³   ṭham³⁵   ṭam¹³   走 zǒu   walk
      phaŋ³⁵   phaŋ⁴⁴   paŋ¹¹   高 gāo   tall

Cognate words among languages of the Dòng–Tái family. Each language of the Dòng–Tái family (cf. §1.3) has undergone its own respective growth since the breaking up of the original 'Dòng–Tái' language. Although the languages have diverged, they still preserve a high proportion of cognate words. A sample is given in (88); a longer list, also including Máonán (毛难) words from the Dòng–Shuǐ branch and Bùyī (布依) words from the Tái branch, is given in appendix 3.

(88) Dòng   Shuǐ   Mùlǎo   Zhuàng   Dǎi   Lí
      侗   水   仫佬   壮   傣   黎

      nɐm³¹   nɐm³³   nəm²⁴   ɣɐm⁴²   nɐm¹¹   nɐm¹¹   water
      pjɐn⁵⁵   vjɐn³¹   fɐn⁴²   fɐn²¹   fɐn⁵¹   fɐn⁵³   tooth
      me⁵⁵   ʔmi¹³   mɛ⁴²   mui²⁴   mi⁵⁵   mui⁵³   bear (n)
      lam²¹²   lam³¹   lam¹²¹   lŭm²¹   lum⁵¹   lum⁵⁵   forget
      na⁵⁵   ʔna¹³   na⁴²   na²⁴   na⁵⁵   na⁵³   thick

Dòng, Shuǐ, and Mùlǎo all belong to the Dòng–Shuǐ language branch. The number of cognate words within this group is greater than for languages from different branches of the same language family. See (89) for some examples, including Zhuàng and Dǎi words from the Tái branch, and Lí words from the Lí branch; see appendix 3 for a more extensive list, including Máonán words and Bùyī words.

(89) Dòng   Shuǐ   Mùlǎo   Zhuàng   Dǎi   Lí
      侗   水   仫佬   壮   傣   黎

      loŋ²¹²   loŋ³¹   lŏŋ¹²¹   tuŋ⁴²   tɔŋ¹¹   pok⁵⁵   belly
      ma²¹²   ma³¹   ma¹²¹   lĭn⁴²   lĭn¹¹   ṭin¹¹   tongue
      mun³³   mon⁵⁵   mun¹¹   lĭŋ²¹   liŋ⁵¹   nok⁵⁵   monkey
      ja²¹²   ya³¹   ya¹²¹   soŋ²⁴   sɔŋ⁵⁵   ṭău¹¹   two
      sui⁵³   hui³¹   tui¹¹   năŋ³³   năŋ³³   tsoŋ¹¹   sit

3.5 Loan words

For many generations, Dong people have been living together with people from sister nationalities: Hàn, Miáo, Yáo, Shuǐ, Zhuàng, and others. The Dong assimilated aspects of the Hàn people's systems of government, economics, and education, and in the process borrowed many words from Chinese. Some words were also borrowed from other minority languages, but relatively few compared with loan words from Chinese.

For centuries Dong has been continually absorbing words from Chinese. By and large, these loan words can be divided into two large classes: Ancient and Modern loans. There are fairly clear differences in pronunciation between the two classes (for details, see §2.5). From the point of view of vocabulary, each also has its own distinctive points. Ancient loans are practically all monosyllabic. They have usually adapted to the patterns of word-formation in Dong and can be used in deriving new words. Most Modern Chinese loans are polysyllabic and usually cannot be used in deriving new words. The great majority of the Modern loan syllables cannot be analyzed as Dong syllables, but their use is extremely widespread and frequent. Ancient loan words relate more to everyday life; Modern loans relate more to government, economics, education, and scientific techniques.

Structural types of Chinese loan words in Dong. There are four basic types.

Direct transliteration. Both Chinese pronunciation and word order are accepted. Two examples are given in (90).

(90) $koŋ^{55}$ $than^{31}$ $taŋ^{31}$
gòng chǎn dǎng (共产党)
the Communist Party

to^{33} hu^{33}
dòu fu (豆腐)
tofu

Borrowed with Dong word order. Chinese loan morphemes are used in a word-formation pattern which is characteristic of Dong, not Chinese, to generate compound words. Usually the loan morphemes are Ancient loans, as in (91).

(91) hai^{212} pi^{212}
shoe leather
leather shoes (cf. 皮鞋 pí xié)

ʔan⁵⁵   ma³¹
saddle horse
saddle (cf. 马鞍 *mǎ ān*)

Borrowed with Dong prefix. A transliterated loan word is used as a special term, with a Dong morpheme prefixed as a generic term. This generates a 'generic-specific' modification type composite compound word (cf. §3.2).

(92) ma⁵⁵   po³³tshai³⁵
      vegetable   spinach
      spinach (cf. 菠菜 *bō cài*)

      mak³¹   hu²¹²ɲi²¹²
      soil   silt
      silt (cf. 淤泥 *yū ní*)

Hybrids of Chinese and Dong. One loan morpheme plus one Dong morpheme are put together in a Dong word-formation pattern to generate a compound word. For example:

(93) nɐm³¹   mɐk²¹
      water   black
      ink (cf. 墨水 *mò shuǐ*)

      pən²¹²   mɐi³¹
      basin   wood
      wooden basin (cf. 木盆 *mù pén*)

Use of Chinese loan words in Dong. Generally, the following four phenomena exist.

Simultaneous use of native Dong words and Modern Chinese loans. When new ideas arise in society, the transliterated Chinese is immediately introduced, but expressions using native Dong phonemes and structure are also used. These two different approaches increase vocabulary and lead to new synonyms. Two examples are given in (94).

(94) ɲən²¹²   sak³²³   ja⁵³   noŋ²¹²mjən²¹²
      person   plant (v) land   peasant
      peasant   peasant (cf. 农民 *nóng mín*)

Lexicon   75

    lit³¹   *loŋ²¹²*   *than³¹pe²¹²*
    take^apart belly   honest
    honest   honest (cf. 坦白 *tǎn bái*)

Simultaneous use of native Dong words and Ancient Chinese loans. In this case, the two words are different in either meaning or usage. Four examples are given in (95).

(95)   Native Dong   Ancient Chinese loan

        ʔi⁵⁵   *ʔet⁵⁵*
        one   one

        ja²¹²   *ɲi³³*
        two   two

        ʔit³²³   *pjiŋ³³*
        be slightly ill   have a disease

        ɲa⁵⁵   *ʔaŋ⁵⁵ha²¹²*
        river   river (used in poems and songs)

Simultaneous use of Ancient Chinese loans and Modern Chinese loans. Modern Chinese loan words are often used to express contemporary new meaning. Four examples are given in (96).

(96)   Ancient Chinese loan   Modern Chinese loan

        we³¹ʔoŋ⁵⁵   *lau³¹toŋ⁵⁵*
        labor (v, cf. 做工 *zuò gōng*)   labor (v, cf. 劳动 *láo dòng*)

        ɲən²¹²mjek³²³   *fu³⁵ɲui³¹*
        woman (cf. 女人 *nǔ rén*)   woman (cf. 妇女 *fù nǚ*)

        ʔa⁵⁵   *ko³³*
        folk song (cf. 歌 *gē*)   modern song (cf. 歌 *gē*)

        kwak⁵⁵   *kwe²¹²*
        country, state (cf. 国家 *guó jiā*) country, state (cf. 国 *guó*)

Replacement of native Dong words by Chinese loan words. When Chinese loan words are introduced, Dong words are less used, and some are eventually abandoned. This phenomenon can be detected by comparing

Dong with other languages from the same language family. Some examples are given in (97).

(97)
	Dòng 侗	Shuǐ 水	Zhuàng 壮	Dǎi 傣	Lí 黎	Chinese	
	pi^{212}	pi^{31}	$năŋ^{24}$	$năŋ^{51}$	$ŋoŋ^{53}$	皮肤 *pí fū*	skin
	$çai^{33}$	ban^{33}	ban^{55}	ban^{13}	bou^{11}	寨子 *zhài zi*	village
	$ɲin^{212}$	$^{m}be^{13}$	pi^{24}	pi^{55}	pou^{55}	年 *nián*	year
	$ʑui^{323}$	$maŋ^{13}$	$faŋ^{21}$	phi^{55}	$tiŋ^{55}$	鬼 *guǐ*	ghost

4

Grammar

4.1 Lexical categories

Dong is an analytical language. It has no standard morphology that can be used to differentiate lexical categories. Thus, differentiation can only be according to special structural features of words, their compatability with other words, and their syntactic functions. Since grammatical features of lexical categories seem to overlap so much, we can only furnish a rough classification here according to the main grammatical features of each lexical category.

Dong words divide into two general classes: content words and function words. Content words have semantic meaning, while function words have only grammatical meaning.

Content words include nouns, classifiers, numerals, pronouns, verbs, adjectives, adverbs, and sound descriptive words. Nominals (nouns, classifiers, numerals, or pronouns) form one subgroup, and predicative words (verbs or adjectives) form another. The main role of nominals is to serve as subjects or objects, not predicates. The main role of predicative words is to serve as predicates, not subjects or objects.

Function words include prepositions, conjunctions, auxiliary words, and interjections.

The main features of each lexical category are given in §§4.1.1–4.1.12.

4.1.1 Nouns

Dong nouns can be divided into five classes: common nouns, time nouns, place nouns, locative nouns, and proper nouns.

Common nouns. These are nouns that indicate everyday things. Some examples are presented in (98).

(98) mən⁵⁵   ma³²³
      sky   cloud

      ɲa⁵⁵   lo⁵⁵
      river   boat

      mɐi³¹   ma⁵⁵
      tree   vegetable

      ȶən²¹²   ʔɐu³¹
      mountain   rice

      le²¹²   pau²¹²
      book   algae

      ŋwət²¹   ɲon²¹²
      loach   story

      jan²¹²
      house

Common nouns are modified by numeral phrases. When expressing quantities, common nouns are usually modified by numeral phrases, with numeral plus classifier, placed before the nouns. They cannot directly take numerals as modifiers—exceptions to this are some nouns that can themselves be used as classifiers, and some kinship terms.

(99) ʔi⁵⁵   pən³²³   le²¹²   si⁴⁵³   ȶiu²¹²   mɐi³¹
      one   CLF   book   four   CLF   tree
      one book   four trees

      ŋo³¹   ɲin²¹²   ljok²¹ ɲan⁵⁵
      five   year   six   month
      five years   six months

      ʔi⁵⁵   ɕoŋ²¹²   pet³²³ jan²¹²
      one   point   eight   house
      one o'clock   eight houses

Grammar 79

>   *ja²¹² noŋ³¹*   *sam³⁵ pu³¹*
>   two   younger^brother   three   father
>   two younger brothers   three men of father's generation

When talking about numbers of relatives, the northern and southern dialects differ. In the northern dialect, a classifier is inserted between the numeral and the kinship term to make up a numeral phrase. The example in (100) is from the Dong spoken in Tiānzhù Shídòng (天柱石洞).

(100) *sam¹¹ pu³⁵ ko³³   ja²²   pu³⁵ noŋ³¹*
       three   CLF   older^brother two   CLF   younger^brother
       three older brothers and two younger brothers

Nouns are normally not modified by adverbs. The negative adverb *kwe²¹²* 'not', however, can modify nouns.

(101) *jau²¹² kwe²¹² sin²¹²*
       1s   not   money
       I don't have any money.

>   *kwe²¹² ma⁵⁵   ţi⁵⁵*
>   not   dish   eat
>   There is no food to eat.

>   *ma⁵⁵ nai³³ kwe²¹² jim²¹²*
>   dish   this   not   salt
>   This dish has no salt.

The negative adverb usually has the form *kwe²¹² li³²³* 'do not have' in Zhānglǔ (章鲁) and *kwe²² me²²* 'do not have' in Shídòng. The phenomenon whereby *kwe²¹²* can modify nouns can be viewed as the omission of the words *li³²³* or *me²²* after *kwe²¹²*. Or alternatively, *kwe²¹²* can be thought of as having dual properties: when it modifies nouns, it is like a verb; and when it modifies verbs or adjectives, it is like an adverb (cf. §4.1.7).

Common nouns cannot reduplicate, except in the following situations
1. Monosyllabic nouns which are used like classifiers can reduplicate. After reduplication of 'A', the meaning becomes 'all the As'.

(102) *ţən²¹²   ţən²¹²   tu⁵⁵   li³²³   mɐi³¹*
       mountain   mountain all   have   tree
       All the mountains have trees.

*jan*²¹²	*jan*²¹²	*li*³²³	*nən*²¹²	*tok*²¹	*le*²¹²
house	house	have	person	read	book

All the homes have people who attend school.

*ʔe*⁵⁵	*ʔe*⁵⁵	*tu*⁵⁵	*li*³²³	*ʔɐu*³¹	*ɬi*⁵⁵
household	household	all	have	rice	eat

All the households have enough food to eat.

2. Two monosyllabic nouns A and B from the same class of things can reduplicate for emphasis as AABB, indicating large numbers of the things designated.

(103)
*ʔai*⁵³	*ʔai*⁵³	*pət*⁵⁵	*pət*⁵⁵	*tik*³²³	*jan*²¹²
chicken	chicken	duck	duck	fill	house

The shed is full of chickens and ducks.

The monosyllabic noun A can likewise reduplicate as AA, with the meaning 'much A' or 'many As'.

(104)
*ʔɐu*³¹	*ʔɐu*³¹	*tik*³²³	*so*³¹
rice	rice	fill	barn

The barn is full up with rice.

*mɐi*³¹	*mɐi*³¹	*tik*³²³	*tən*²¹²
tree	tree	fill	mountain

The mountain is full of trees.

After reduplication, nouns in the northern dialect can still modify other nouns, expressing the meaning 'covered in'.

(105)
*zən*¹¹	*kau*³³	*ʔən*³³	*ʔən*³³
CLF	head	soil	soil

whole head is covered in soil

*tau*⁴⁴	*mja*²²	*ju*²²	*ju*²²
pair	hand	oil	oil

both hands are covered in oil

*za*²²	*na*³³	*muʔ*³¹	*muʔ*³¹
CLF	face	nasal^mucus	nasal^mucus

whole face is covered in nasal mucus

ʐoŋ²² ʔo²² t̪ai⁵⁵ t̪ai⁵⁵
CLF neck sweaty^dirt sweaty^dirt
whole neck is covered in sweaty dirt

wən²² ɕən¹¹ tat¹³ tat¹³
all^over body blood blood
whole body is covered in blood

In the northern dialect, the words *kau³¹* 'father', *nəi³¹* 'mother', and *ʔun³³* 'child' can all reduplicate. When they do, their meanings change: *kau³¹kau³¹* means 'old man', *nəi³¹nəi³¹* means 'woman', and *ʔun³³ʔun³³* means 'child-like'.

Dong nouns do not have distinct singular and plural forms. When expressing the plural, the word *mɐn⁵³* 'some' can be added before the noun. The northern dialect equivalent of *mɐn⁵³* is *loi³⁵* or *ləu³¹*.

(106)   Southern   Northern

mɐn⁵³ ŋən²¹²   loi³⁵ jən²²   some people
mɐn⁵³ khwa⁴⁵³   ləu³¹ ho²⁵   some goods

Simple animal names in Tiānzhù Shídòng speech must all be preceded by the classifier *to²²* (equivalent to the Chinese 个 *ge*). Here, *to²²* can be viewed as an affix.

(107) *to²²ljai¹³*   *to²²ʔai⁵⁵*
       sparrow   chicken

       to²²pət⁵⁵   *to²²lei²⁵*
       duck   monkey

       to²²lai⁵⁵   *to²²ta³⁵*
       wild boar   fish

       to²²məm³¹   *to²²to²²*
       tiger   ox

Some nouns in some northern dialect areas are subject to phonetic change. Under the conditions indicated in (108) and (109) (which use Tiānzhù Shídòng speech), syllable initials change to fricatives or approximants at the same place of articulation.

(108) Nouns combine to form compound words, the second morpheme changes

noŋ³¹   →   *tai³¹zoŋ³¹*
younger brother   brothers (older brother/younger brother)

pən³⁵   →   *kau³³wən³⁵*
day   midday (head/day)

sa¹¹   →   *pha¹¹ʐa¹¹*
shoulder   shoulder (upper arm/shoulder)

naŋ³⁵   →   *na³³ʐaŋ³⁵*
nose   facial features (face/nose)

(109) Nouns change and function as verbs

ɕoŋ⁵⁵   →   *təi²² ɕoŋ⁵⁵ joŋ²⁵ pai³⁵*
gun   take   gun   shoot   go
                 Take the gun and shoot (it).

pjet³⁵   →   *təi²² pjet³⁵ wjet³⁵ pai³⁵*
whip   take   whip (n) whip (v) go
                 Take the whip and slash (it).

tin³⁵   →   *nəm³⁵ tin³⁵ jin³⁵ pai³⁵*
stone   grasp   stone bash   go
                 Take the stone and bash (it).

kwan³⁵   →   *təi²² kwan³⁵ wan³⁵ pai³⁵*
ax   take   ax   chop   go
                 Take the ax and chop (it).

ʔan²²   →   *təi²² ʔan²²   yan²²   pai³⁵*
shoulder pole   take   shoulder^pole carry   go
                 Take the shoulder pole and carry (the load).

Certain words also change tones. For example, *ɕoŋ⁵⁵* 'gun' in (109) changes to *joŋ²⁵* 'shoot', the Quán Yīn tone 5 changing to Cì Yīn tone 5'.

Time nouns. Examples of time nouns are given in (110).

(110) ɲin²¹²   ɲin²¹²sa²¹²
       year   next year

       ɲin²¹²pe⁵⁵   ɲin²¹²nai³³
       last year   this year

       ɲan⁵⁵   mɐn⁵⁵
       month   day

       mɐn⁵⁵mu³²³   ɕi²¹²
       tomorrow   hour

       hət³⁵   ɲɐm⁵³
       morning   evening

Time nouns do not take adverbs or classifiers as modifiers. Monosyllabic time nouns can be used like classifiers, can reduplicate, and can also be directly modified by numerals. Compound time nouns cannot be used like classifiers, do not reduplicate, and very rarely take modification.

(111) tok²¹   sam³⁵   ɲin²¹²   le²¹²
       read   three   year   book
       study for three years

       mɐn⁵⁵   mɐn⁵⁵   li³²³   mɐn⁵⁵mu³²³
       day   day   have   tomorrow

       ɲin²¹²   ɲin²¹²   li³²³   ɲin²¹²sa²¹²
       year   year   have   nextˆyear
       Every day has a tomorrow, every year has a next year.

       sak³²³   ja²¹²   ɲin²¹²   ja⁵³
       plant   two   year   field
       work the land for two years

In most situations, monosyllabic time nouns can only be integrated in a sentence after combining to give compound words or phrases

(112) kau³²³   hət³⁵   pai⁵⁵   ʈən²¹²   ʔau⁵⁵   ʈət⁵⁵
       head   morning go   mountain take   firewood
       go to the mountain in the morning to collect firewood

ɲin²¹² ta⁵⁵ ɲa²¹² nɐŋ⁵⁵ ʔun³²³
year that 2s still small
That year you were still small.

mɐn⁵⁵ nai³³ mɐn⁵⁵ maŋ²¹²
day this day what
What day is today?

In Dong there are two words for 'month'. One is *ɲan⁵⁵* and comes from the word for 'moon'. The other is *ŋwet³¹* and is borrowed from the Chinese word for 'moon'. The word *ɲan⁵⁵* can be used to indicate the month of the year (according to the lunar calendar) and can also be used in counting months. Apart from a few fixed phrases—for example, *ɲin²¹² tɐŋ⁵⁵ ŋwet³¹ jai³²³*, literally 'year/long/month/long', meaning 'after a very long time'—the word *ŋwet³¹* can only be used to indicate the month of the year (according to the solar calendar). It cannot be used in counting months. In indicating the month of the year, *ɲan⁵⁵* is used according to Dong's own natural word order, while *ŋwet³¹* is used with Chinese word order.

(113) Lunar calendar   Solar calendar

ɲan⁵⁵ɕiŋ⁵⁵   ɕiŋ⁵⁵ŋwet³¹
first month   January

ɲan⁵⁵ɲi³³   ɲi³³ŋwet³¹
second month   February

ɲan⁵⁵sam³⁵   sam³⁵ŋwet³¹
third month   March

ɲan⁵⁵si⁴⁵³   si⁴⁵³ŋwet³¹
fourth month   April

ɲan⁵⁵tu³²³   tu³²³ŋwet³¹
ninth month   September

ɲan⁵⁵ɕət²¹/ɲan⁵⁵ɕəp²¹   ɕəp²¹ŋwet³¹
tenth month   October

ɲan⁵⁵ɕəp²¹ʔat⁵⁵   ɕəp²¹ʔat⁵⁵ŋwet³¹
eleventh month   November

Grammar   85

   ȵan⁵⁵ɕəp²¹ȵi³³   ɕəp²¹ȵi³³ŋwet³¹
   twelfth month   December

Other examples are presented in (114).

(114)   ȵan⁵⁵nai³³   ȵan⁵⁵toŋ⁵⁵
        this month   winter

        ȵan⁵⁵ȵin²¹²   sam³⁵ ȵan⁵⁵
        twelfth month (lunar)   three months

        ɕəp²¹ȵi³³ ȵan⁵⁵
        twelve months

Place nouns. Examples of place nouns are: təm²¹², toi⁵³, ki⁵⁵, ʔo²¹², and sa³¹ (a Shídòng word). All these words mean 'place'. Some people maintain that place names also belong in this category of nouns.
   Place nouns cannot take classifiers or adverbs as modifiers.
   Some can reduplicate.

(115) **toi⁵³**   toi⁵³   tu⁵⁵   li³²³   nən²¹²   paŋ⁵⁵
       place   place   all   have   person   help
       Everywhere there are people who are helping.

       ki⁵⁵   ki⁵⁵   tu⁵⁵   we³¹   li³²³   jan²¹²   mei⁴⁵³
       place   place   all   make   have   house   new
       Everywhere there are new houses being built.

       ȵən²²   nai⁴⁴   **sa³¹**   sa³¹   tu³⁵   yau³⁵   lai³⁵   ʔeu³¹
       year   this   place   place   all   entire good   rice
       This year everywhere is growing good rice. (Shídòng)

Locative nouns. Examples of locative nouns are given in (116).

(116)   ta⁵³   ʔeu³¹
        among   in

        nuk³²³   ʔu⁵⁵
        outside   up

        te³²³   ɕe³²³
        down   left

wa^{35}
right

$ta^{53}na^{323}$
in front of

$ljem^{13}lən^{212}$
behind

$toŋ^{55}$
east

si^{35}
west

nam^{212}
south

pek^{55}
north

Simple and compound locative nouns. Compound locative nouns are made up of simple words. The component parts of the compound words are not always the same from place to place. The prefix $maŋ^{53}$ meaning 'side' is the most commonly encountered.

(117) $ʔu^{55}$ → $maŋ^{53}ʔu^{55}$
up   above, top part

te^{323} → $maŋ^{53}te^{323}$
down   below, bottom part

$ʔun^{53}$ → $maŋ^{53}ʔun^{53}$
front   in front, front part

$lən^{212}$ → $maŋ^{53}lən^{212}$
behind   at the back, back part

$ʔɐu^{31}$ → $maŋ^{53}ʔɐu^{31}$
in   inside

nuk^{323} → $maŋ^{53}nuk^{323}$
out   outside

$ɕe^{323}$ → $maŋ^{53}ɕe^{323}$
left   left side

wa^{35} → $maŋ^{53}wa^{35}$
right   right side

$toŋ^{55}$ → $maŋ^{53}toŋ^{55}$ or $toŋ^{55}waŋ^{35}$
east   east side

Grammar

si^{35} → $maŋ^{53}si^{35}$ or $si^{35}waŋ^{35}$
west west side

nam^{212} → $maŋ^{53}nam^{212}$ or $nam^{212}waŋ^{35}$
south south side

$pɐk^{55}$ → $maŋ^{53}pɐk^{55}$ or $pɐk^{55}waŋ^{35}$
north north side

wan^{44} → $maŋ^{53}wan^{44}$
outside outside (Shídòng)

ta^{55} → $taŋ^{35}ta^{55}$
among middle (Shídòng)

The word $kən^{11}$ from the northern dialect meaning 'road, path, way' is a locative word prefix arising from a common noun. It can combine with the words 'up, down, front, behind, in, left, right, this, that', as in (118).

(118) $kən^{11}ʔu^{35}$ $kən^{11}te^{33}$
above, top part   below, bottom part

$kən^{11}sun^{35}$ $kən^{11}sən^{22}nai^{44}$
in front, front part   at the back, back part

$kən^{11}ʔau^{31}$ $kən^{11}ɕe^{33}$
inside   left side

$kən^{11}wa^{11}$ $kən^{11}nai^{44}$
right side   this side

$kən^{11}ka^{55}$
that side

Some of the locative nouns in Dong can either use the simple form or the compound form of (117); for example, the words meaning front, up, down, behind, inside, outside, beside, and middle. Examples using the simple form with such locative nouns are given in (119).

(119) $muŋ^{31}$ $ʔun^{53}$ pu^{35} sun^{35}
CLF   front   CLF   front
the one in front (Zhānglǔ)   the one in front (Shídòng)

ʔu⁵⁵   tən²¹²   tha⁴⁵³   ʔu⁵⁵   ma³⁵
up   mountain   go^up   up   come
on top of the mountain   Come up to the top.

çai³³   te³²³   ʔɐu³¹   jan²¹²
village down   in   house
the village downstream   in the house

jan²¹²   ʔɐu³¹   ke⁵⁵   ɲa⁵⁵
house   in   side   river
the inner room   by the river

ta⁵³   ɲan⁵⁵
among   month
the middle of the month

Some locative nouns, however, can only use the compound form; for example, the words meaning left, right, east, west, south, and north. An example is given in (120).

(120) toŋ⁵⁵   waŋ³⁵   ŋe⁵³   kwaŋ⁵⁵   si³⁵   waŋ³⁵   ljaŋ³³
      east   place   open   light   west   place   bright
      Dawn breaks in the east, and the west brightens up.

Monosyllabic locative nouns of the southern dialect can reduplicate for emphasis. A demonstrative pronoun appears after reduplication.

(121) jan²¹²   mau³³   ɲau³³   ʔu⁵⁵   ʔu⁵⁵   ta⁵⁵
      house   3s   at   top   top   that
      His house is at the very top.

      muŋ³¹   ʔun⁵³   ʔun⁵³   ta³³
      CLF   front   front   that
      that person nearest the front

In Shídòng (northern) speech, the adverb of degree is used to express the meaning given by reduplication in (121).

(122) mau⁴⁴   jan²²   ɲau⁴⁴   sa³¹   paŋ¹¹   ʐau²⁵   ka⁵⁵
      3s   house   at   place high   most   that
      His house is at the very top.

pu³⁵ ɕi³¹ sun³⁵ **ʐau²⁵** ka⁵⁵
CLF face front most that
that person nearest the front

Locative nouns do not take adverbs or numeral-classifier phrases as modifiers.

Proper nouns. Proper nouns include names of people, deities, places, books, and so on, as in (123).

(123) ɕaŋ⁵⁵ ljaŋ²¹² ɕaŋ⁵⁵ mui⁵³
Zhāng Liáng Zhāng Mèi (章良章妹, names of two people)

ȶaŋ³³ jən¹³faŋ³³
Jiāng Yìngfāng (姜映芳, a woman's name)

wu²² mjən³¹
Wú Miǎn (吴勉, a man's name)

sa³¹ pja³²³
Léi Pó (雷婆, the thunder goddess)

sa³¹si³²³
a female deity

ɕai³³waŋ¹¹
Wángzhài (王寨, the Dong name for Jǐnpíng, 锦屏)

ʔo²¹²paŋ⁵⁵
Bāngdòng (邦洞, a place name)

ȶu³²³toŋ³³
Jiǔdòng (九洞, a place name)

ʔa⁵⁵tʉŋ⁵³tən³²³
Song of Origins (起源之歌)

le²¹²kʉm⁵⁵
Dong literature (侗文)

Modification. Proper nouns, except for place names, are not generally modified by other lexical categories. The name of a place which is encompassed by a larger place can be modified by the name of the larger place. The name of the larger place appears first.

(124) ku⁵⁵ɕu⁵⁵   sam³⁵pau³²³
       Gǔzhōu   Sānbǎo
       Gǔzhōu Sānbǎo (古州三宝)

       ȶhen³⁵ɕui³³   ʔo²¹²paŋ⁵⁵
       Tiānzhù   Bāngdòng
       Tiānzhù Bāngdòng (天柱邦洞)

       kui⁵³ɕu⁵⁵   kwan⁵³
       Guìzhōu   Guàndòng
       Guìzhōu Guàndòng (贵州贯洞)

       kwaŋ³²³si³⁵   kwan⁵³
       Guǎngxī   Guàndòng
       Guǎngxī Guàndòng (广西冠洞)

Monosyllabic versus disyllabic place names. In the north, the word ʔo²² 'place, location' or the word ɕai⁴⁴ 'village' is prefixed to any monosyllabic place name.

(125) ʔo²²ʔai²²   ʔo²²ȶəu²²
       Huáizhài (怀寨)   Huángqiáo (黄桥)

       ʔo²²han²⁵   ʔo²²pjoŋ³¹
       Hànzhài (汉寨)   Tūdòng (凸洞)

       ʔo²²koŋ³⁵   ʔo²²ʔam³⁵
       Bāngzhài (邦寨)   Gāndòng (甘洞)

       ɕai⁴⁴han²⁵   ɕai⁴⁴koŋ³⁵
       Hànzhài (汉寨)   Bāngzhài (邦寨)

The southern dialect has some disyllabic place names, as in (126).

(126) ljoŋ²¹²tu²¹²   ɕai³³ɕa³⁵
       Lóngtú (龙图)   Chēzhài (车寨)

The majority of southern dialect place names, however, are monosyllabic.

Grammar 91

(127)　sau³⁵　　　　　　　　ʔam⁵⁵
　　　Zhàoxīng (肇兴)　　　　Gāntuán (干团)

　　　lo²¹²　　　　　　　　　tuk³²³
　　　Luóxiāng (罗香)　　　　Dúdòng (独洞)

　　　thəi⁴⁵³　　　　　　　　ləm²¹²
　　　Xīshān (西山)　　　　　Lúndòng (伦洞)

　　　pji³³　　　　　　　　　mau²¹²
　　　Pílín (皮林)　　　　　　Máugòng (茅贡)

　　　kwan⁵³
　　　Guàndòng (贯洞)

It seems that, originally, Dong place names were mostly monosyllabic, and there has been a shift towards disyllabic names. Now, the first syllable of a disyllabic place name is frequently ʔo²¹² 'place', ɕai³³ 'village', kau³²³ 'head', pjiŋ²¹² 'level ground', or waŋ²¹² 'square'.

4.1.2 Classifiers

Dong is rich in classifiers. There are two types: nominal and verbal.

Nominal classifiers. Nominal classifiers indicate units of people and things. They can be divided into the following five classes.

Classifying. These classifiers are used in distinguishing different categories of things.

(128)　Southern　Northern
　　　dialect　　dialect

　　　muŋ³¹　　pu³⁵　　　people (cf. 位 wèi, 个 gè)
　　　tu²¹²　　 to²²　　　animals (cf. 只 zhī, 个 gè)
　　　ʔoŋ⁵⁵　　ȶiu²²　　　plants (cf. 棵 kē, 条 tiáo)
　　　mɐi³¹　　məi³¹　　　upper outer garments (cf. 件 jiàn)
　　　ȶiu²¹²　　ȶiu²²　　　long thin things (cf. 条 tiáo)

Grouping. These classifiers are used for groups or pairs of things.

(129) Southern   Northern
       dialect   dialect

       ȶɐu³³   ȶəu⁴⁴   pair (cf. 双 shuāng)
       toi⁵³   təi⁵⁵   team (cf. 队 duì)
       tɐu³¹   təu³³   crowd (cf. 群 qún, 夥 huǒ)
       pjat³²³   kau⁵⁵   bunch (e.g., of grapes, cf. 串 chuàn)

General. These are classifiers that can be used for a wide range of things, and do not indicate a specific kind of object. For example, in the southern dialect area the words ȶɐk²¹ or ȵan⁵⁵ sometimes correspond to Chinese classifiers 个 gè, 只 zhī, 根 gēn, and 条 tiáo, and in the northern dialect area the word ta²² (or ʐa²²) corresponds to the Chinese 个 gè.

(130) ȶɐk²¹   ȵən²¹²   nai³³
       CLF (cf. 个) person   this
       this person

       ja²¹²   ȶɐk²¹   ɕo²¹²sən³³
       two   CLF (cf. 个) student
       two students

       ʔi⁵⁵   ȶɐk²¹   tɐŋ⁵³
       one   CLF (cf. 根) stool
       one stool

       ja²¹²   ȶɐk²¹   kwaŋ³²³
       two   CLF (cf. 只) bowl
       two bowls

       ʐa²²   mja³¹   nai⁴⁴
       CLF (cf. 把) knife   this
       this knife (Shídòng)

       ja²²   ta²²   nəi³¹
       two   CLF (cf. 个) woman
       two women (Shídòng)

Measuring. These are classifiers representing units of measurement, such as those in (131).

(131) ɕik¹³   sən⁴⁵³
       0.333 meter (cf. 尺 chǐ)   0.033 meter (cf. 寸 cùn)

ɕaŋ³³
3.333 meters (cf. 丈 zhàng)

phe⁴⁵³
arm spread (cf. 庹 tuò)

ɕe³⁵
handspan (cf. 拃 zhà)

ʔum³²³
armful (cf. 抱 bào)

tɐu³²³
ten liters (cf. 斗 dǒu)

tam⁵³
100 liters (cf. 石 dàn)

ȶɐn⁵⁵
0.5 kilogram (cf. 斤 jīn)

ljaŋ³¹
0.05 kilogram (cf. 两 liǎng)

sin²¹²
money (cf. 钱 qián)

lji³¹
0.5 kilometer (cf. 里 lǐ)

Most of the measuring classifiers in Dong are borrowed from Chinese. Only a few length measuring classifiers, such as ʔəm³³ (Shídòng), phe⁴⁵³, and ɕe³⁵, are native Dong words. The word toŋ³²³ 'bucket' (cf. 桶 tǒng) is used for capacity measurements, and kwiu⁵³ 'balance' (cf. 秤 chèng) is used for weights.

Borrowed from other lexical categories. Certain nouns or verbs can be used as classifiers to indicate amounts of things.

(132) ʔi⁵⁵   **tui³¹**   ʔɐu³¹
       one   bowl   rice
       one bowl of rice

ja²¹²   **ɕai³³**   ȵən²¹²
two   village   person
people of two villages

sam³⁵   **tɐi³³**   taŋ²¹²
three   bag   candy
three bags of candy

si⁴⁵³   **loŋ³¹**   ʔuk³²³
four   box   clothing
four boxes of clothing

ʔi⁵⁵   **tap³²³**   ȶət⁵⁵
one   pole   firewood
one load of firewood

sam³⁵   **pa³²³**   ma⁵⁵
three   grip   vegetable
three bundles of vegetables

ʔi⁵⁵   **ȵɐm⁵⁵**   ʔiu³²³
one   grip   aˆvegetable
one bundle of *jué cài* (蕨菜)

Grammatical characteristics of nominal classifiers

Numeral-classifier phrases. When nominal classifiers are used to indicate numbers of things, they combine with numerals to form numeral-classifier phrases which come before the nouns they modify.

(133) $\textit{ʔi}^{55}$ $\textit{muŋ}^{31}$ $\textit{ŋən}^{212}$
         one   CLF   person
         one person

         $\textit{ja}^{212}$ $\textit{ʔoŋ}^{55}$ $\textit{mɐi}^{31}$
         two   CLF   tree
         two trees

         $\textit{sam}^{35}$ $\textit{tɐu}^{33}$ $\textit{ço}^{33}$
         three   CLF   chopstick
         three pairs of chopsticks

Modifiers. Nominal classifiers have properties and usage similar to nouns. They can be modified by nouns, pronouns, adjectives, and verbs.

(134) $\textit{ja}^{212}$ $\textit{tu}^{212}$ $\textit{jan}^{212}$ $\textit{çau}^{35}$ $\textit{ta}^{33}$
         two   CLF   house   2p   that
         those two (animals) from your house

         $\textit{nɐn}^{55}$ $\textit{man}^{13}$ $\textit{lai}^{55}$ $\textit{nɐn}^{55}$ $\textit{su}^{35}$ $\textit{kwe}^{212}$ $\textit{lai}^{55}$
         CLF   yellow   good   CLF   green   not   good
         The yellow one is good, the green one is not good.

         $\textit{tu}^{212}$ $\textit{pən}^{323}$ $\textit{phaŋ}^{35}$ $\textit{ta}^{33}$ $\textit{taŋ}^{323}$ $\textit{tu}^{212}$ $\textit{mak}^{323}$
         CLF   fly   high   that   be   CLF   big
         That one that's flying high is a big one.

Classifiers can generally reduplicate, as illustrated in (135).

(135) $\textit{muŋ}^{31}\textit{muŋ}^{31}$ $\textit{tu}^{212}\textit{tu}^{212}$
         everyone   each one (animals)

         $\textit{nɐn}^{55}\textit{nɐn}^{55}$ $\textit{tɐu}^{33}\textit{tɐu}^{33}$
         each one (things)   each pair

Grammar

In some places in the northern dialect area, the word ji^{35} 'one' is added before reduplicated classifiers to indicate a small amount. The examples in (136) are from Shídòng speech.

(136) ji^{35} wu^{25} wu^{25} $ʔəu^{31}$ nai^{44} kwe^{22} ten^{35} $ţe^{35}$
one   CLF   CLF   rice   this   not   enough   eat
This small mouthful of rice is not enough to eat.

ji^{35} $jəm^{11}$ $jəm^{11}$ $çoŋ^{33}$ ma^{35} nai^{44} kwe^{22} ten^{35} to^{33}
one   CLF   CLF   seed   vegetable   this   not   enough   plant
These few vegetable seeds are not enough for planting.

ji^{35} ji^{31} ji^{31} $nəm^{31}$ nai^{44} nan^{22} $saŋ^{31}$ ja^{55}
one   CLF   CLF   water   this   difficult   keep   field
This small amount of water is insufficient to provide for the field.

When there is no modifying numeral, the classifier itself expresses the meaning 'one'

(137) $muŋ^{31}$ $ņən^{212}$ $ţa^{53}$
CLF   person   that
that person

jan^{212} tu^{212} jan^{212} tu^{212}
house   CLF   house   CLF
one (animal) to each house

$nɐn^{55}$ nai^{33} $nɐn^{55}$ $ņa^{212}$ $nɐn^{55}$ $ţa^{53}$ $nɐn^{55}$ jau^{212}
CLF   this   CLF   2s   CLF   that   CLF   1s
This one is yours, that one is mine.

Verbal classifiers. Verbal classifiers indicate units of action. They can be divided into the following two subclasses.

Number of times. These are classifiers which are used to indicate the number of times an action occurs.

(138) $çon^{33}$ tau^{53}
time (cf. 次 cì, 趟 tàng)   time (cf. 次 cì)

$çən^{33}$ mat^{323}
gust, outburst (cf. 阵 zhèn, 次 cì)   time (cf. 次 cì)

ha^{35}
time (cf. 下 xià, 次 cì)

zau^{55}
time (Shídòng, cf. 次 cì)

Borrowed from nouns. These are words, such as body organs, names of tools, and time nouns, borrowed into use as verbal classifiers. They typically occur in a numeral-classifier phrase following a verb.

(139) nu^{53} $\mathfrak{z}i^{55}$ ta^{55}
       look   one   CLF^eye
       glance

       $\underline{t}hik^{13}$ $\mathfrak{z}i^{55}$ tin^{55}
       kick   one   CLF^foot
       kick (once)

       te^{53} $\mathfrak{z}i^{55}$ mja^{31}
       chop   one   CLF^knife
       chop (once)

       $ŋau^{33}$ $\mathfrak{z}i^{55}$ $ɲin^{212}$
       live   one   CLF^year
       live for one year

       we^{31} sam^{35} $ɲan^{55}$
       do   three   CLF^month
       do for three months

       pai^{55} sam^{35} $ɕon^{33}$
       go   three   CLF^time
       go three times

Phonetic change of classifiers in the northern dialect. In most areas where the northern dialect is spoken, when classifiers follow the numerals ji^{35} 'one' and $ɕi^{33}$ 'ten' to form numeral-classifier phrases, the classifiers' syllable initials, and occasionally also the tones, change. Changes basically follow the same pattern in different areas. Normally, the syllable initial changes to the voiced fricative or approximant at the same place of articulation (initials which are already voiced fricatives or approximants do not change). Some tones change from Quán Yīn to Cì Yīn of the same tone category. Phonetic and tone change patterns are illustrated in (140)–(146), using speech from Shídòng in Tiānzhù.

Bilabial and labialized sounds change to the bilabial voiced approximant *w* and some of the corresponding tones change from Quán Yīn to Cì Yīn tones.

(140) $ja^{22} po^{33}$ → $ji^{35} wo^{33}$
two bowls (cf. 碗 *wǎn*)   one bowl

$ja^{22} paŋ^{22}$ → $ji^{35} waŋ^{22}$
two buckets (cf. 桶 *tǒng*)   one bucket

$ja^{22} məi^{31}$ → $ji^{35} wəi^{31}$
two (e.g.) coats (cf. 件 *jiàn*)   one coat

$ja^{22} mən^{55}$ → $ji^{35} wən^{25}$ tone change
two (sliced) pieces (cf. 片 *piān*)   one piece

$ja^{22} kwai^{25}$ → $ji^{35} wai^{25}$
two Rénmínbì (cf. 块 *kuài*)   one Rénmínbì

$ja^{22} kwaŋ^{22}$ → $ji^{35} waŋ^{22}$
two sections (cf. 股 *gǔ*)   one section

$ja^{22} mju^{44}$ → $ji^{35} wju^{44}$
two lines (cf. 行 *háng*)   one line

$ja^{22} mjan^{35}$ → $ji^{35} wjan^{11}$ tone change
two months (cf. 月 *yuè*)   one month

$ja^{22} wən^{11}$ → $ji^{35} wən^{11}$ no change
two cents (cf. 分 *fēn*)   one cent

$ja^{22} wut^{33}$ → $ji^{35} wut^{33}$ no change
two tufts (of hair, cf. 撮 *zuǒ*)   one tuft

Alveolar sounds and palatalized laterals change to the retroflex voiced fricative $z̢$, and some of the corresponding tones change from Quán Yīn to Cì Yīn tones.

(141) $sam^{11} to^{22}$ → $ji^{35} z̢o^{22}$
three (e.g.) pigs (cf. 只 *zhī*)   one pig

$sam^{11} təu^{33}$ → $ji^{35} z̢əu^{33}$
three nests (cf. 窝 *wō*)   one nest

ɕəp³⁵ nən³⁵ → ji³⁵ z̦ən¹¹ tone change
ten (e.g.) shops (cf. 个 gè) one shop

ɕəp³⁵ naŋ³⁵ → ji³⁵ z̦aŋ¹¹ tone change
ten bags (cf. 兜 dōu) one bag

sam¹¹ səm⁴⁴ → ji³⁵ z̦əm⁴⁴
three generations (cf. 辈 bèi) one generation

sam¹¹ sin¹¹ → ji³⁵ z̦in¹¹
three thousand (cf. 千 qiān) one thousand

ŋo³¹ ljo³¹ → ji³⁵ z̦o³¹
five (e.g.) beds (cf. 张 zhāng) one bed

ŋo³¹ ljaŋ³¹ → ji³⁵ z̦aŋ³¹
five liang (cf. 两 liǎng) one liang

Coronals, nasals, and voiceless fricatives change to the palatal voiced approximant *j*. The tones of some words change from Quán Yīn to Cì Yīn tones.

(142) si²⁵ ta⁴⁴ → ji³⁵ ja⁴⁴
four steps (cf. 步 bù) one step

si²⁵ təu⁴⁴ → ji³⁵ jəu⁴⁴
four pairs (cf. 双 shuāng) one pair

ljoʔ¹³ ȵəm³⁵ → ji³⁵ jəm¹¹ tone change
six (e.g.) handfuls (cf. 把 bǎ) one handful

ljoʔ¹³ ȵəm⁵⁵ → ji³⁵ jəm²⁵ tone change
six nights (cf. 夜 yè) one night

ja²² ɕeu³³ → ji³⁵ jeu¹³ tone change
two (e.g.) bundles (cf. 束 shù) one bundle

ɕəp³⁵ ɕaŋ⁴⁴ → ji³⁵ jaŋ⁴⁴
ten zhang (cf. 丈 zhàng) one zhang

ja²² jan²² → ji³⁵ jan²² no change
two houses (cf. 家 jiā) one house

Grammar   99

      ja²² jau¹¹　　　　　　　→　*ji³⁵ jau¹¹*　　　no change
      two bowls (cf. 碗 *wǎn*)　　　　one bowl

Velar stops and glottal stops change to the velar voiced fricative *ɣ* and some corresponding tones change from Quán Yīn to Cì Yīn tones.

(143) *ja²² kau³³*　　　　　　　→　*ji³⁵ ɣau¹³*　　　tone change
       two bundles (cf. 把 *bǎ*)　　　one bundle

       ja²² kau⁵⁵　　　　　　　→　*ji³⁵ ɣau²⁵*　　　tone change
       two clusters (cf. 串 *chuàn*)　one cluster

       ja²² ʔun³⁵　　　　　　　→　*ji³⁵ ɣun¹¹*　　　tone change
       two shoulder-loads (cf. 扛 *káng*)　one load

       sət³⁵ ʔan³⁵　　　　　　　→　*ji³⁵ ɣan³⁵*
       seven evenings (cf. 晚 *wǎn*)　one evening

       ȵu³³ yo²²　　　　　　　→　*ji³⁵ yo²²*　　　no change
       nine boxes (cf. 盒 *hé*)　　　one box

       si²⁵ yau¹¹　　　　　　　→　*ji³⁵ yau¹¹*　　　no change
       four valleys (cf. 冲 *chōng*)　one valley

The bilabial palatalized stop *pj* changes to the bilabial palatalized voiced approximant *wj*.

(144) *ja²² pjen¹¹*　　　　　　　→　*si²⁵ɕi³³ wjen¹¹*
       two pages (cf. 页 *yè*)　　　forty pages

       ja²² pjiu¹¹　　　　　　　→　*si²⁵ɕi³³ wjiu¹¹*
       two baskets (cf. 篓 *lǒu*)　　forty baskets

       ja²² pjən²²　　　　　　　→　*ŋo³¹ɕi³³ wjən²²*
       two bottles (cf. 瓶 *píng*)　　fifty bottles

       ja²² pji²²　　　　　　　→　*sam¹¹ɕi³³ wji²²*
       two pieces (of cloth, cf. 匹 *pǐ*)　thirty pieces

Phonetic changes of Dong classifiers only occur after the numerals *ji³⁵* 'one' and *ɕi³³* 'ten'; after the equivalent numerals *jat³⁵* 'one' and *ɕəp³⁵* 'ten', there is no phonetic change.

(145) ŋo³¹ **toŋ**²²   ji³⁵ ʐoŋ²²
five tong (where tong is tube-shaped, cf. 筒 *tǒng*)   one tong

ɕi³³jət³⁵ **toŋ**²²   ɕəp³⁵ **toŋ**²²
eleven tong   ten tong

If phonetic change is continuous over time, it may simply be classified as phonetic change. When the numeral *ji³⁵* 'one' is omitted, however, the phonetic change of the following classifier still persists.

(146) ji³⁵   wu³⁵ , ƚe³⁵   ji³⁵   yən¹¹   =   wu³⁵   ƚe³⁵   yən¹¹
      one   CLF   eat   one   CLF   CLF   eat   CLF
      one (person) eats one (here do not use *bu³⁵* person classifier or *nən³⁵* general classifier)

      ji³⁵   wən³⁵   pai³⁵   ji³⁵   ʐau⁵⁵   =   wən³⁵   pai³⁵   ʐau⁵⁵
      one   CLF   go   one   CLF   CLF   go   CLF
      go once a day (here do not use *pən³⁵* 'day' or *tau⁵⁵* 'time')

      jau²²   me²²   ji³⁵   wa³³   kwan³⁵   =   jau²²   me²²   wa³³   kwan³⁵
      1s   have   one   CLF   ax   1s   have   CLF   ax
      I have an ax (here do not use *pa³³* classifier for 'ax').

The examples in (146) illustrate how the phonetic change in classifiers of the northern dialect is no longer purely a change in pronunciation but has become a grammatical feature.

4.1.3 Numerals

Numerals in Dong can be divided into cardinal and ordinal numbers on the one hand and approximates, multiples, fractions, and whole amounts on the other.

Cardinal and ordinal numbers

Cardinal numbers in Dong include the words in (147).

(147) ʔi⁵⁵   ja²¹²
      one   two

      sam³⁵   si⁴⁵³
      three   four

ŋo³¹	ljok²¹
five	six
sət³⁵	pet³²³
seven	eight
tu³²³	ɕap²¹
nine	ten
pek³²³	sin³⁵
100	1,000
wen³³	ljiŋ²¹²
10,000	zero
maŋ⁵³	
half	

Some numerals have two forms in Dong. For example, ʔi⁵⁵ and ʔət⁵⁵ both mean 'one', ja²¹² and ɲi³³ both mean 'two', and ɕap²¹ and ɕi⁵⁵ both mean 'ten'. In each of these cases the two different forms have different uses.

Ordinal numbers in Dong are normally made up of the affix ti³³ plus cardinal numbers, as illustrated in (148).

(148) ti³³ ʔət⁵⁵   ti³³ ɲi³³
       the first   the second

       ti³³ sam³⁵   ti³³ ɕap²¹ŋo³¹
       the third   the fifteenth

This way of expressing the ordinals is borrowed from Chinese. Dong's own natural way of expressing an ordinal is to omit ti³³ and place a cardinal number after a classifier, as in (149).

(149) a. muŋ³¹   ɲi³³
           CLF   two
           the second person (Dong way of expressing ordinal)

           muŋ³¹   ti³³   ɲi³³
           CLF   the   two
           the second person (mixed Chinese/Dong way of expressing ordinal)

    ȶi³³   ȵi³³   muŋ³¹
    the   two   CLF
    the second person (Chinese way of expressing ordinal)

b. *nɐn⁵⁵*   *sam³⁵*
    CLF   three
    the third thing (Dong way of expressing ordinal)

    nɐn⁵⁵   *ȶi³³*   *sam³⁵*
    CLF   the   three
    the third thing (mixed Chinese/Dong way of expressing ordinal)

    ȶi³⁵   *sam³⁵*   *nɐn⁵⁵*
    the   three   CLF
    the third thing (Chinese way of expressing ordinal)

Dong numerals are decimal. Compound numerals are expressed in the same way as for other languages in the same language branch and also in the same way as for Chinese.

Apart from certain set phrases, such as *sin³⁵ sin³⁵ wen³³ wen³³* 'millions and millions', numerals cannot reduplicate.

Except for the two situations following, numerals usually cannot take modification from other lexical categories.

1. When a numeral is the predicate in a sentence, it can be modified by time nouns (or phrases expressing time) or by adverbs.

(150) *jau²¹²* *ȵin²¹²* *nai³³* **ȵi³³** *ɕəp²¹* *mau³³* *ɕi³³* *ɕəp²¹* *ljok²¹*
       1s   year   this   two   ten   3s   just   ten   six
       This year I am twenty (years old), he is only sixteen.

2. Numerals can be modified by plural personal pronouns, representing a number of people.

(151) *ja²¹²* *tau⁵⁵*
       two   1pˆinc
       we two

       sam³⁵ *ɕau³⁵*
       three   2p
       you three

Different forms for the same numeral
1. ʔi⁵⁵ and ʔət⁵⁵ meaning 'one'; ja²¹² and ɲi³³ meaning 'two'. ʔi⁵⁵ and ja²¹² are used as cardinals, not as ordinals; while ʔət⁵⁵ and ɲi³³ are used as ordinals and only used as cardinals in compound numbers. Normally the two pairs cannot be interchanged. The words ʔi⁵⁵ 'one' and ja²¹² 'two' can be placed before classifiers to form numeral-classifier phrases, but ʔət⁵⁵ 'one' and ɲi³³ 'two' cannot. The words ʔət⁵⁵ and ɲi³³ can be placed after classifiers to become ordinal numbers, but ʔi⁵⁵ and ja²¹² cannot.

(152) ʔi⁵⁵ muŋ³¹   one person   *ʔət⁵⁵ muŋ³¹
       ja²¹² nɐn⁵⁵   two things   *ɲi³³ nɐn⁵⁵
       muŋ³¹ ʔət⁵⁵   the first person   *muŋ³¹ ʔi⁵⁵
       nɐn⁵⁵ ɲi³³   the second thing   *nɐn⁵⁵ ja²¹²

When forming compound numerals, only ʔi⁵⁵ and ja²¹² can precede the numerals pek³²³ '100', sin³⁵ '1,000', or wen³³ '10,000'; ʔet⁵⁵ and ɲi³³ cannot. Before the word ɕap²¹ 'ten', usually ʔi⁵⁵ and ɲi³³ are used; after ɕap²¹, ʔət⁵⁵ and ɲi³³ are used. For the last digit of compound numerals, ʔət⁵⁵ and ɲi³³ are used; ʔi⁵⁵ and ja²¹² cannot be used. The ʔi⁵⁵ is frequently dropped from the front in compound numerals whose first digit is one. Examples are given in (153).

(153) ʔi⁵⁵   wen³³   ʔi⁵⁵   sin³⁵   ʔi⁵⁵   pek³²³   ʔi⁵⁵   ɕap²¹   ʔət⁵⁵
       one   10,000 one   1,000   one   100   one   ten   one
       eleven thousand, one hundred eleven (11,111)

       ja²¹² wen³³   ja²¹² sin³⁵   ja²¹² pek³²³   ɲi³³   ɕap²¹   ɲi³³
       two   10,000 two   1,000   two   100   two   ten   two
       twenty-two thousand, two hundred twenty-two (22,222)

       wen³³   ʔət⁵⁵
       10,000   one
       eleven thousand (11,000)

       sin³⁵   ɲi³³
       1,000   two
       one thousand, two hundred (1,200)

       pek³²³   ɲi³³
       100   two
       one hundred twenty (120)

ni^{33} $çəp^{21}$ ni^{33} $muŋ^{31}$
two   ten   two   CLF
twenty-two people

2. $çəp^{21}$ and $çi^{55}$ meaning 'ten'. The southern dialect has the two words $çəp^{21}$ 'ten' and $çi^{55}$ 'ten'; in the north these are pronounced $çəp^{35}$ and $çi^{33}$, respectively. In the south, $çi^{55}$ is seldom used, and it can always be exchanged for $çəp^{21}$. The word $çi^{55}$ can only be used as a place number, for counting the number of tens, and a number must follow it, e.g., $çəp^{21}wen^{33}$ '100,000', *$çi^{55}wen^{33}$; $sam^{35}çəp^{21}$ 'thirty', *$sam^{35}çi^{55}$, but one can say $sam^{35}çi^{55}ŋo^{31}$ 'thirty-five'.

The word $çi^{55}ʔət^{55}$ 'eleven' can be said $çəp^{21}ʔət^{55}$ in the southern dialect, but not in the northern dialect. Apart from this, $çəp^{35}$ and $çi^{33}$ of the northern dialect can be interchanged freely.

3. $maŋ^{53}$, pan^{53}, and tot^{31} meaning 'half'. In the southern dialect there are three words which express the idea of 'half': $maŋ^{53}$, pan^{53}, and tot^{31}. In the northern dialect, there are four: $maŋ^{55}$ ($waŋ^{25}$), pan^{55} (wan^{55}), tot^{31} (jot^{31}), and $zaŋ^{44}$.

The word $maŋ^{53}$ can stand alone as part of a sentence or be placed before the name of a thing, meaning a half of the whole thing.

(154) $toŋ^{212}$ sin^{212} la^{53} ta^{53} **$maŋ^{53}$** sai^{35} na^{212}
       copper   money   cut   middle   half   give   2s
       cut the coin in half and give half to you (evidence of romantic love)

na^{212} $phje^{453}$ **$maŋ^{53}$** liu^{212} sai^{35} $noŋ^{31}$
2s   share   half   tangerine   give   younger^brother
Give half of the tangerine to your younger brother.

The word pan^{53} is placed before a classifier (except for time classifiers), meaning half the amount, or after a numeral-classifier phrase, meaning an addition of half of the amount.

(155)   **pan^{53}** $tɛn^{55}$
       half   CLF^0.5^kilogram
       0.25 kilogram

       pan^{53} tau^{55}
       half   CLF^pot
       half a pot full

Grammar 105

    sam³⁵   tui³¹   **pan⁵³**
    three   CLF^bowl half
    three and a half bowls

The word *ṭot³¹* is placed before time classifiers, meaning half the amount of time, or after time classifiers, meaning an addition of half the amount of time.

(156) **ṭot³¹**   mɐn⁵⁵
       half   CLF^day
       half a day

       mɐn⁵⁵   **ṭot³¹**
       CLF^day half
       a day and a half

       ŋo³¹   ɲin²¹²   **ṭot³¹**
       five   CLF^year half
       five and a half years

In the northern dialect, when the word *pan⁵⁵* appears before a classifier, or when *ṭot³¹* appears before a time classifier, their syllable initials change, becoming voiced approximants at the same places of articulation: the words become *wan⁵⁵* and *jot³¹*, respectively.

(157) sam¹¹   tui³¹   **pan⁵⁵** → wan⁵⁵ tui³¹
       three   CLF^bowl half   half   CLF^bowl
       three and a half bowls   half a bowl

       ja²²   ṭən³⁵   **pan⁵⁵** → wan⁵⁵ ṭən³⁵
       two   CLF^0.5^kilogram half   half   CLF^0.5^kilogram
       1.25 kilograms   0.25 kilogram

       sam¹¹   ɲin²²   **ṭot³¹** → jot³¹ ɲin²²
       three CLF^year half   half   CLF^year
       three and a half years   half a year

       ja²²   mjan³⁵   **ṭot³¹** → jot³¹ mjan³⁵
       two   CLF^month half   half   CLF^month
       two and a half months   half a month

In the northern dialect, there is a difference between the uses of *maŋ⁵⁵* and *ʑaŋ⁴⁴*. The word *maŋ⁵⁵* is placed before the name of an individual thing and indicates half of the whole thing. The word ʐaŋ⁴⁴ is placed before a plural noun and indicates half of the total number of things.

(158)   wən¹¹   waŋ²⁵   (maŋ⁵⁵)   ti³⁵   sai¹¹   noŋ³¹
        share   half   (half)   pear   give   younger^brother
        Give half the pear to your younger brother.

        wən¹¹   ʐaŋ⁴⁴   ti³⁵   sai¹¹   noŋ³¹
        share   half   pear   give   younger^brother
        Give half of the pears to your younger brother.

Approximates, multiples, fractions, and whole amounts

Approximates are words representing amounts that are not clear-cut. In Dong, the words *mjeŋ²¹²* 'several', *kuŋ²¹²* 'many', *ta³³* 'over', and *pa³²³* 'roughly' are used, among others. Some examples are given in (159)–(162).

1. The word *mjeŋ²¹²* appears before classifiers and place numbers.

(159)   **mjeŋ²¹²**   **mɐn⁵⁵**
        several   day
        several days

        mjeŋ²¹²   **ɲin²¹²**
        several   year
        several years

        mjeŋ²¹²   **sin³⁵**
        several   thousand
        several thousand

        mjeŋ²¹²   **tu²¹²**
        several   CLF
        several (e.g.) pigs

        mjeŋ²¹²   **tu²¹²**   **ŋu⁴⁵³**
        several   CLF   pig
        several pigs

In Shídòng speech of the northern dialect, the approximates *ʐoi³⁵* 'a big number' or *ɣa²²ɮuŋ²²* 'very many' can be added before classifiers or nouns.

Grammar 107

(160) mau⁴⁴ pai³⁵ ẓoi³⁵ (ya²²ṭuŋ²²) pən³⁵ lja³¹
     3s   go   a^big^number (very^many) day PAST
    He went many days ago.

    mau⁴⁴ tou⁵⁵ ɕaŋ²² ṭəi³³ li³³ ẓoi³⁵
    3s   go^to market buy get a^big^number

    (ya²²ṭuŋ²²) yo²⁵ ha¹¹
    (very^many) goods come
    He went to the market, bought lots of goods, and came back.

2. The words kuŋ²¹² 'many, more than' (ṭuŋ²² in the north), ta³³ 'over', and pa³²³ 'roughly' (pa³¹ in the north) appear after numerals. The word kuŋ²¹² is not often used in the southern dialect, in contrast to the word ṭuŋ²² which is often used in the north. The word ta³³ cannot be added after numerals in general, only after round numbers (consisting of a digit followed only by zeros). The word pa³²³ is added after round numbers greater than or equal to 100. Examples are given in (161).

(161) ȵi³³ ɕəp²¹ ta³³ mɐn⁵⁵
     two ten over day
    more than twenty days

    ȵi⁴⁴ ɕi³³ ṭuŋ²² pən³⁵
    two ten more^than day
    more than twenty days (Shídòng)

    pek³²³ ta³³ muŋ³¹
    100 over CLF
    more than 100 people

    peʔ³¹ ṭuŋ²² pu³⁵
    100 more^than CLF
    more than 100 people (Shídòng)

    ɕəp²¹ kuŋ²¹² tau⁵³
    ten more^than time
    more than ten times

    ɕəp³⁵ ṭuŋ²² tau⁵⁵
    ten more^than time
    more than ten times (Shídòng)

ȥin¹¹   ɬuŋ²²   lji³¹   kən¹¹
1,000   more^than 0.5^kilometer road
more than 500 kilometers (Shídòng)

wen⁴⁴   pa³¹   ɬən³⁵   ʔəu³¹
10,000 roughly 0.5^kilogram   rice
roughly 5,000 kilograms of rice (Shídòng)

3. The verbs ɬha⁴⁵³ lui³³ 'go up, come down' or pai⁵⁵ ɕon⁴⁵³ 'go, come back' appear after numerals (mostly used in connection with age) to indicate the meaning 'more or less'; or two consecutive numbers are placed side by side before nominals for a similar effect.

(162) ŋo³¹   ɕəp²¹   ɬha⁴⁵³   lui³³
       five   ten   go^up   come^down
       fifty (years old), more or less

       sam³⁵   ɕep²¹   pai⁵⁵   ɕon⁴⁵³
       three   ten   go   come^back
       thirty (years old), more or less

       pai⁵⁵   ja²¹²   sam³⁵   ȵɐm⁵³
       go   two   three   evening
       go for two or three evenings

       li³²³   si⁴⁵³   ŋo³¹   ɬən⁵⁵
       have   four   five   0.5^kilogram
       have four or five jīn (one jīn = 0.5 kilogram)

       ljok²¹   sat³⁵   pek³²³   muŋ³¹
       six   seven   100   CLF
       six or seven hundred people

Multiples, fractions, and whole amounts. Words expressing multiples and fractions, such as *poi³³* 'times' (cf. 倍 *bèi*), *ɕən²¹²* 'tenth' (cf. 成 *chéng*), and *pən³³* 'portion' (cf. 份 *fèn*), are borrowed from Chinese.

(163) pet³²³   pi³²³   si⁴⁵³   kuŋ²¹²   ʔi⁵⁵   poi³³
       eight   compare   four   more   one   time
       Eight is two times four.

Grammar

$\wp{\partial}p^{21}$ $\wp{\partial}n^{212}$ $\wp{u}^{35}$ pet^{323} $\wp{\partial}n^{212}$
ten   CLF   receive eight   CLF
get eight out of ten

sam^{35} $p{\partial}n^{33}$ li^{323} ja^{212} $p{\partial}n^{33}$
three   part   get   two   part
get two out of three parts

$te\eta^{212}$ $\wp{ai}^{33}$ $l{\partial}t^{35}$ li^{323} $p{\partial}n^{33}$
whole   village   all   have   share
Everyone in the village has a share.

The word $te\eta^{212}$ means 'the whole amount' (cf. 整 zhěng, 全 quán). In Shídòng of the northern dialect the equivalent word is yau^{35}.

(164) toi^{35} nai^{44} yau^{35} $\wp{i}^{55}$ ηa^{22} li^{33}
    pile   this   whole   be   2s   REL
    This whole pile is yours. (Shídòng)

Phonetic change in numerals of the northern dialect. In most northern dialect areas, the syllable initials of some numerals undergo phonetic change in combining with other numerals: they change to voiced fricatives or approximants at identical or similar places of articulation. The tones of some words also change. Examples below are taken from Shídòng speech in Tiānzhù.

When the numerals sam^{11} 'three', si^{25} 'four', $ljo?^{13}$ 'six', $s{\partial}t^{35}$ 'seven', pet^{33} 'eight', and tu^{33} 'nine' follow the numeral $\wp{i}^{33}$ 'ten' in two-digit numerals, their syllable initials undergo phonetic change.

(165) sam^{11} three → $\wp{i}^{33}zam^{11}$ thirteen
    si^{25} four → $\eta i^{44}\wp{i}^{33}zi^{25}$ twenty-four
    $ljo?^{13}$ six → $sam^{11}\wp{i}^{33}zo?^{13}$ thirty-six
    $s{\partial}t^{35}$ seven → $si^{25}\wp{i}^{33}z{\partial}t^{35}$ forty-seven
    pet^{33} eight → $\eta o^{31}\wp{i}^{33}wet^{33}$ fifty-eight
    tu^{33} nine → $tu^{33}\wp{i}^{33}ju^{33}$ ninety-nine

In Shídòng speech the words for one, two, and five do not undergo any phonetic change after $\wp{i}^{33}$ 'ten', but in Tiānzhù's Zhùxī (注溪) speech, the word ηo^{31} 'five' changes to wo^{31}.

Some syllable initials undergo phonetic change either when the word sam^{11} 'three' follows the word ja^{22} 'two' or precedes the words $pe?^{31}$ '100' or sin^{11} '1,000' expressing an approximate number; or when $\wp{\partial}p^{35}$ precedes the words *ṯuŋ²²* 'many' or *pa³¹* 'roughly' expressing an approximate number, or when *peʔ³¹* or *sin¹¹* follow the word *ji³⁵* 'one'.

(166)   *sam¹¹* three   →   *ja²² ẓam¹¹ pu³⁵*   two or three people
                     or *ja²² ẓam¹¹ məi³¹*   two or three (e.g., matches)
                     or *ja²² ẓam¹¹ to²²*   two or three (e.g., pigs)
                     or *ẓam¹¹ peʔ³¹*   300, roughly (special usage)
                     or *ẓam¹¹ sin¹¹*   3,000, roughly (special usage)

        çəp³⁵ ten   →   *jəp³⁵ ṯuŋ²² pən³⁵*   ten or more days
                     or *jəp³⁵ pa³¹ ṯiu²²*   ten or more (e.g., trees)

        peʔ³¹ 100   →   *ji³⁵ weʔ³¹*   100
        sin¹¹ 1,000   →   *ji³⁵ ẓin¹¹*   1,000

4.1.4 Pronouns

With respect to grammatical function, pronouns in Dong can be divided into two broad categories: nominal (taking the place of nouns and numerals) and verbal (taking the place of verbs and adjectives). It is customary, however, to classify them as personal, demonstrative, and interrogative pronouns.

Personal pronouns

Commonly occurring personal pronouns in Dong are presented in (167).

(167)   *jau²¹²*   *ŋa²¹²*
         1s[15]   2s

         mau³³   *ṯiu⁵⁵*
         3s   1p, exclusive

         çau³⁵   *ṯa³³mau³³*
         2p   3p

         tau⁵⁵   *ṯən⁵⁵*
         1p, inclusive   other person (cf. 人家 *rén jiā*)

---

[15] As in chapter 3 (cf. footnote 14, §3.1) '1s' represents first-person singular, etc.

si³³ ʔa⁵⁵ oneself	*ʔe³⁵* others/they (cf. 人家 *rén jiā*, 他们 *tā men*)
ʔak³²³ oneself	*tɐŋ²¹²tɐu³¹* other person (cf. 人家 *rén jiā*)

Difference between pronouns and nouns. Grammatical characteristics of personal pronouns are more or less the same as the content words or phrases which they replace. One difference is that, whereas nouns can be modified by adjectives, personal pronouns cannot.

(168) *nən²¹²   phaŋ³⁵   lai⁵⁵   heu³⁵   tɐu²¹²*
person   tall   good   hit   ball
Tall people can play basketball well.

jən²²   çau¹¹   we³¹   si⁵⁵   wa³¹
person   foolish   do   thing   stupid
Fools do stupid things. (Shídòng)

The words *nən²¹²* and *jən²²* in the two sentences in (168) cannot be substituted by personal pronouns. The two words *jau²¹² phaŋ³⁵* 'I am tall' can stand together. But this is a subject-predicate construction different from the above two sentences. The structure *nən²¹² phaŋ³⁵ ta³³* is admissable, but **jau²¹² phaŋ³⁵ ta³³* is inadmissable.

Modification. Personal pronouns generally cannot take modification from numerals. Exceptions are the plural personal pronouns in the southern dialect, as exemplified in (169).

(169) *sam³⁵   çau³⁵*
three   2p
you three

ja²¹²   ʔe³⁵
two   3p
those two

ja²¹²   tau⁵⁵
two   1p^inc
we two

Pronouns do not reduplicate.

Dialect differences in personal pronouns

1. In the southern dialect, the first-person plural pronoun has two forms: exclusive *ȶiu⁵⁵* and inclusive *tau⁵⁵*. The northern dialect does not differentiate these.

(170) Southern speech from Zhānglǔ in Róngjiāng

ȶiu⁵⁵	*ȶaŋ³²³*	*ȵən²¹²*	*ʔu⁵⁵ɕu⁵⁵*	*ɕau³⁵*	*ȶaŋ³²³*	*ȵən²¹²*
1p^exc	be	person	Róngjiāng	2p	be	person

ɕai³³waŋ²¹²	*tau⁵⁵*	*lət³⁵*	*ȶaŋ³²³*	*ȵən²¹²*	*kui⁵³ɕu⁵⁵*
Jǐnpíng	1p^inc	all	be	person	Guìzhōu

We (exc) are Róngjiāng people, you are Jǐnpíng people, we (inc) are all Guìzhōu people.

(171) Northern speech from Shídòng in Tiānzhù

tau³⁵	*ɕi⁵⁵*	*tən¹¹ɕui³¹*	*jən²²*	*ɕau¹¹*	*ɕi⁵⁵*	*juŋ¹¹ȶaŋ²²*
1p	be	Tiānzhù	person	2p	be	Róngjiāng

jən²²	*tau³⁵*	*ɣau²⁵*	*ɕi⁵⁵*	*kui⁵⁵ɕu³⁵*	*jən²²*
person	1p	all	be	Guìzhōu	person

We are Tiānzhù people, you are Róngjiāng people, we are all Guìzhōu people.

2. In the northern dialect, the first- and second-person plural pronouns both have two forms, depending on whether two or more than two people are indicated. If only two people are indicated, the words *ma²²* 'we two' and *ja¹¹* 'you two' are used. Alternatively, the forms in (172) can be used.

(172)

ma²²	*ja²²*	*ʔəu³¹*
we^two	two	CLF
we two		

ja¹¹	*ja²²*	*ʔəu³¹*
you^two	two	CLF
you two		

In the southern dialect area there are also some places that have special words for two people (first- and second-person plural). For example, Róngjiāng has the words *mja²²* 'we two' and *ja³⁵* 'you two'. However, these are reserved for use in songs and poems. The origin of the special pronouns for two people in the northern and southern dialects is the same. In the Dǎi

Grammar 113

(傣) language from the same language family, a complete set of singular, double, and plural personal pronouns still exists. It is probable then that the distinction between personal pronouns for two and more than two people also used to exist in spoken southern Dong.

3. In the southern dialect there is only one word for the third-person singular pronoun: mau^{33} 'he/she/it'. In the northern dialect there are two words: mau^{44} 'he/she' and $mən^{22}$ 'it'. By comparison with related languages, it can be seen that $mən^{22}$ is an intrinsically Dong word: currently, all the other languages in the same language family as Dong retain this word—in Shuǐ (水) it is $mɐn^{1}$, in Máonán (毛南) $mɐn^{2}$, in Dǎi $mɐn^{2}$, and in the Zhuàng (壮) spoken in Guǎngxī Lóngzhōu (广西龙州) min^{2}—although it has disappeared in southern Dong.

The meaning and use of mau^{44} and $mən^{22}$ in the northern dialect differ: mau^{44} refers to people, while $mən^{22}$ refers to animals and other things.

(173) tau^{35} tu^{35} **mau^{44}** we^{31} $mən^{22}$ kwe^{22} ma^{11} $ʔu^{31}$
       1p   uncle 3s   do   what   not   come EX
Our uncle—why is he not coming!?

       to^{22} kwa^{11} nai^{44} $ʔei^{55}$ $lja ʔ^{13}$ $ʔo^{33}$ $ɕi^{55}$
       CLF dog this like steal mouth extremely

       $ʔeu^{11}$ **$mən^{22}$** tai^{35} lo^{33}
       hit   3s   die   EX
This dog really likes stealing food, beat it to death!

The words mau^{44} and $mən^{22}$ in the two sentences in (173) cannot be interchanged.

When feelings of an indignant or derogatory nature are being conveyed, the word $mən^{22}$ can also be used to refer to people. It has a connotation of short life. Examples of its use are given in (174) and (175). Under no circumstances can it be used to refer to elders.

(174) Expressing indignation

       $tən^{13}$ $miŋ^{22}$ mau^{44} **$mən^{22}$** tai^{22} jau^{22} jiu^{22} ja^{55}
       short life 3s   3s   PTC 1s   CLF field

       ta^{35} γau^{25} $ʔəu^{25}$ pai^{35} lju^{31}
       fish all   catch go   PTC
May he have a short life—he caught all the fish in my field and took them away.

(175) Expressing derogatory feelings, denouncing bad behavior

mən²²	pai³⁵	jaŋ⁴⁴	kwaŋ³¹	ȵin²²	ha¹¹	ɣau²⁵	kwe²²	ma¹¹
3s	go	way	many	year	come	all	not	come

sən⁵⁵	lau³⁵	ɣau²⁵	ko³¹	mən²²	we³¹	məŋ²²
letter	not	all	not^know	3s	do	what

He went away many years ago and has never sent a letter; nobody knows what he is doing.

4. When personal pronouns are used to express possession of nouns, the pronoun comes after the noun in the southern dialect but before the noun in the northern dialect. In the northern dialect, the word *ti³³* (corresponding to the Chinese 的 *de*) is added between the modifying pronoun and the noun, except in phrases that express kinship relations, or with place nouns or with proper nouns (cf. §4.1.1).

(176) Southern dialect

ţai³¹	mau³³
older^brother	3s

his older brother

mai³¹	ȵa²¹²
wife	2s

your wife

taŋ²¹²jo¹³	ţa³³mau³³
school	3p

their school

çai³³ça³⁵	çau³⁵
Chēzhài	2p

your Chēzhài (车寨)

pjət⁵⁵	jau²¹²
pen	1s

my pen

le²¹²	ţiu⁵⁵
book	1p

our book

(177) Northern dialect

mau⁴⁴	ko³³
3s	older^brother

his older brother

ȵa²²	mai³¹
2s	wife

your wife

mau⁴⁴ʔe¹¹	ʔo²²jo¹¹
3p	school

their school

çau¹¹	çaŋ³³han⁵⁵
2p	Hànzhài

your Hànzhài (汉寨)

jau^{22}	*ti*^{33}	*pjət*^{55}	*tau*^{35}	*ti*^{33}	*le*^{22}
1s	REL	pen	1p	REL	book
my pen			our book		

5. In the southern dialect, plural personal pronouns can combine with numerals or numeral-classifier phrases to form appositional phrases. When such phrases are made up of numerals and pronouns, the numerals must precede the pronouns, as in (178). When they are made up of pronouns and numeral-classifier phrases, the numeral-classifier phrases can either precede or follow the pronouns, as in (179).

(178) *sam*^{35} *çau*^{35}
three   2p
you three

ja^{212} *tau*^{55}
two   1p^inc
we two

(179) *ta*^{33}*mau*^{33} *ŋo*^{31} *muŋ*^{31} = *ŋo*^{31} *muŋ*^{31} *ta*^{33}*mau*^{33}
3p   five   CLF   five   CLF   3p
those five people

In the northern dialect, personal pronouns normally cannot be modified by numerals or by numeral-classifier phrases; only pronouns indicating two people can.

(180) a. *ma*^{22} *pai*^{35} =   *ma*^{22} *ja*^{22} *pu*^{35} *pai*^{35}
we^two   go   we^two   two   CLF   go
we two go   we two go

=   *ma*^{22} *pu*^{35} *pai*^{35}
we^two   CLF   go
we two go

b. *ja*^{11} *ma*^{11} =   *ja*^{11} *ja*^{22} *pu*^{35} *ma*^{11}
you^two   come   you^two   two   CLF   come
you two come   you two come

=   *ja*^{11} *pu*^{35} *ma*^{11}
you^two   CLF   come
you two come

Demonstrative and interrogative pronouns. Commonly used demonstrative and interrogative pronouns in Dong include the pronouns in (181).

(181) nai³³   ta³³
       this   that (near)

       ta⁵³   ʔi⁵⁵nai³³
       that (far)   this way, like this

       ʔi⁵⁵ta³³   ʔi⁵⁵ta⁵³
       that way, like that   that way

       nʙu²¹²   maŋ²¹²
       who   what

       nu³⁵   ʔi⁵⁵nu³⁵
       which   how

       nu³⁵jaŋ³³   nu³⁵haŋ²¹²
       how   why

Dialect differences in demonstrative and interrogative pronouns are given below.

1. In the southern dialect, there are three demonstrative pronouns: *nai³³* 'this', *ta³³* 'that (nearby)', and *ta⁵³* 'that (distant)'. These words, and the interrogative pronouns *nʙu²¹²* 'who', *nu³⁵* 'which', and so on, can all stand alone as subjects or objects. In Shídòng speech of the northern dialect, there are only two demonstrative pronouns, indicating things near at hand and things far away, respectively. The pronoun referring to things near at hand has two forms: *nai⁴⁴* and *ʔai⁴⁴* 'this'; the one referring to things further away is *ka⁵⁵* 'that'.

The northern dialect's *nai⁴⁴* and *ʔai⁴⁴* are used in different ways. The word *nai⁴⁴* can only function as a modifier, while *ʔai⁴⁴* can stand alone as a subject or object.

(182) pu³⁵   **nai⁴⁴**   ɕi⁵⁵   nəu¹¹
       CLF   this   be   who
       Who is this person?

       ʔai⁴⁴   mja²²   məi³¹   **nai⁴⁴**
       this   plant (v)   CLF   this
       Plant this (tree) here.

Grammar

$\textit{ɕau}^{11}$ $\textit{ma}^{11}$ $\textit{sui}^{55}$ $\textit{ʔai}^{44}$
2p   come   sit   this
You come and sit here.

The word $\textit{ʔai}^{44}$ comes from combining the two words $\textit{ʔo}^{22}$ 'place' and $\textit{nai}^{44}$ 'this': $\textit{ʔo}^{22}$ + $\textit{nai}^{44}$ becomes $\textit{ʔai}^{44}$. Everywhere $\textit{nai}^{44}$ is used to indicate a place, the word $\textit{ʔo}^{22}$ can be prefixed; in contrast, $\textit{ʔo}^{22}$ cannot be prefixed to $\textit{ʔai}^{44}$. When the interrogative pronoun $\textit{nəu}^{11}$ 'which' is used alone as a subject or object, its pronunciation also changes, to $\textit{ʔəu}^{11}$. The change comes about as: $\textit{ʔo}^{22}$ + $\textit{nəu}^{11}$ becomes $\textit{ʔəu}^{11}$.

(183) $\textit{ʔəu}^{11}$ $\textit{ma}^{11}$ $\textit{ti}^{33}$ ($\textit{li}^{33}$) $\textit{ʔeʔ}^{13}$
       where   come   REL   (REL)   guest
       guest from where?

$\textit{ʔo}^{22}$ $\textit{nəu}^{11}$ $\textit{ma}^{11}$ $\textit{ti}^{33}$ $\textit{ʔeʔ}^{13}$
place   which   come   REL   guest
guest from where?

$\textit{n̩a}^{22}$ $\textit{pai}^{35}$ $\textit{ʔəu}^{11}$
2s   go   where
Where are you going?

$\textit{n̩a}^{22}$ $\textit{pai}^{35}$ $\textit{ʔo}^{22}$ $\textit{nəu}^{11}$
2s   go   place   which
Where are you going?

With other languages in the same language family as Dong, there are analogous phenomena. When indicating places, some languages generally combine a place morpheme with a pronoun to form a compound word; only after doing so can the word serve as the subject or object of a sentence. In combining, the word frequently becomes monosyllabic.

(184) Zhuàng (壮)
       $\textit{ki}^{2}$ place + $\textit{nei}^{6}$ this   → $\textit{kei}^{6}$ here
       $\textit{ki}^{2}$ place + $\textit{kɐn}^{4}$ that   → $\textit{kjɐn}^{4}$ there
       $\textit{ki}^{2}$ place + $\textit{lɐɯ}^{2}$ which → $\textit{kjɐɯ}^{2}$ where

       Máonán (毛南)
       $\textit{ɕi}^{6}$ place + $\textit{nai}^{6}$ this   → $\textit{ɕai}^{6}$ here
       $\textit{ɕi}^{6}$ place + $\textit{ka}^{5}$ that   → $\textit{ɕa}^{5}$ there
       $\textit{ɕi}^{6}$ place + $\textit{nɐu}^{1}$ which → $\textit{ɕɐu}^{1}$ where

2. In the southern dialect, before demonstrative pronouns and before the interrogative pronoun nu^{35}, the word $ʔi^{55}$ is added (and sometimes can be omitted) to form predicate-type pronouns. The northern dialect, on the other hand, uses different words to do the same thing: $jaŋ^{44}$ 'way', $ja^{55} jaŋ^{44}$ 'that way', $jən^{22} jaŋ^{44}$ 'how'. These predicate-type pronouns are used to indicate the manner of an action and are often used as adverbial expressions, complements, or attributes. Under certain conditions they can also be used as subjects or predicates.

(185) Southern dialect

$ʔi^{55}$ **nai^{33}** we^{31} = we^{31} **$ʔi^{55}$** **nai^{33}**
way this do   do way this
Do (it) this way.

$ʔi^{55}$ **nu^{35}** kai^{55} = kai^{55} **$ʔi^{55}$** **nu^{35}**
many few distant   distant many few
How far?

$muŋ^{31}$ $ȵən^{212}$ **$ʔi^{55}$** **nai^{33}**
CLF person way this
this kind of person

$ȵeŋ^{212}$ **$ʔi^{55}$** **ta^{53}** $ʔa^{55}$
really way that Q
(Is he/she/it) really that way?

(186) Northern dialect (Shídòng)

$ɕau^{11}$ **ja^{55}** **$jaŋ^{44}$** $ɕei^{33}$ sin^{22} $ʔa^{35}$
2p that way spend money EX
That is the way you spend money!

mau^{44} **ja^{55}** **$jaŋ^{44}$** we^{31} kwe^{22} $ɕen^{22}$ le^{22}
3s that way do not okay EX
It is not good that he does it that way!

jau^{22} kwe^{22} $ɕi^{55}$ **$jaŋ^{44}$** ti^{33} $jən^{22}$
1s not be kind REL person
I am not that kind of person.

Grammar

>
> *jaŋ⁴⁴ ɕu³¹ lai³⁵ ȶaŋ²² lja³¹*
> way just good more PAST
> This way was a lot better.

Demonstrative pronouns as function words. Demonstrative pronouns can act as function words in the following situations.

After time nouns. When demonstrative pronouns are placed after time nouns, they express the meaning 'this/that time'.

(187) *kau³²³ mɐn⁵⁵ **nai³³** tha⁴⁵³ ȶən²¹² pai⁵⁵ ʔau⁵⁵ ȶət⁵⁵*
head day (this) go^up mountain go want firewood
Go up the mountain in the daytime to collect firewood.

kau³²³ ȵɐm⁵³ ȶa³³ kwe²¹² joŋ³³ ȶa⁵⁵ to⁵⁵
head night (that) not use close door
There's no need to close the door at night.

After common or locative nouns. When demonstrative pronouns are placed after common nouns or locative nouns, they express the meaning 'this/that place'.

(188) *ʔu⁵⁵ ɕən³⁵ **nai³³** wet¹³ tun⁵⁵*
on body (this) become hot
he (his body) has a fever

ʔɐu³¹ ȶa³³ to³²³ pui⁵⁵
in (that) put fire
light a fire inside

After reduplicated adjectives or verbs. When demonstrative pronouns are placed after reduplicated adjectives or verbs, they have the same meaning as the Chinese 的 *de* or 地 *de* in the structures 'AA的' or 'VV地' (where A and V represent adjective and verb, respectively).

(189) *ma³²³ ma³²³ ȶa³³*
soft soft (that)
very soft

thɐm⁴⁵³ thɐm⁴⁵³ ȶa³³
short short (that)
very short (of stature)

ljɐk²¹   *ljɐk²¹*   *ta³³*
stealthily stealthily (that)
very stealthily

nɐi³⁵   *nɐi³⁵*   *ta³³*
move (v) move (v) (that)
constantly moving

At the beginning of a sentence. When demonstrative pronouns are placed at the beginning of a sentence, they express a turning point in the conversation or a change of topic.

(190) *ta⁵³*   *ja²¹²*   *tau⁵⁵*   *toŋ²¹²*   *pai⁵⁵*   *ma³¹*
(that) two   1p^inc   together go   EX
Well then, let's (both) go together!

ta⁵³   *mɐn⁵⁵mu³²³*   *ma³⁵*   *we³¹*
(that) tomorrow   come   do
Well then, come and do it tomorrow.

4.1.5 Verbs

Classification of verbs. Verbs function in sentences as predicates. They are commonly divided into five classes.

Common verbs. For example, *tham¹³* 'walk', *nu⁵³* 'look', *ti⁵⁵* 'eat', and *pən³²³* 'fly'.

Modal verbs. These are also called auxiliary verbs. For example, *wo³¹* 'know', *ju⁵³* 'want', *haŋ¹³* 'agree', and *ɲon³³* 'be willing'.

Directional verbs. For example, *pai⁵⁵* 'go', *ma³⁵* 'come', *ʔuk³²³* 'go or come out', and *lau³²³* 'come or go into'.

Stative verbs. For example, *taŋ³²³* 'be', *ɕiŋ⁵³* 'be', *ɕi⁵⁵* 'be', and *ɕoŋ³²³* 'resemble'.

Predicate nouns. These occur predominantly in the northern dialect: e.g., *joŋ²⁵* 'shoot with gun', *jo⁵⁵* 'saw (v)', *zɐn³⁵* 'cut with knife', *wjet³⁵* 'slash with whip', *waŋ³³* 'hit with cudgel', *yan²²* 'strike with carrying pole', and *wan³³* 'strike with palm of hand'.

The southern dialect also has some predicate nouns: e.g., *khɐi³⁵* 'plow (n)', *kwiu⁵³* 'weighing scale', *so¹³* 'lock (n)', and *siu⁵³* 'chisel (n)'.

Grammatical characteristics of verbs

Verbs can take modification from adverbs and from time nouns

(191) *kop³²³   we³¹*
       just   do
       done just now

   lət³⁵   pai⁵⁵
   all   go
   all go

   ʔɐi³²³   ɳon³³
   not   beˆwilling
   unwilling

   mɐn⁵⁵mu³²³   ma³⁵
   tomorrow   come
   come tomorrow

Dong verbs normally cannot take modification from adverbs of degree. For example, you cannot say *hən³¹ tham¹³ 'very go' or *the³⁵ ma³⁵ 'too come'. Some adverbs of degree, however, like *nɐŋ²¹²* 'really' and *ɕaŋ³³* 'even more, anyway', can modify verbs. For example, *nɐŋ²¹² tan⁵⁵* 'really eat', *nɐŋ²¹² ju⁵³ tan⁵⁵* 'really want to eat', *nɐŋ²¹² ma³⁵* 'really come', and *nɐŋ²¹² we³¹* 'really do'; *ɕaŋ³³ pai⁵⁵* 'go anyway', *ɕaŋ³³ ju⁵³ pai⁵⁵* 'want to go even more', and *ɕaŋ³³ we³¹* 'do even more'.

Verbs generally cannot reduplicate. Under the influence of Chinese, however, some verbs can reduplicate, expressing the meaning 'of short duration' or 'try out'. When expressing the meaning 'try out', the word *nu⁵³* 'see' is usually added after the reduplicated verb. Two examples are given in (192).

(192) *ɳa²¹²   thiŋ⁴⁵³   thiŋ⁴⁵³   nu⁵³   ɕok²¹   mi³¹*
       2s   taste   taste   see   cooked not
       You taste a little and see whether it's cooked or not.

        ja²¹²   tau⁵⁵   pai⁵⁵   **tham¹³**   **tham¹³**
        two   1p^inc   go   walk (v)   walk (v)
        Let's (the two of us) go for a short walk.

The above two sentences are often said alternatively as in (193).

(193) ȵa²¹²   ɕi⁴⁵³   **thiŋ⁴⁵³**   nu⁵³   ɕok²¹   mi³¹
        2s   try   taste   see   cooked   not
        You taste a little and see whether it's cooked or not.

        ja²¹²   tau⁵⁵   pai⁵⁵   **tham¹³**   teŋ³¹   (ȵi⁵⁵)
        two   1p^inc   go   walk (v)   a^little   (some)
        Let's (the two of us) go for a short walk.

In addition to the above kind of reduplication, two antonymous monosyllabic verbs A and B may reduplicate in the form AABB to express the meaning of doing something again and again; but there are very few phrases like this in Dong. Two examples are given in (194).

(194) **tha⁴⁵³**   **tha⁴⁵³**   lui³³   lui³³
        go^up   go^up   go^down   go^down
        go up and down, again and again

        pai⁵⁵   pai⁵⁵   ɕon⁵³   ɕon⁵³
        go   go   turn   turn
        keep going back and forth

Modal verbs generally appear before other verbs.

(195) **haŋ¹³**   pai⁵⁵
        agree   go
        agree to go

        ʔam³²³   ma³⁵
        dare   come
        dare to come

        li³²³   tɐn³²³
        have   wear
        have (clothes) to wear

Under particular circumstances, however, modal verbs can carry nouns or pronouns as objects of their own.

(196) wo³¹   le²¹²
      know   book
      be literate

      ɳon³³   mau³³
      willing 3s
      want to marry him

Directional verbs. Apart from possessing the usual grammatical characteristics and uses of verbs, directional verbs can also be used as complements for other verbs. When the other verbs have objects, the directional verbs appear after the objects.

(197) lui³³   tən²¹²   ma³⁵
      come^down   mountain   come
      come down from the mountain

      pjeu⁵³   ʔuk³²³   pai⁵⁵
      run   go^out   go
      run outside

      tok⁵⁵   lau³²³   ɳa⁵⁵   pai⁵⁵
      fall   enter   river   go
      fall into the river

      jan²¹²   ta⁵³   ʔut¹³   tən²¹²   ma³⁵
      house   that   burn   start   come
      That house is starting to burn.

Stative verbs. In Dong there are three verbs, taŋ³²³, ɕiŋ⁵³, and ɕi⁵⁵, all meaning 'to be'. The verbs taŋ³²³ and ɕiŋ⁵³ are used in most places in the southern dialect area. The verb ɕi⁵⁵ is seldom used in the south and then only for poems and songs.

(198) phaŋ³⁵   ɕi⁵⁵   thɐm⁴⁵³
      high   be   low
      High is (still) low.

      jɐm⁵⁵   ɕi⁵⁵   lin⁵³
      deep   be   shallow
      Deep is (still) shallow.

In the south ȶaŋ³²³ can be used in answering questions. When answering in the negative, the word kwe²¹² 'not' precedes ȶaŋ³²³.

(199)   mau³³   ȶaŋ³²³   ȵən²¹²   ɕai³³   ȶiu⁵⁵
         3s   be   person   village   1p
         He is from our village.

        muŋ³¹   ȵən²¹²   ȶa⁵³   kwe²¹²   ȶaŋ³²³   ta⁵⁵   pha³⁵
        CLF   person   that   not   be   eye   gray
        That person is not blind.

In contrast to its rare usage in the southern dialect, ɕi⁵⁵ is the most-used stative verb in the northern dialect. There are two ways of expressing the negative: kwe²² ɕi⁵⁵ and ʔaŋ³³.

(200)   to²²   mu²⁵   nai⁴⁴   ɕi⁵⁵   na²²   li³³   kwe²²   ɕi⁵⁵
        CLF   pig   this   be   2s   REL   not   be
        Is this pig yours or not?

       ɕi⁵⁵
       be
       Yes, it's mine.

       to²²   mu²⁵   nai⁴⁴   ɕi⁵⁵   na²²   li³³   ʔaŋ³³
       CLF   pig   this   be   2s   REL   not^be
       Is this pig yours or not?

       ʔaŋ³³
       not^be
       No, it's not mine.

Stative verbs cannot reduplicate and cannot express tense. When there is no subject, or when the predicate is not a predicate noun, ȶaŋ³²³ or ɕi⁵⁵ at the beginning of a phrase do not link anything, but express a kind of emphasis.

(201)   ȶaŋ³²³   jau²¹²   ʔau⁵⁵   pai⁵⁵   jaŋ³¹
       be   1s   take   go   STM
       It was **I** who took (it).

       jau²¹²   ɕi⁵⁵   ʔɐi³²³   li³²³   maŋ²¹²   mje³³   la³¹
       1s   be   not   have   anything   consider   EX
       I do not have anything to think over!

Predicate nouns. In the northern dialect predicate nouns derive from physical objects of one kind or another. For example, ţin³⁵ 'stone', məi³¹ 'branch', mja³¹ 'knife', pjət³⁵ 'whip', ɕoŋ⁵⁵ 'gun', kwan³⁵ 'ax', paŋ⁴⁴ 'wooden cudgel', and so on. When these nouns serve as verbs, their syllable initials and some of their tones are subject to change. A predicate noun expresses the action the given noun is used to perform.

(202)   təi²²   ţin³⁵   **jin³⁵**   mən²²
          take   stone   'stone'   3s
          Take the stone to bash it.

          təi²²   məi³¹   **wəi³¹**   pai³⁵
          take   stick   'stick'   go
          Take the stick and hit (it).

          təi²²   ɕoŋ⁵⁵   **joŋ²⁵**   mən²²
          take   gun   'gun'   3s
          Take the gun to shoot it.

          təi²²   paŋ⁴⁴   **waŋ⁴⁴**   pai³⁵
          take   cudgel   'cudgel'   go
          Take the cudgel and strike (it).

Predicate nouns add a sense of intensity, with their associated action being of a resolute and decisive nature.

(203)   jau²²   təi²²   mja³¹   **wja³¹**   pai³⁵
          1s   take   knife   'knife'   go
          I'll take the knife to cut (it).

          jau²²   **wja³¹**   pai³⁵
          1s   'knife'   go
          I'll cut (it).

Predicate nouns can be replaced by verbs, but when they are, the verbs use phonetically changed forms.

(204)   ņa²²   təi²²   ţin³⁵   ya¹¹   (*ta¹¹)   pai³⁵
          2s   take   stone   pound   go
          You take the stone and pound (it).

jau²² təi²² mja³¹ won¹¹ (*pon¹¹) pai³⁵
1s   take knife chop   go
I'll take the knife and chop (it).

mau⁴⁴ təi²² paŋ⁴⁴ wən¹¹ (*pən¹¹) pai³⁵
3s   take cudgel fly   go
He flung the cudgel.

Phonetic change of some verbs in the northern dialect. The syllable initials of some verbs in some northern dialect areas, in certain situations, undergo phonetic change. The rules for change are the same as for classifiers (cf. (140)–(146)). The examples in (205) are from Shídòng speech.

(205) **pet¹³** → **wet¹³** ka¹¹
      beat   beat   ear
                 slap ear

pit³³ → **wit³³** pai³⁵
run   run   go
            run

tui³³ → **ʐui³³** pai³⁵
ladle   ladle (v) go
            ladle (it)

to³⁵ → **ʐo³⁵** tin³⁵
bind   bind   foot
           Tie the shoe.

sun¹¹ → **ʐun¹¹** mən²² təi³⁵
pierce   pierce   3s   die
             Pierce it to death.

tai¹³ → **jai¹³** mən²¹ təi³⁵
trample   trample 3s   die
             Trample it to death.

tiŋ²⁵ → kwe²² lai³⁵ **jiŋ²⁵**
listen   not   good   listen
           not good-sounding

Grammar 127

  kəi³⁵ → yəi³⁵ pai³⁵
  hit   hit go
       hit (v)

 The scope and significance of such phonetic change is not yet completely clear. It seems that in most cases it is connected with the occasion and speed of the associated action, and implies a sense of intensity, indicating the action is faster and more resolute than usual.

4.1.6 Adjectives

Grammatical characteristics of adjectives

 Adjectives in Dong can reduplicate. The monosyllabic adjective A reduplicates as AA, expressing emphasis. In the southern dialect, the 'empty' demonstrative pronoun *ta³³* is added after reduplication. (Some Dong intellectuals like to add the word *ti³³* borrowed from the Chinese 的 *de*, instead of *ta³³*.) This kind of reduplication gives rise both to complements appearing after a noun and adverbial expressions appearing before a verb.

(206) Southern dialect

   na³²³ ja⁴⁵³ ja⁴⁵³ ta³³ (ti³³)
   face red red PTC (PTC)
   very red face

   nɐm³¹ lu³⁵ lu³⁵ ta³³ (ti³³)
   water clear clear PTC (PTC)
   very clear water

   lai⁵⁵ lai⁵⁵ ta³³ (ti³³) we³¹
   good good PTC (PTC) do
   do very well

(207) Northern dialect (instead of *li³³* below, can also use *ti³³*)

   zou³³ ʔai⁵⁵ lau³¹ lau³¹ li³³
   CLF hen big big PTC
   brood of very big hens

   wəi³¹ tuʔ³¹ məi²⁵ məi²⁵ li³³
   CLF clothing new new PTC
   item of brand new clothing

lai³⁵ lai³⁵ li³³ to?¹³ le²²
good good PTC read book
study very well

In both the southern and northern dialects, disyllabic adjectives AB usually reduplicate in the form AABB.

(208) Southern dialect

khwan³⁵ţi³³ → khwan³⁵khwan³⁵ţi³³ţi³³
happy   elated

ţet²¹ţhut¹³ → ţet²¹ţet²¹ţhut¹³ţhut¹³
hasty   extremely hasty

noŋ²¹²ņen³³ → noŋ²¹²noŋ²¹²ņen³³ņen³³
pleased   delighted

lu³³la³³ → lu³³lu³³la³³la³³
in a mess   in terrible disorder

(209) Northern dialect

wan¹¹ņi¹³ → wan¹¹wan¹¹ņi¹³ņi¹³
happy   elated

woŋ¹¹ņoŋ²² → woŋ¹¹woŋ¹¹ņoŋ²²ņoŋ²²
lively   extremely lively

ljo²⁵ţo⁵⁵ → ljo²⁵ljo²⁵ţo⁵⁵ţo⁵⁵
hasty   extremely hasty

nai³³wən²² → nai³³nai³³wən²²wən²²
patient   extremely patient

Two antonymous adjectives A and B generally reduplicate as AABB, though some can also reduplicate as ABAB; in either case, reduplication expresses diversity.

(210) phaŋ³⁵ phaŋ³⁵ thɐm⁴⁵³ thɐm⁴⁵³
       tall   tall   short   short
       (many) tall and short, all heights

mak^{323} mak^{323} ni^{53} ni^{53}
big   big   small   small
(many) big and small, all sizes

lau^{31} lau^{31} $ɲi^{31}$ $ɲi^{31}$
old   old   young   young
(many) old and young, all ages

Stative adjectives in Dong can take objects. In such cases, the verb 'to be' is implicit.

(211) ja^{453} na^{323} ja^{453} ta^{55}
       red   face   red   eye
       face is red   eye is red

       wa^{53} $ʔuk^{323}$ wa^{53} $jaŋ^{33}$
       dirty   clothing   dirty   quilt
       clothing is dirty   quilt is dirty

       $lʲɐk^{35}$ tin^{55} lai^{55} $ʔɐu^{31}$
       cold   foot   good   rice
       feet are cold   rice is good

       $kwaŋ^{55}$ $mən^{55}$ $kwaŋ^{55}$ pui^{55}
       bright   sky   bright   light
       sky is bright (dawn has broken)   light is lit

This kind of phrase has the same form as predicate-complement type compound words (cf. (58)–(63)). The difference is that the compound words have fixed extended meanings. For example, the word $ɕeŋ^{11}sai^{33}$ 'raw/intestines' from Tiānzhù's Shídòng speech does not mean 'raw intestines', but has an extended meaning of 'bitterly disappointed'. It is impossible to take this and derive meanings by analogy for $ɕeŋ^{11}tin^{35}$ 'raw/foot', $ɕeŋ^{11}kau^{33}$ 'raw/head', or $ɕeŋ^{11}tu^{33}$ 'raw/belly'. By contrast, the meaning of a predicate-object type phrase is a composite of the meanings of the component parts. Thus, the phrase $səm^{33}jeu^{35}$ 'ache/back' means 'backache', a synthesis of the two individual components. In this case it is possible to derive meanings for the new phrases $səm^{33}tin^{35}$ 'foot-ache' or $səm^{33}mja^{22}$ 'hand-ache'.

Predicate-complement type compound words of some places in the northern dialect area can take objects. The examples in (212) are from Tiānzhù speech.

(212) ɕeŋ¹¹ sai³³ mən²²
raw intestines 3s
bitterly disappointed in him

kit³³ sai³³ na²²
be^ill intestines 2s
long for you

ɕaŋ⁵⁵ ɬi²⁵ mau⁴⁴
expand air 3s
dislike him

so³³ ʔo²² nəm³¹
dry throat water
thirsty for water

Suffixes. After some monosyllabic adjectives, a suffix expressing different intensity or quality can be added to form a suffixed compound word. The adjectives can only be words which vary on a relatively concrete scale; for example, adjectives which express the color, length, height, taste, or sharpness of things. Adjectives which are more abstract, such as *lai⁵⁵* 'good', *ja³¹* 'bad', *ʔe³²³* 'foolish', or *ɕɐi³⁵* 'intelligent', do not take such suffixes.

These suffixed compound words can take one of three forms: AB, ABB, or ABC, where A represents the adjective and B and C represent suffixes. The form ABC is seldom used. A given adjective can frequently take several different suffixes, expressing different intensities and qualities. Below are some examples from both southern and northern dialects. (Because of the complexity and subtlety of the meanings of these compound words, only the meanings of the original adjectives are indicated.)

(213) Southern dialect

pak³¹ → pak³¹moŋ⁵⁵   pak³¹moŋ⁵⁵moŋ⁵⁵
white   pak³¹sep³²³   pak³¹sep³²³sep³²³
          pak³¹siŋ³³   pak³¹siŋ³³siŋ³³

nɐm⁵⁵ → nɐm⁵⁵tum³²³   nɐm⁵⁵tum³²³tum³²³
black

jai³²³ → jai³²³je³¹   jai³²³je³¹je³¹
long

jai^{33} → $jai^{33}jep^{31}$ $jai^{33}jep^{31}jep^{31}$
sharp

(214) Northern dialect

ja^{25} → $ja^{25}wu^{55}$ $ja^{25}wu^{55}wu^{55}$
red $ja^{25}ljei^{33}$ $ja^{25}ljei^{33}ljei^{33}$
         $ja^{25}ljaŋ^{31}$ $ja^{25}ljaŋ^{31}ljaŋ^{31}$
         $ja^{25}lji^{55}ljaŋ^{31}$

$səm^{13}$ → $səm^{13}pjat^{33}$ $səm^{13}pjat^{33}pjat^{33}$
sour $səm^{13}ɲəm^{31}$ $səm^{13}ɲəm^{31}ɲəm^{31}$

$paŋ^{11}$ → $paŋ^{11}ɕaŋ^{22}$ $paŋ^{11}kot^{33}ɲot^{33}$
tall

$taŋ^{35}$ → $taŋ^{35}pən^{35}$ $taŋ^{35}pən^{35}pən^{35}$
fragrant

Usually, the AB form is stronger in intensity than the original adjective, and the ABB and ABC forms are even stronger than AB. After adding a suffix, adjectives can only serve as predicates and not as attributes, adverbial expressions, or complements.

Similarities and differences between adjectives and verbs

Adjectives and verbs in Dong can both be modified by adverbs. One of the characteristic differences between adjectives and verbs in Chinese is whether or not they can take modification from the adverb of degree 很 *hěn* (in general, only adjectives can take this intensifier in Chinese). In Dong, adjectives can take modification from the borrowed adverbs of degree $hən^{31}$ (很 *hěn*) and the^{35} (太 *tài*); but apart from some verbs expressing feeling and emotion, verbs in Dong are not usually modified by these borrowed adverbs. However, Dong's own adverbs of degree $nəŋ^{212}$ 'really' and $ɕaŋ^{33}$ 'even more, anyway' can modify both adjectives and verbs (cf. paragraph after (191)).

Chinese adjectives cannot take objects. Dong adjectives and verbs can both take objects.

(215) mau^{33} pai^{55} $ɕuk^{323}$ na^{323}
       3s   go   wash (v)   face
       He is going to wash his face. (verb)

mau³³ **nɐm⁵⁵** na³²³ ljeu³¹
3s black face PAST
He became unhappy. (adjective)

ȵan⁵⁵ nai³³ ju⁵³ pai⁵⁵ to³²³ ma⁵⁵
month this want go plant (v) vegetable
This month (I) will go and plant vegetables. (verb)

ȵan⁵⁵ nai³³ nɐŋ²¹² **jun³²³** ma⁵⁵ nɐŋ²¹²
month this really little vegetable really
This month there are very few vegetables. (adjective)

Grammatical function. With respect to grammatical function, adjectives and verbs are very much alike: both can serve as subjects, predicates, attributes, complements, and objects. Adjectives, however, in contrast to verbs, can also play the part of adverbial modifiers, as in (216).

(216) ȵa²¹² **hoi⁴⁵³** ȶi⁵⁵
2s fast eat
You eat quickly.

Adjectives can reduplicate, while verbs generally cannot. In some places in the southern dialect area, there are some monosyllabic verbs that can reduplicate (cf. (192)). After reduplication, they often add the 'empty' verb *nu⁵³* 'look'. After reduplication, monosyllabic adjectives usually add the 'empty' demonstrative pronoun *ta³³* 'that' (cf. (206)).

Adjectives, in contrast to verbs, can add suffixes to make compound words (cf. (213), (214)). The only descriptive words which can follow verbs are sound descriptive words (cf. (228)–(230)).

4.1.7 Adverbs

Adverbs are words which restrict, modify, or supplement verbs and adjectives.

Classification of adverbs. In this section, northern dialect words are indicated in parentheses after the English gloss or after all the southern dialect examples.

Adverbs of degree: e.g., *hən³¹* 'very' (*ta³¹*), *ʈhe³⁵* 'excessively' (*tai²⁵*), *nɐŋ²¹²* 'really' (*ɕin³⁵*), *ɕaŋ³³* 'even more, anyway', and *ɕi⁴⁵³*, *khɐn⁴⁵³*, *sau⁴⁵³*, and *lau³¹ho³³* 'extremely' (*ʐau²⁵*).

Adverbs of scope: e.g., *lət³⁵* 'all, completely' (*ɣau²⁵* and *hau³⁵*), *tu⁵⁵* and *ɕet¹³* 'all' (*tu³⁵*), *pən³²³* and *lau¹³* 'only' (*ɕi²²*), and *pu³³* and *ja³³* 'also' (*ja³³*). (In the northern dialect: *ʈuŋ²²* 'many'.)

Adverbs of time: e.g., *su³³* 'at once' (*ɕu⁴⁴*), *kop³²³* 'just now' (*ja⁵⁵ɕi²²*, *ka¹³ka¹³*, *ʔau¹³nai³³*, *ja⁵⁵ʔau¹³*, and *ja⁵⁵sai²²*), *nʋŋ⁵⁵* 'still' (*han¹¹*), *lʋŋ³¹* 'immediately', and *wan²¹²* 'already'. (In the northern dialect, adverbs of time include *jən²²* and *ɕaŋ²²ɕi²²* 'often, frequently', *ju⁴⁴* 'again', and *taŋ⁵⁵taŋ⁵⁵* 'gradually'.)

Adverbs of negation: e.g., *kwe²¹²*, *ʔʋi³²³*, and *ljan³¹* 'not' (*kwe²²* and *ʔei³³*), *mi³¹* 'have not, did not' (*me³¹*, *me³¹jaŋ²²*, or *mjaŋ²²*), *ʔoŋ³⁵* 'not have', *pi³¹* 'do not' (*pe³¹* or *pi³¹*), and *ʔi³²³* 'cannot' (*ki³³* and *nan²²*).

Adverbs of manner: e.g., *pen³³* 'so long as...' (*ɕi²²ju³⁵*), *hoŋ²¹²he²¹²* 'anyway' (*hoŋ²²he²²*), and *phjen³⁵* 'stubbornly, contrary to what was expected' (*pjen¹¹*).

Grammatical characteristics of adverbs

Normally adverbs cannot reduplicate, though there are a few which can, such as *kop³²³* 'just now', *sau⁴⁵³* 'extremely', and in the northern dialect *ʔau¹³* 'just now'. With these few, reduplication is used for increased emphasis.

(217) jau²¹² kop³²³ ma³⁵ → jau²¹² kop³²³ kop³²³ ma³⁵
1s just come 1s just just come
I just came. I only just came.

kwe²¹² lai⁵⁵ sau⁴⁵³ → kwe²¹² lai⁵⁵ sau⁴⁵³ sau⁴⁵³
not good very not good very very
very bad terrible

jau²² ʔau¹³ ʈe³⁵ → jau²² ʔau¹³ ʔau¹³ ʈe³⁵
1s just eat 1s just just eat
I just ate. (Shídòng) I only just ate. (Shídòng)

The northern dialect has some other reduplicating adverbs. The two examples in (218) are from Shídòng speech.

(218) jau²² **ka¹³ ka¹³** ʈe³⁵ kən¹¹ ʔəu³¹
1s just just eat whole meal
I only just finished eating a meal.

jau²² pai³⁵ **ha³³ ha³³** ɕu³¹ ɕon⁵⁵ ma¹¹
1s go while while just turn come
I am going for a little while and will come straight back.

Questions. Adverbs cannot be used alone to answer questions, except for adverbs of negation.

Modifiers and complements. In the southern dialect of Dong, most adverbs can only act as adverbial modifiers.

(219)   **lət³⁵** khwan³⁵   **pu³³** lai⁵⁵
       all   sweet   also   good
       all are sweet   also good

       pən³²³ wo³¹   **tu⁵⁵** pai⁵⁵
       only   know   all   go
       only know   all go

       kwe²¹² jai³²³   **ʔɐi³²³** we³¹
       not   long   not   do
       not long   not do

Some adverbs, such as ɕi⁴⁵³, khɐn⁴⁵³, sau⁴⁵³, and lau³¹ho³³ (all meaning 'extremely') can act only as complements.

(220)   ni⁵³   **ɕi⁴⁵³**
       small   extremely
       extremely small

       kwe²¹² pai⁵⁵ **sau⁴⁵³**
       not   go   very
       never go

       ja³¹   **khɐn⁴⁵³**
       bad   extremely
       extremely bad

Grammar   135

    kwe²¹²   *lai⁵⁵*   *sau⁴⁵³*
    not   good   very
    very poor (quality)

Other adverbs, such as *ʔun⁵³* 'in front' and *nɐŋ²¹²* 'really', can act as either modifiers or complements. In fact, *nɐŋ²¹²* can appear before and after a verb in the same phrase.

(221) *n̠a²¹²* *ʔun⁵³*   *pai⁵⁵* = *n̠a²¹²* *pai⁵⁵* *ʔun⁵³*
      2s   in^front go   2s   go   in^front
      You go first.

      nɐŋ²¹²   *taŋ⁵⁵*   *nɐŋ²¹²*
      really   fragrant really
      really very fragrant

      nɐŋ²¹² *we³¹* *li³²³* *lai⁵⁵* *nɐŋ²¹²*
      really   do   PTC   good   really
      really do extremely well

In the northern dialect, except for adverbs borrowed from Chinese and adverbs of negation, which are placed before verbs or adjectives and act as adverbial modifiers, adverbs are normally placed after verbs or adjectives and act as complements.

(222) *tai²⁵* *lai³⁵*   *tu³⁵* *pai³⁵*
      too   good   all   go
      great!   all go

      ɕu⁴⁴   *t̠am¹³*   *kwe²²* *t̠ai³³*
      at^once walk (v)   not   buy
      go at once   not buy

      t̠e³⁵ *tok³¹*   *woi²⁵* *ɕi⁵⁵*
      eat   alone   fast   extremely
      eat alone (selfishly)   extremely fast

      pəi³⁵ *t̠uŋ²²*   *taŋ³⁵* *ʐau²⁵*
      near   much   fragrant most
      much nearer   the most fragrant

Emphasis. Two synonymous adverbs may sometimes be said together for emphasis.

(223) tau⁵⁵   çet¹³   lət³⁵   tən²¹²   ma³⁵   su³³   lɐŋ³¹   pai⁵⁵
      1p   all   all   up   come   at^once immediately   go
      Let's all get up and go immediately!

      jau²¹²   pən³²³   lau¹³   wo³¹   tɐm³²³   tak³²³   tok²¹   tok²¹
      1s   only   barely   know   weave   cloth   alone   alone
      I only know how to weave (I don't know anything else)!

      ka³²³   nai³³   nɐŋ²¹²   lai⁵⁵   kuŋ²¹²
      seedling   this   really   good   much
      These seedlings are really very good!

Adverbs with verbal function. Adverbs sometimes possess grammatical characteristics of verbs or adjectives.

In the southern dialect, most native Dong monosyllabic adverbs can modify nominals; when they do, they precede the nouns.

(224) çai³³   nai³³   lət³⁵   kɐm⁵⁵   tən⁵⁵   tən⁵⁵
      village   this   all   Dong   all   all
      Everyone in this village is Dong (nationality).

      pən³²³   mau³³   ka³¹
      only   3s   Hàn
      Only he is Hàn (nationality).

      lɐŋ³¹   nɐn⁵⁵   nai³³   lai⁵⁵
      just   CLF   this   good
      It's this one that's good.

      kui³²³   kwe²¹²   pa⁵⁵   ɲo²¹²   we³¹   mak³²³
      stream   not^have   fish   shrimp   do   big
      When the stream has no fish, the shrimp is called the biggest. (Dong song)

      ʔoŋ³⁵   wa³⁵   ʔɐi³²³   wən³⁵   pha³⁵
      not^have   pattern   not   be   scarf

      ʔoŋ³⁵   jən⁵⁵   ʔɐi³²³   wən³⁵   ʔa⁵⁵
      not^have   rhyme   not   be   song
      Without a pattern, there is no scarf; without rhyme, there is no song.

In the northern dialect, there are several pairs of adverbs with very similar meaning, e.g., *kwe²²* and *ʔəi³³* 'not', *nən²²* and *ki³³* 'out of the question, not able', *wan¹¹* and *men¹¹* 'entirely', and *ta³³* and *ŋən¹¹* 'determinedly'. These have some differences in usage.

The words *kwe²²* and *ʔəi³³* are adverbs of negation: *kwe²²* can double-up as a verb and combine directly with nominals, while *ʔəi³³* can only function as an adverb.

(225) *kwe²² jən²²* *kwe²² sin²²*
 not person not money
 there are no people there is no money

 kwe²² we³¹ *kwe²² ȶui⁵⁵*
 not do not expensive
 have not done/will not do not expensive

 ʔəi³³ we³¹ *ʔəi³³ ȵau⁴⁴*
 not do not stay
 (will) not do (will) not stay (overnight)

 ʔəi³³ pai³⁵ *ʔəi³³ ȶe³⁵*
 not go not eat
 (will) not go (will) not eat

The meanings of the words *kwe²²* and *ʔəi³³* are also a bit different: *kwe²²* corresponds to the Chinese 'not' (不 *bù*), while *ʔəi³³* corresponds to the Chinese 'not agree, not be willing' (不肯 *bù kěn*).

(226) *kwe²² pai³⁵* *mau⁴⁴ kwe²² toŋ³⁵ ʔəu³¹*
 not go 3s not boil rice
 not go He is not boiling rice.

 ʔəi³³ pai³⁵ *mau⁴⁴ ʔəi³³ toŋ³⁵ ʔəu³¹*
 not^willing go 3s not^agree boil rice
 not willing to go He does not want to boil rice.

The words *nən²²* and *ki³³* are both adverbs of negation, but there are some differences in their usage: *nən²²* can only be placed before a predicate, functioning as an adverbial modifier, while *ki³³* is just the opposite and can only be placed after a predicate, functioning as a complement. In the eight examples in (227), the expressions translated 'not able to' have the connotation 'do not want to', whereas the expressions translated 'cannot' have the connotation 'afraid to'.

(227) **nən²²**   ȶəi³³   ȶəi³³   **ki³³**
       not^able buy   buy   cannot
       not able to buy   cannot buy

       nən²²   we³¹   we³¹   **ki³³**
       not^able do   do   cannot
       not able to do   cannot do

       nən²²   ȶoŋ³⁵   ȶoŋ³⁵   **ki³³**
       not^able point   point   cannot
       not able to point   cannot point

       nən²²   ȶe³⁵   ȶe³⁵   **ki³³**
       not^able eat   eat   cannot
       not able to eat   cannot eat

4.1.8 Sound descriptive words

Sound descriptive words are words which simulate real-life sounds or convey imagery associated with real-life actions.

Classification of sound descriptive words

Onomatopoeic words. These are imitative of the sound of the action or noise designated.

(228) ko⁵⁵   hi⁵⁵   hi⁵⁵
       laugh xī (嘻)   xī (嘻)
       laugh—hee, hee

       heu³⁵ pat²¹   pat²¹
       hit   bā (叭)   bā (叭)
       hit—bat, bat

Descriptive words. These can be either monosyllabic or polysyllabic. They are used to convey imagery associated with an action or to add a certain modification of meaning. A given sound descriptive word can frequently only describe a specific verb, though occasionally one may apply to a number of verbs. On the other hand, a given verb may be described by several sound descriptive words, used to describe different sounds or images associated with different stages of the action in question. There is not necessarily any phonetic link between the descriptive words and the actions of the verbs they describe.

(229) **pjiu⁵⁵** → **pjiu⁵⁵ sat³²³sat³²³**
jump   jump, again and again

pjeu⁵³ → **pjeu⁵³ lət⁵⁵lət⁵⁵**
run   run, huffing and puffing

ʔui³⁵ → **ʔui³⁵ tɐt⁵⁵tɐt⁵⁵** or **ʔui³⁵ təp⁵⁵təp⁵⁵**
flow   babble along

Grammatical characteristics of sound descriptive words

Function. Sound descriptive words can either be placed after verbs and function as complements or before verbs and function as adverbial modifiers.

(230) **hem³¹ ljoŋ³¹ljoŋ³¹** = **ljoŋ³¹ljoŋ³¹ ta³³ hem³¹**
shout (v) loudly   loudly   PTC shout (v)
shout loudly

pɐm²¹² lui³³ nɐm³¹ pai⁵⁵
splash go^down water go
splash into the water

In some idiomatic phrases, sound descriptive words can function as predicates.

(231) **lak³¹ pja³²³ hu³¹hu³¹ ʔu³¹ thik¹³ su³⁵**
son thunder (n) sound^of^thunder hail kick autumn
In autumn, the thunder rumbles and the hail falls.

pan⁵⁵ sak³²³ tin²¹² ti³³ mjek³²³ weu²¹²weu³⁵
male plant (v) field earth female sound^of^spinning
Men plow the fields, women weave.

Verb with object. In the southern dialect, if a verb carries an object, the sound descriptive word usually comes after the object.

(232) **tok⁵⁵ pjən⁵⁵ tɐt⁵⁵tɐt⁵⁵**
fall rain sound^of^rain
continuously raining

pai⁵⁵ ȶən²¹² khweŋ⁴⁵³khweŋ⁴⁵³
go   mountain sound^of^marching
(many people are) going up the mountain

In the northern dialect, sound descriptive words can be placed either after direct objects or before predicates.

(233) ʔəi¹¹   mu⁵⁵   ŋa³³ŋa³³ = ŋa³³ŋa³³ li³³ ʔəi¹¹ mu⁵⁵
       open   mouth   SD   SD   REL   open   mouth
       stupid, stunned

       tui¹¹   nəm³¹   tje³¹tje³¹
       flow   water   sound^of^water^flowing
       murmuring stream

       kıt³¹   pjən³⁵   kɐp¹¹kɐp¹¹
       bite   tooth   sound^of^teeth^grinding
       grinding teeth

Monosyllabic sound descriptive words. Sound descriptive words are usually disyllabic with repeated syllables and usually follow verbs. In the southern dialect, however, there are still some monosyllabic sound descriptive words which precede verbs and function as adverbial modifiers. They indicate the associated action is sudden.

(234) **pat³²³** la⁵³   ȶak²¹   ʔaŋ⁵⁵
       SD   break CLF   big^jar
       suddenly smash the big jar

       thot¹³ jɐm⁵⁵ lui³³   pai⁵⁵
       SD   sink   go^down go
       suddenly sink down

       ɕat¹³   jən⁵⁵ ȶən²¹² ma³⁵
       SD   lift   up   come
       suddenly raise up

4.1.9 Prepositions

Grammatical characteristics of prepositions

In prepositional phrases. Prepositions are not used alone, nor do they allow reduplication. Normally they occur before nouns, pronouns, or noun phrases, functioning as heads of prepositional phrases.

Prepositional phrases can modify the verbs or adjectives that follow them.

(235) jau²¹²   ta³³   pa²¹²tən³³   ma³⁵
      1s   pass (v)   Běijīng   come
      I am coming from Běijīng.

      mau³³   pi³²³   na²¹²   phaŋ³⁵
      3s   compare   2s   tall
      He is taller than you.

      ɲim³⁵   ҫau³⁵   wa³³   kem⁵⁵
      with   2p   talk   Dong
      speaking Dong with you

      sok²¹   na⁵⁵   tha⁴⁵³   pai⁵⁵
      along   river   go^up   go
      go up along the river

Prepositional phrases can also function as complements to preceding verbs or adjectives.

(236) sui⁵³   nau³³   te³²³   mei³¹   ta³³
      sit   at   below   tree   that
      Sit underneath that tree.

      jam⁵⁵   sai³⁵   noŋ³¹   ҫau³⁵   ʔi⁵⁵   pən³²³   le²¹²
      lend   give   younger^brother   2p   one   CLF   book
      Lend your younger brother a book.

As predicates. Prepositions and prepositional phrases generally cannot function as predicates nor serve alone in answering questions. In Dong, however, many prepositions developed from verbs. These prepositions can have a dual role. In one situation they are prepositions; and in another situation they are verbs, able to function as predicates and to be used in answering questions.

(237) jau²¹² ȵau³³ kui⁵⁵jaŋ²¹² tok²¹ le²¹²
1s in Guìyáng read book
I am studying in Guìyáng. (preposition)

jau²¹² ȵau³³ kui⁵⁵jaŋ²¹²
1s be^in Guìyáng
I am in Guìyáng. (verb)

mau³³ ȵau³³ kwe²¹² ȵau³³ jan²¹²
3s be^at not be^at home
Is he at home or not? (verb)

ȵau³³
at/be^at
Yes, he's at home. (preposition/verb)

Non-predicate prepositions. In Dong, there are very few prepositions which only function as prepositions and not as verbs. Examples are wi³³ 'for' in the southern dialect and ȶaŋ³³ 'by' in the northern dialect.

(238) wi³³ ȵa²¹² heu³⁵ jau²¹² wi³³ jau²¹² heu³⁵ ȵa²¹²
for 2s hit 1s for 1s hit 2s
hit me for you, hit you for me (riddle, referring to hitting mosquitoes)

ȶaŋ³³ məm³¹ kit³¹
PASS tiger bite
bitten by a tiger (Shídòng)

ȶaŋ³³ mja³¹ te³⁵
PASS knife chop
chopped by a knife (Shídòng)

Usage of some particular prepositions

tʋu³³ 'by' (cf. 被 bèi). This is used in passive sentences. The following noun or pronoun is the agent of the verb. (If there is no noun or pronoun representing the agent following tʋu³³, then tʋu³³ is not in that case a preposition but rather an auxiliary word expressing the passive voice; cf. (251)). In the northern dialect, passive sentences can either use ȶaŋ³³ or təu⁴⁴, both meaning 'by'.

Grammar

(239) Southern dialect

pu^{33}	$ɬiu^{212}$	$mɐi^{31}$	$ʈa^{53}$	$tɐu^{33}$	$nɐm^{31}$	lau^{31}
CLF	bridge	wooden	that	PASS	water	big

$khuk^{13}$	wai^{33}	$jaŋ^{31}$
wash^away	damage (v)	STM

That wooden bridge was damaged by the flood.

(240) Northern dialect

pu^{44}	$ɬiu^{22}$	$məi^{31}$	ka^{55}	$ʈaŋ^{33}$	$(təu^{44})$	$nəm^{31}$
CLF	bridge	wooden	that	PASS	(PASS)	water

lau^{31}	$ɕu^{31}$	wai^{44}	lja^{31}
big	wash^away	damage (v)	PAST

That wooden bridge was damaged by the flood.

$tɐi^{212}$ 'take' (cf. 把 *bǎ*). Usage of this word is the same in southern and northern dialects. As with the word 把 *bǎ* in Chinese, $tɐi^{212}$ lifts the object in front of the verb, expressing emphasis and conveying the idea of 'handling' the object in some way.

(241)

mau^{33}	$tɐi^{212}$	jau^{212}	kai^{212}	lau^{323}	jan^{212}	pai^{55}
3s	take	1s	pull	enter	house	go

He pulled me into the house.

In (242), a sentence with the same meaning as in (241) is presented, without using $tɐi^{212}$.

(242)

mau^{33}	kai^{212}	jau^{212}	lau^{323}	jan^{212}	pai^{55}
3s	pull	1s	enter	house	go

He pulled me into the house.

$ljen^{212}$ 'even' (cf. 连 *lián*). This word also lifts the object in front of the verb or can be placed in front of the subject for emphasis.

(243)

mau^{33}	$ljen^{212}$	$ʔɐu^{31}$	tu^{55}	kwe^{212}	$ʈi^{55}$	su^{33}	pai^{55}	la^{31}
3s	even	meal	all	not	eat	just	go	EX

He left straight away without even eating any food!

ljen²¹² nɐn⁵⁵ si³³ nai³³ tu⁵⁵ kwe²¹² wo³¹me⁵⁵
even CLF character this even not know
do(es) not even know **this** character!

ljen²¹² jau²¹² tu⁵⁵ kwe²¹² wo³¹ mau³³ we³¹ maŋ²¹²
even 1s all not know 3s do what
Even **I** don't know what he's doing!

There are some sentences which in Chinese normally require the use of prepositions, but in Dong do not

(244)   su³³   soŋ⁴⁵³   (ȵau³³)   ʔɐu³¹   pən²¹²   ta³³
        just   place   (in)   inside   basin   that
        just put (it) into that basin (ȵau³³ is optional)

4.1.10 Conjunctions

Conjunctions cannot stand alone as constituents of a sentence. They cannot modify other words nor be modified. They can normally only serve as links at the clause or phrase level.

Many conjunctions in Dong have been borrowed from Chinese. Only a few are native to Dong. These come from verbs. Some still retain distinct verbal meaning.

(245)   jau²¹²   **ȵim³⁵**   mau³³   kan³¹si²¹²   pai⁵⁵
        1s   with   3s   together   go
        I am going together with him. (conjunction)

        jau²¹²   **ȵim³⁵**   mau³³   kuŋ²¹²   ȵin²¹²
        1s   beˆwith   3s   many   year
        I have been with him for many years. (verb)

        kuŋ⁵⁵   **tɐŋ³³**   la²¹²   jau²¹²   tu⁵⁵   wo³¹   heu³⁵
        drum   and   gong   1s   both   know   hit
        I can play both the drum and the gong. (conjunction)

        kuŋ⁵⁵   **tɐŋ³³**   la²¹²
        drum   accompany   gong
        drum accompanying gong (verb)

        nu⁵³   ȵa²¹²   pai⁵⁵   jau²¹²   ja³³   pai⁵⁵
        see/if   2s   go   1s   also   go
        Seeing as you are going, I'll go too. *or* If you go, I'll go too.

In the first translation of the last sentence in (245), nu^{53} is a verb; in the second, it is a conjunction. The meaning can only be judged from the context. For the sake of precision in expression, the conjunction nu^{53} 'if' is frequently said as $nu^{53}pau^{53}$. In the northern dialect, the words for 'see' and 'if' are two different words, nu^{55} and nu^{11}, respectively.

Coordinate and subordinate conjunctions

Coordinate conjunctions are presented in (246).

(246) $tɐŋ^{33}$ $ɲim^{35}$
        and   with

        jin^{35} $ho^{212}kai^{55}$
        and   or (as in either/or)

        $ɕi^{33}$ $toŋ^{22}$
        or (as in questions) with (Shídòng)

        jin^{11} to^{33}
        and (Shídòng)   and (Shídòng)

        $ɕi^{44}$
        or (as in either/or) (Shídòng)

Some sentences illustrating the use of coordinate conjuctions are given in (247).

(247) $ʔoŋ^{323}$ $tɐŋ^{33}$ sa^{31} tu^{55} $sət^{35}$ $ɕəp^{21}$ ta^{33} la^{31}
       grandfather   and   grandmother   both   seven   ten   more   EX
       Grandfather and grandmother are both over seventy years old!

       mau^{33} $pən^{323}$ $ʔɐi^{53}$ $tɐŋ^{53}$ $ʔa^{55}$ jin^{35} $tɐŋ^{53}$ $ɕi^{55}$
       3s   only   like (v)   create   song   and   create   play
       He only likes making up songs and plays.

       $ɲa^{212}$ we^{31} $ho^{212}kai^{55}$ tai^{31} $ɲa^{212}$ we^{31} tu^{55} li^{33}
       2s   do   or   older^brother   2s   do   both   okay
       You do (it) or your brother do (it)—either is okay.

       $mɐn^{55}$ nai^{33} $ɕu^{35}$ $ʔət^{55}$ $ɕi^{33}$ $ɕu^{35}$ $ɲi^{33}$
       day   this   month   one   or   month   two
       Is today the first or second (of the month)?

Subordinate conjunctions join clauses which are logically connected. Examples of subordinate conjunctions are given in (248).

(248)   kai^{53} jən^{55}jui^{33}
        because   because

        nu^{53} nu^{53}pau^{53}
        if   if

        so^{31}ji^{31} sɐi^{33}lan^{212}...tan^{55}si^{35}
        therefore   although...still

        lɐŋ^{31}ɕaŋ^{323}
        even if

Two examples showing use of subordinate conjunctions are given in (249).

(249)   **kai^{53}**   ɲa^{212} ʈhau^{13} kuŋ^{212} to^{323} noŋ^{31}
       because   2s   noisy   much   make   younger^brother

             jau^{212} ljo^{35} jaŋ^{31}
             1s   wake^up   STM
Because you were very noisy, my younger brother woke up.

    sɐi^{33}lan^{212}   khwən^{35} kai^{55} lu^{33} jai^{323} **tan^{55}si^{35}**
    although   way   distant   way   long   still

        mau^{33} mɐn^{31} sai^{323} pai^{55} nu^{53} mau^{33}
        3s   decide   intestines   go   see   3s
Although it's a very long way, he's still determined to go and see her.

4.1.11 Auxiliary words

Auxiliary words cannot function independently but can only modify other words or be appended to the end of a sentence expressing a particular mood. Auxiliary words in Dong can be divided into three classes: structural, aspect, and modal auxiliaries.

Grammar

Structural auxiliaries

li³²³. This word developed from a verb meaning 'have' or 'get'. It is like the Chinese 得 *de* and comes between verbs and their complements, linking the two.

(250)   mau³³   ça³²³   **li³²³**   lai⁵⁵
      3s   write   PTC   good
      He writes well.

      sɐk⁵⁵   **li³²³**   mjeŋ²¹²   mɐn⁵⁵   nɐŋ⁵⁵   mi³¹   so³²³
      wash   PTC   some   day   still   not   dry
      washed several days ago and still not dry

ti³³. This word is assimilated from Chinese and corresponds to the Chinese 的 *de*. It is used to link a head and its preceding modifier, indicating that the head in a sense belongs to the modifier. It is referred to here as a relational auxiliary and is marked REL in the examples.

In the northern dialect, personal pronouns expressing the meaning of 'possession' can only be placed before the head, and the word *ti³³* is placed between the personal pronoun and the noun. If the head is a kinship term, a place noun, or a proper noun, *ti³³* is normally not added (cf. (177)).

tɐu³³. This word means 'receive, suffer' (cf. 受 *shòu*, 挨 *ái*, 被 *bèi*). It is placed before a verb to express the passive mood.

(251)   ***tɐu³³***   heu³⁵
      PASS   hit
      suffered a beating

      tɐu³³   kwa⁵³
      PASS   scold
      endured a scolding

      tɐu³³   sɐp⁵⁵
      PASS   catch (v)
      was caught

      tɐu³³   hai³³
      PASS   hurt (v)
      was hurt

Aspect auxiliaries. Aspect auxiliaries are words which indicate the sequence in time of given actions. In Dong verbs do not indicate tense. Tense is shown by aspect auxiliaries and time nouns. Commonly used aspect auxiliaries are presented in (252).

(252) *to^{323}*
indicates an action in progress; cf. 着 *zhe*

ta^{33}
indicates a completed action; cf. 过 *guò*

ljeu^{31}
indicates completion, change, or past event; cf. 了 *le*

khwən^{35} or *khwən^{35}ljeu^{31}*
indicates an action is finished; cf. 完 *wán*, 完了 *wán liǎo*

ȶən^{212}ma^{35}
indicates the beginning and continuation of an action; cf. 起来 *qǐ lái*

to^{323} (cf. 着 *zhe*). This generally occurs after a verb and indicates an action is continuing.

(253) *sui^{53}*   ***to^{323}***
 sit   CONT
 sitting

 sap^{323} ***to^{323}***
 meet   CONT
 meeting

In the northern dialect, the word *ȶhi^{13}* is frequently added after *to^{33}*, also indicating action in progress. In the north, the two examples in (253) are rendered as in (254).

(254) *sui^{55}*   ***to^{33}ȶhi^{13}***
 sit   CONT
 sitting

 sap^{31}   ***to^{33}ȶhi^{13}***
 meet   CONT
 meeting

ta³³ (cf. 过 *guò*). This is added after a verb to indicate that the action has been experienced before. In the southern dialect, if the verb carries an object, the word *ta³³* follows the object. In the northern dialect, *ta⁴⁴* may come before or after an object and it may even occur before and after an object at the same time.

(255) Southern dialect

    jau²¹²   *pai⁵⁵*   *pe²¹²ʈən³³*   ***ta³³***
    1s   go   Běijīng   before
    I have been to Běijīng.

    mau³³   *sai³⁵*   *jau²¹²*   ***ta³³***
    3s   give   1s   before
    he gave (it) to me

(256) Northern dialect

    a. *jau²²*   *pai³⁵*   *pe¹¹ʈən³³*   ***ta⁴⁴***
       1s   go   Běijīng   before
       I have been to Běijīng.

       jau²²   *pai³⁵*   ***ta⁴⁴***   *pe¹¹ʈən³³*
       1s   go   before   Běijīng
       I have been to Běijīng.

       jau²²   *pai³⁵*   ***ta⁴⁴***   *pe¹¹ʈən³³*   ***ta⁴⁴***
       1s   go   before   Běijīng   before
       I have been to Běijīng.

    b. *mau⁴⁴*   *sai¹¹*   *jau²²*   ***ta⁴⁴***
       3s   give   1s   before
       he gave (it) to me

       mau⁴⁴   *sai¹¹*   ***ta⁴⁴***   *jau⁴⁴*
       3s   give   before   1s
       he gave (it) to me

       mau⁴⁴   *sai¹¹*   ***ta⁴⁴***   *jau²²*   ***ta⁴⁴***
       3s   give   before   1s   before
       he gave (it) to me

ljeu³¹ (cf. 了 *le*) and *khwən³⁵ljeu³¹* (cf. 完了 *wán liǎo*). These can both be added after verbs to indicate the completion of an action.

(257) mau³³   pai⁵⁵   **ljeu³¹**   sam³⁵   mɐn⁵⁵   la³¹
       3s   go   PAST   three   day   STM
       He left three days ago.

       pən³²³   le²¹²   nai³³   jau²¹²   nu⁵³   **khwən³⁵ljeu³¹**
       CLF   book   this   1s   read   PAST
       I have finished reading this book.

In the northern dialect, when *lja³¹* (the equivalent of *ljeu³¹*) is placed at the end of a sentence, it expresses mood as well as indicating the end of some action. Sometimes it is added after the verbal attribute *kən¹¹* (which indicates an action is finished), adding emphasis. The examples in (258) are from Shídòng speech.

(258) mau⁴⁴   pai³⁵   **lja³¹**
       3s   go   PAST
       He has gone!

       mau⁴⁴   pai³⁵   **kən¹¹lja³¹**
       3s   go   PAST
       He has already gone!

       jau²²   we³¹   **lja³¹**
       1s   do   PAST
       I did it!

       jau²²   we³¹   **kən¹¹lja³¹**
       1s   do   PAST
       I finished it!

ṭən²¹²ma³⁵ (cf. 起来 *qǐ lái*). This is added after a verb to indicate the beginning and continuation of an action.

(259) ʔaŋ³²³   **ṭən²¹²**   **ma³⁵**
       speak   begin   come
       begin speaking

       ʔut¹³   **ṭən²¹²**   **ma³⁵**
       burn   begin   come
       begin burning

Modal auxiliaries. Most modal auxiliaries appear at the end of a sentence. They can also be used at pauses in the middle of a sentence, when things are being listed. They can express all kinds of moods.

Statement. In the southern dialect, statement auxiliaries include $jaŋ^{31}$ and la^{31}. They focus on the actuality of a statement. The word $jaŋ^{31}$ also carries a tone of emphasis.

(260) $ʔek^{13}$ ma^{35} $\mathbf{jaŋ^{31}}$
 guest come STM
 The guest has arrived.

 tok^{55} $pjən^{55}$ ma^{35} $\mathbf{jaŋ^{31}}$
 fall rain come STM
 It is starting to rain.

In the northern dialect, frequently used statement auxiliaries include lo^{31} and $ʔe$ (spoken with neutral tone).

(261) jau^{22} $ɕeŋ^{11}$ sai^{33} $mən^{22}$ $təi^{35}$ $\mathbf{lo^{31}}$ $\mathbf{(ʔe)}$
 1s raw intestines 3s die STM (STM)
 I'm bitterly disappointed in him.

In the northern dialect, there is another statement auxiliary $ɕi^{55}ẓa^{31}$.

(262) $toʔ^{55}$ $mjən^{35}$ ma^{11} $\mathbf{ɕi^{55}ẓa^{31}}$
 fall rain come STM
 It is starting to rain.

 $laʔ^{31}$ nai^{44} lai^{35} wu^{35} $\mathbf{ɕi^{55}ẓa^{31}}$
 child this good CLF STM
 This child is good.

When the $ẓa^{31}$ is omitted, however, $ɕi^{55}$ changes to become an emphatic negative auxiliary.

(263) $toʔ^{55}$ $mjən^{35}$ $\mathbf{ɕi^{55}}$
 fall rain NEG^STM
 It is not raining!

 $laʔ^{31}$ nai^{44} lai^{35} wu^{35} $\mathbf{ɕi^{55}}$
 child this good CLF NEG^STM
 This child is not good!

Question. In the southern dialect, question auxiliaries include $\textipa{P}a^{55}$ (transforming a statement into a question; cf. 吗 *ma*), $\textipa{P}a^{31}$ (indicating surprise; cf. 呀 *yā*), and pa^{31} (assuming the answer will be affirmative; cf. 吧 *ba*). The northern dialect uses the words *ʔa*, *ʔo*, and *ʔe* (all with neutral tone).

(264) ȵa²¹² pai⁵⁵ ʔa⁵⁵
2s go Q
Are you going?

mau³³ ju⁵³ we³¹ maŋ²¹² ʔa³¹
3s want do what Q
What does he want to do? (expressing surprise)

ɕau³⁵ kwe²¹² ma³⁵ la³¹ **pa³¹**
2p not come EX Q
You are not coming, right(?) (may or may not be a question)

Imperative. In the southern dialect, imperative auxiliaries include pa^{31} and lo^{33}; in the northern dialect, *ma*.

(265) ȵa²¹² pi³¹ we³¹ **lo³³**
2s doˆnot do IMP
Don't do that!

ɕau¹¹ ɕu³¹ ta⁴⁴ ma¹¹ **ma**
2p atˆonce cross (v) come IMP
(You all) come over immediately! (Shídòng)

Exclamation. In the southern dialect, exclamation auxiliaries include lo^{31}, la^{31} (expressing exclamation; cf. 啦 *la*), and $\textipa{P}o^{31}$ (expressing surprise; cf. 啊 *ā*); in the northern dialect, they include $ẓa^{22}$ (cf. 啦 *la*).

(266) ʔeu³¹ nai³³ ȵeŋ²¹² lai⁵⁵ kuŋ²¹² **ʔo³¹**
rice this really good very EX
This rice is really very good!

ʔo²² kui³³ ȶuŋ²² ta³⁵ ɕi⁵⁵ **ẓa²²**
place stream many fish very EX
This stream has so very many fish! (Shídòng)

List. When listing things, natural pauses can be filled by the modal auxiliaries $\textipa{P}a^{33}$ or $\textipa{P}a^{31}$.

(267) ʔɐu³¹ɕu⁵⁵   ʔa³³   ʔɐu³¹pjaŋ³²³   ʔa³³   tu⁵⁵   ɕu³⁵
       maize   LIST   millet   LIST   all   store^up

       ljeu³¹   la³¹
       PAST   STM

The maize, the millet—both have been harvested.

       jan²¹²   mau³³   nan³¹   ʔa³³   pa⁵⁵   ʔa³³   haŋ²¹²   haŋ²¹²
       house   3s   meat   LIST   fish   LIST   type   type

       li³²³
       have

In his house there are all kinds of meat and fish.

Many modal auxiliaries are unstable, with the vowels or tones undergoing change. Sometimes they are spoken loudly, sometimes softly.

4.1.12 Interjections

Interjections include shouts where no name is specified and all kinds of sounds expressing feeling, especially in moody moments. They are often used as independent constituents of a sentence or as one-word sentences.

(268) **he⁵⁵**   hoi⁴⁵³   ma³⁵   ʔo³¹
       INT   quickly come   EX
       Hey! Come quickly!

       hai³¹   loŋ³⁵   la³¹
       INT   wrong   EX
       Aaagh! Wrong!

       ʔen³¹   su³³   ma³⁵   la³¹
       INT   just   come   EX
       Yeah! I'm just coming!

       ʔo⁵³   lɐŋ³¹   ȵau³³   nai³³   ʔo³¹
       INT   just   at   here   EX
       Ah! (it's) just here!

4.2 Phrases

Words and word groups form phrases. Phrases in Dong can be divided into different classes according to structural and semantic differences. The classes include head-modifier, head-complement, predicate-object, coordinate, subject-predicate, appositional, serial-verb, object-raising, and set phrases.

Head-modifier phrases

Noun as head. Typically, except for numerals and classifiers, modifiers come after the head, as in (269) where the head is bolded.

(269) **ȷan^{212}**   ŋwe^{31} **ȶən^{212}**   phaŋ^{35}
       house   tile   mountain high
       tile-roofed house   high mountain

       pa^{55}   tɐi^{55} **lak^{31}**   saŋ^{31} tu^{212}
       fish   dead   child   raise   ox
       dead fish   child who takes care of oxen

       ja^{212} tu^{212} **ma^{31}**   ʔi^{55} ȶiu^{212} **ȵa^{55}**
       two   CLF   horse   one   CLF   river
       two horses   one river

In the northern dialect, the word order in this kind of head-modifier phrase is in the process of change. Personal pronouns which indicate possession must come before the head (some need also to add the relational auxiliary word *ti^{33}*, cf. 的 *de*) and other modifiers may also be placed before the head.

(270) **ȶau^{35}**   **noŋ^{31}**
       1p   younger^brother
       our younger brother

       wa^{11} ja^{25} = ja^{25} ti^{33} wa^{11}
       flower   red   red   REL   flower
       red flower

Classifier as head. The basic pattern in this case is the same as for noun as head. Apart from ordinal numbers, which must precede classifiers, and cardinal numbers, which can sometimes also precede classifiers, modifiers normally follow the head. With this structure, the demonstrative pronoun

Grammar 155

ta^{33} 'that' is frequently added; in the northern dialect, ka^{55} 'that' or nai^{44} 'this' is added.

(271) **nɐn⁵⁵** *mɐi³¹* *ta³³*
       CLF   wood   that
       that log

       muŋ³¹ *tap³²³*   *ta³³*
       CLF   carry^with^pole that
       that person who is carrying (a load on the pole)

       nən³⁵ *ŋu¹¹* *ka⁵⁵*
       CLF   green that
       that green one (Shídòng)

       to²² *tət³¹*   *nai⁴⁴* *lai³⁵*
       CLF   run^away this   good
       This one (e.g., pig) that ran away is good. (Shídòng)

Verb or adjective as head. In this case the modifier comes before the head. The form 'adverb + verb' is the most common.

(272) **kwe²¹²** **sai³⁵**
       not   give
       not give

       kwe²¹² **pat³²³**
       not   tart (adj)
       not tart

       lət³⁵ **pai⁵⁵**
       all   go
       all are going

       lət³⁵ **man¹³**
       all   yellow
       all are yellow

When time nouns or demonstrative pronouns modify verbs or adjectives, they are also generally placed before the verbs or adjectives.

(273)   mɐn⁵⁵mu³²³   ma³⁵
        tomorrow   come
        come tomorrow

        ɲin²¹²sa²¹²   we³¹
        next^year   do
        do next year

        ʔi⁵⁵   nai³³   mɐi⁴⁵³
        way   this   new
        new like this

        ʔi⁵⁵   ta⁵³   jɐm⁵⁵
        way   that   deep
        deep like that

Head-complement phrases

Verb as head. In this case the complement is generally an adverb, a verb, an adjective, a sound descriptive word, or a numeral-classifier phrase.

(274)   ti⁵⁵   kwe²¹²   li³²³
        eat   not   PTC
        cannot eat

        ma³⁵   li³²³   ja²¹²   ɲan⁵⁵
        come   have   two   month
        came (here) two months ago

        ɕuk³²³   wo³⁵
        wash   clean
        wash clean

        ʔui³⁵   təp⁵⁵təp⁵⁵
        flow   babbling
        babbling along

        jɐn⁵⁵   sam³⁵   tau⁵³
        crow (v)   three   CLF
        crow three times

Adjective as head. In this case the complement is generally an adverb.

(275) **lai⁵⁵   kuŋ²¹²**
good   much
very good

phaŋ³⁵   ɕi⁴⁵³
tall   extremely
extremely tall

In the northern dialect, a nominal complement can be added after some stative adjectives, explaining how the adjectives came to apply.

(276) **wa⁵⁵   ju²²**
dirty   oil
dirtied by oil

ken³⁵   tɔt⁵⁵
tired   firewood
tired from (collecting) firewood

Predicate-object phrases

Verb as predicate. In this case the object is, under most circumstances, a noun phrase or a pronoun. Under certain conditions it can also be a verb or an adjective.

(277) **ɕa³²³   si³³**
write   character
write characters

we³¹   hai²¹²
make   shoe
make shoes

səm³³   mau³³
look^for   3s
look for him

jau¹³   tei⁵⁵
fear (v)   die
fear dying

ʔɐi⁵³   ljan³³
like (v) peppery
like hot (taste)

Stative adjective as predicate. Stative adjectives can take an object. The object may either be described by the adjective, as in (278), or it may be 'acted upon' by the adjective, as in (279).

(278)   so³²³   nɐm³¹
        dry (adj)   water
        water is dried up

        ja⁴⁵³   ta⁵⁵
        red   eye
        eye is red

(279)   jəm⁵⁵   tu²¹²
        thin   ox
        emaciated (by neglect) ox

        ka¹³   ȶau³⁵
        ugly   1p
        make us look like fools (Shídòng)

In predicate-object phrases made up of adjectives and numeral-classifier phrases, a pronoun functioning as an object to be compared, can be placed between the adjective and the numeral-classifier phrase.

(280)   **phaŋ³⁵**   jau²¹²   sam³⁵   sən⁴⁵³
        tall   1s   three   0.033^meter
        ten centimeters taller than me

The phrase in (280) has the same meaning as the one in (281).

(281)   pi³²³   jau²¹²   **phaŋ³⁵**   sam³⁵   sən⁴⁵³
        compare   1s   tall   three   0.033^meter
        ten centimeters taller than me

However, in the phrase in (281), the prepositional construction *pi³²³ jau²¹²* 'compared to me' modifies the adjective *phaŋ³⁵* 'tall', while in (280) *jau²¹²* can be regarded as the object of the adjective *phaŋ³⁵*.

Grammar 159

Coordinate phrases. In a coordinate phrase, except for certain set expressions, the component parts of the phrase are of equal status; they can swap positions without influencing the meaning of the phrase. There are two structural forms.

Direct enumeration. This form does not use conjunctions, nor any modal auxiliaries. Generally the phrase is made up of content phrases with an equal number of syllables, or phrases which have similar internal structure.

(282) tin^{212} $taŋ^{212}$ ti^{33} ton^{33}
      field   dike   land   earth
      farmland

pu^{31} mau^{33} nei^{31} mau^{33} mai^{31} mau^{33} lak^{31} mau^{33}
father   3s   mother   3s   wife   3s   child   3s

   $lət^{35}$ $thon^{453}$ mau^{33} pai^{55}
   all   advise   3s   go
His father, mother, wife, and children are all advising him to go.

$çai^{33}waŋ^{11}$ $thən^{35}çu^{55}$ $çan^{55}çu^{55}$ tu^{55} li^{323} $kɐm^{55}$
Jǐnpíng   Tiānzhù   Jīngzhōu   all   have   Dong
Jǐnpíng, Tiānzhù, and Jīngzhōu all have Dong people.

Linked by conjunctions. When verbs or adjectives make up coordinate phrases, they are generally linked by conjunctions or adverbs.

(283) $jɐm^{55}$ $çi^{33}$ lin^{53}
      deep   or   shallow
      deep or shallow?

      ju^{33} pui^{212} ju^{33} pak^{31}
      also   fat   also   white
      both fat and white

      ju^{33} $ʔaŋ^{323}$ ju^{33} ko^{55}
      also   talk   also   laugh
      both talking and laughing

      $maŋ^{53}$ sin^{13} $maŋ^{53}$ $pjeu^{53}$
      at^once   shout (v)   at^once   run
      shouting and running (at the same time)

tok²¹ le²¹² tɐŋ³³ we³¹ ʔoŋ⁵⁵
read book and do work (n)
study and work

ju³³ tuŋ⁵⁵ ʔɐu³¹ ju³³ mɐi³⁵ ʔɐu³¹
also boil (v) rice also steam (v) rice
both boil and steam rice

Only after being modified by other words can classifiers in Dong make up coordinate phrases.

(284) tu²¹² nai³³ tɐŋ³³ tu²¹² ɬa³³
CLF this and CLF that
this one and that one (e.g., animals)

muŋ³¹ phaŋ³⁵ tɐŋ³³ muŋ³¹ thɐm⁴⁵³
CLF tall and CLF short
the tall person and the short one

Subject-predicate phrases. A subject-predicate phrase is not a sentence, nor does it carry any sentence intonation or modal auxiliaries. It serves as a constituent part of a sentence. Examples of such phrases are bolded in (285).

(285) mau³³ we³¹ saŋ³³mɐi³¹
3s do carpenter
He is a carpenter. (sentence, not phrase; statement intonation)

mau³³ we³¹ saŋ³³mɐi³¹ li³²³ sam³⁵ ɕəp²¹ ɲin²¹² la³¹
3s do carpenter have three ten year EX
He has been a carpenter for thirty years. (phrase; serves as subject)

muŋ³¹ ɲən²¹² nai³³ siŋ⁴⁵³ maŋ²¹²
CLF person this surnamed what
What is this person's surname? (sentence, not phrase; question intonation)

jau²¹² kwe²¹² wo³¹ **muŋ³¹ ɲən²¹² nai³³ siŋ⁴⁵³ maŋ²¹²**
1s not know CLF person this surnamed what
I don't know this person's surname. (phrase; serves as object)

Appositional phrases. The two parts of an appositional phrase are coreferential, and there is no conjunction and normally no pause between the two parts. Commonly occurring appositional phrases include the types in (286).

Grammar 161

(286) ɕai³³ lau³¹ wu²¹²wen³³jɐu³¹
village old WúˆWànyǒu (吴万有)
village advisor, Wú Wànyǒu (noun + noun)

ȶa³³mau³³ ja²¹² nɐi³¹ lak³¹
3p two mother child
the two of them, mother and child (pronoun + noun)

jau²¹² si³³ʔa⁵⁵
1s oneself
I myself (pronoun + pronoun)

sam³⁵ ɕau³⁵
three 2p
you three (numeral + pronoun)

ɕau³⁵ ja²¹² muŋ³¹
2p two CLF
you two (pronoun + numeral-classifier)

ȵa²¹² muŋ³¹ ȵən²¹² nai³³
2s CLF person this
You, this person! (used when complaining, or for emphasis; noun + noun-type head-modifier phrase)

Serial-verb phrases. Serial-verb phrases express the consecutive related actions of a single agent. The actions may be in a given sequence or may express cause and effect. Thus the order of the verbs in a serial-verb phrase cannot usually be altered without changing the meaning of the original phrase.

(287) ʔat³²³ ȵaŋ¹³ saŋ³¹ pa⁵⁵
cut grass raise fish
cut grass, raise fish

lau³²³ jan²¹² pai⁵⁵ səm³³ ȵa²¹²
enter house go lookˆfor 2s
went into the house to look for you

Object-raising phrases. These are phrases for which the object of the first verb serves as the subject of the second verb.

(288) ȵa²¹² ʔeu³²³ **jau²¹²** wa³³ ka³¹
       2s   teach   1s   speak Chinese
       You teach me to speak Chinese.

       sin¹³ ȵa²¹² ma³⁵ ȶi⁵⁵ ʔɐu³¹
       call   2s   come eat rice
       call you to come and eat

Set phrases. Set phrases are phrases which have come to have a fixed form. They frequently have abstract meanings. They are typically old, succinct, expressive, and frequently used. They include idioms, proverbs, and four-word phrases.

(289) Southern dialect

       ʔen⁵³   ta⁵⁵   ʔen⁵³   nɐŋ⁵⁵
       colorful eye   colorful nose
       face is very dirty

       weŋ²¹²   kau³²³ weŋ²¹²   kha³⁵
       horizontal head   horizontal ear
       do not listen to reason

       thau¹³   pɐn⁵⁵ wan³³   ȶi³³   thau¹³   lau³¹
       exchange bamboo exchange generation exchange old

           wan³³   ȵi³¹
           exchange young
       (On the mountains) bamboo shoots take the place of bamboo, (in the villages) the young take the place of the old.

       mɐi³¹ lau³¹ pau³¹   saŋ³⁵ pɐn⁵⁵ lau³¹ pau³¹
       tree old   protect root bamboo old   protect

           naŋ²¹²
           bamboo^shoot
       Old trees protect their saplings, old bamboo protects its shoots.

(290) Northern dialect

       toŋ³⁵ kwa³⁵ lan⁴⁴ ʔau³¹
       winter gourd rot   in
       Pumpkin rots from the inside (out).

ʈin³⁵   pən²²   ta⁵⁵   ɕai⁴⁴
stone   rub   middle   village
the village sharpening stone

to²²   mət³⁵   jim¹¹   to²²   nəi²²
CLF   flea   dislike   CLF   louse
The flea dislikes the louse.

to²²   ni²²   wa⁵⁵   tau³⁵   ma³⁵
CLF   insect dirty   pot   vegetable
One insect can make a whole pot of vegetables dirty.

ʔak³³   ʈən²²   ʔak³³   ʈa²⁵   ʔak³³   la³⁵   ʔak³³   pa²²
each   mountain each   go^up   each   boat   each   row (v)
Everyone has to climb his own mountain, everyone has to row his own boat.

4.3 Sentence composition

Sentences are the basic units of language in practice. They are normally made up of words in different semantic relations, though they sometimes consist of just a single word. They can be divided into different classes according to the interrelations between the different words. Component parts of Dong sentences can generally be divided into subject and predicate, object, complement; attributive and adverbial phrases; and peripheral, vocative, and parenthetical phrases.

Subject and predicate

Subject. Nouns, pronouns, and coordinate or appositional phrases made up of nouns and pronouns generally serve as subjects. In certain cases, verbs, adjectives, and classifiers, or phrases with these word classes as heads, can also serve as subjects. Subject-predicate phrases can also function as subjects.

(291)   **ʔai⁵³**   jɐn⁵⁵   la³¹
        cock   crow (v)   STM
        The cock crowed. (noun as subject)

        mau³³   nu⁵³   le²¹²
        3s   look   book
        He is reading a book. (pronoun as subject)

kɐm⁵⁵   ka³¹   taŋ³²³   ʔi⁵⁵   jan²¹²   n̪ən²¹²
Dong   Hàn   be   one   house   person
The Dong and Hàn people are one family. (coordinate phrase as subject)

ɕau³⁵   sam³⁵   muŋ³¹   toŋ²¹²   pai⁵⁵
2p   three   CLF   with   go
You three go together. (appositional phrase as subject)

ti⁵⁵   ji⁵⁵li³²³   we³¹   nan²¹²
eat   easy   do   difficult
Eating is easy, cooking is difficult. (verb as subject)

jɐk³⁵   lai⁵⁵   khwət³⁵   kwe²¹²   lai⁵⁵
hard-working good   lazy   not   good
Being hard-working is good, being lazy is not good. (adjective as subject)

muŋ³¹   li³²³   nɐn⁵⁵
CLF   have   CLF
Each person gets one. (classifier as subject)

sa¹³   nən²¹²   li³²³   soi³¹
kill   person   have   guilt
Killing people is wrong. (predicate-object phrase as subject)

jau²¹²   thɐu⁴⁵³   ti³³waŋ³⁵   ɕau³⁵   su³³   nan²¹²   la³¹
1s   reach   place   2p   just   difficult STM
For me to reach your place is difficult. (subject-predicate phrase as subject)

Predicate. Verbs, adjectives, numerals, or subject-predicate phrases generally serve as predicates. Under particular conditions, nouns or noun phrases can also serve as predicates.

(292) *n̪a²¹²   we³¹*
       2s   do
       You do (it). (verb as predicate)

       le²¹²   nai³³   lai⁵⁵
       book   this   good
       This book is good. (adjective as predicate)

jau²¹² ɲi³³ çəp²¹ mau³³ ɲi³³ çi⁵⁵ ʔət⁵⁵
1s   two ten   3s   two ten one
I'm twenty (years old), he's twenty-one. (numeral as predicate)

mɐn⁵⁵ nai³³ çu³⁵   sam³⁵
day   this   beginning   three
Today's the third (of the month). (ordinal number as predicate)

lak³¹ nai³³ nɐm³¹ ta⁵⁵ ʔui³⁵ təp⁵⁵təp⁵⁵
child this   water eye   flow   SD
This child's tears are flowing quietly. (subject-predicate phrase as predicate)[16]

mau³³ tai³¹   jau²¹² noŋ³¹
3s   older^brother 1s   younger^brother
He's the older brother, I'm the younger. (noun as predicate)

Relationship between subject and predicate. The subject can be either the agent or the patient of an action. When it is the patient, the verb sometimes needs to be preceded by the passive auxiliary tɐu³³ (in the northern dialect, taŋ³³).

(293) tu²¹² ŋwa³⁵ ta³³ tɐu³³ heu³⁵ tɐi⁵⁵ pai⁵⁵ la³¹
      CLF   dog   that PASS   hit   die   go   EX
      That dog was beaten to death!

When the subject is obviously a patient, the auxiliary tɐu³³ can be omitted.

(294) jan²¹² sət⁵⁵   sin³⁵   ljeu³¹
      house   sweep   clean   PAST
      The house was swept clean.

Object. Words or phrases which can serve as subjects in a sentence can also serve as objects.

Relationship between predicate and object. There are all kinds of notional relations between predicate and object.
Some objects are the targets of the action indicated by the predicate.

---

[16]This is a topic comment sentence, with lak³¹ nai³³ serving as the topic. The comment is treated by the authors as a predicate.

(295) sɐk⁵⁵ ʔuk³²³
　　　 wash　clothing
　　　 wash clothes

　　　 pɐn²¹² mja³¹
　　　 sharpen knife
　　　 sharpen knife

Some objects are the results of the action indicated by the predicate.

(296) ʔɐi³⁵ mjeŋ⁵⁵
　　　 open (v) ditch
　　　 dig a ditch

　　　 ɕa³²³ le²¹²
　　　 write character
　　　 write characters

Some objects express the medium for the action indicated by the predicate.

(297) phjeu³⁵ pui⁵⁵
　　　 toast fire
　　　 warm up (by the fire)

　　　 ṭham¹³ khwən³⁵
　　　 walk path
　　　 walk (on the path)

Some objects are agents of the action indicated by the predicate.

(298) ṭhi¹³ ləm²¹²
　　　 rise wind (n)
　　　 wind gets up

Some objects explain why the action indicated by the predicate is necessary.

(299) lɐŋ³³ ka³¹
　　　 flee Hàn
　　　 flee from government troops

From the perspective of the agent, objects can be divided into three types: the patient, the agent, and a neutral object.

(300) ma³¹ ʂhik¹³ ȵən²¹²
horse kick person
The horse kicks the person. ('person' is the patient of the action)

mɐn⁵⁵ nai³³ pai⁵⁵ ʔi⁵⁵ tɐu³¹ ȵən²¹²
day this go one partner person
Today one partner resigned. ('one partner' is the agent of the action)

pak³²³ jan²¹² ta³³ taŋ³²³ ja⁵³ nɐm³¹
mouth house that be field water
Outside the house is a paddy field. ('paddy field' is both the patient and the agent of the action 'is')

Indirect object. When a verb has two objects, normally the indirect object comes first, followed by the direct object.

(301) mau³³ sun³¹ jau²¹² / ʔi⁵⁵ pak³²³ kwan⁵⁵
3s give 1s one CLF ax
He gave me an ax.

Sentences with two objects also frequently appear in the form subject/ predicate/direct object/complement. This happens when the indirect object is part of a prepositional phrase, including the preposition *sai³⁵* 'give', that acts as the complement.

(302) mau³³ / sun³¹ / ʔi⁵⁵ pak³²³ kwan⁵⁵ / sai³⁵ jau²¹²
3s give one CLF ax give 1s
He gave me an ax.

Position with respect to predicate. Objects normally come after the predicate, but under certain conditions, can also come before it (cf. (239)–(243)).

Complement. Complements are mostly comprised of adjectives, verbs, or numeral-classifier phrases. Prepositional phrases or phrases with predicates as heads can also function as complements.

Position with respect to predicate and object. If a sentence has both a complement and an object, the typical order is: predicate/object/complement.

(303) sət⁵⁵   jan²¹²   wo³⁵
      sweep   house   clean (adj)
      Sweep the house clean.

      ȶi⁵⁵   ʔeu³¹   ȶɐŋ⁵³
      eat   rice   full
      full (from eating)

In the northern dialect, the complement can sometimes come between the predicate and the object.

(304) ȶe³⁵   ʔəu³¹   ȶəŋ⁵⁵   =   ȶe³⁵   ȶəŋ⁵⁵   ʔəu³¹
      eat   rice   full   eat   full   rice
      full (from eating)

      te⁵⁵   mən²²   tai³⁵   =   te⁵⁵   tai³⁵   mən²²
      chop   3s   die   chop   die   3s
      Chop it to death.

Deep structure. Sentences of the type subject/predicate/object/complement appear identical in form to those of the type subject/predicate/object (with subject-predicate phrase as object). However, the two deep structures are different.

(305) tau⁵⁵   ɕen³¹   mau³³ / we³¹   tai⁵⁵pjau³¹
      1p   choose   3s   do   representative
      We elect him to be a representative. (subject/predicate/object/complement, predicate-object phrase as complement)

      tau⁵⁵   wo³¹   / mau³³   we³¹   tai⁵⁵pjau³¹
      1p   know   3s   do   representative
      We know he is a representative. (subject/predicate/object, subject-predicate phrase as object)

Attributive and adverbial phrases

Attributive phrases. Subjects or objects which are nouns or classifiers are modified by attributive phrases (or attributes). Content words and all kinds of phrases, except adverbs, can serve as attributes.

Attributes come after the head, except for numeral-classifier phrases, which come before the head.

In the northern dialect, personal pronouns expressing possession must come before the head, and the word *ti*^{33} (parallelling the Chinese 的 *de*) is placed between the pronoun and the subject or object.

If there are pre- and post-modifiers, the usual word order is numeral/ classifier/noun (head)/predicate/phrase (any)/personal pronoun/demonstrative pronoun.

(306) *ja*^{212} / *tu*^{212} / *ŋwa*^{35} / *man*^{13} *lau*^{31} / *jan*^{212} / *ṭiu*^{55} / *ṭa*^{33}
 two   CLF   dog   yellow   big   house   1p   that
 those two big yellow dogs belonging to our family

Adverbial phrases. Predicates are modified by adverbial phrases, which are generally adverbs, time nouns, adjectives, sound descriptive words, demonstrative pronouns indicating the manner of an action, or prepositional phrases. Adverbial phrases generally precede predicates.

(307) **kwe**^{212} **kai**^{55}
 not   far
 not far

 mɛn^{55}**mu**^{323} **pai**^{55}
 tomorrow   go
 go tomorrow

 hoi^{453} **we**^{31}
 quick   do
 do quickly

 sat^{323}**sat**^{323} **pjiu**^{55}
 SD   jump
 jump, again and again

 ʔi^{55} **nai**^{33} **phaŋ**^{35}
 way   this   tall
 this tall

 ta^{33} **kui**^{55}**jaŋ**^{212} **ma**^{35}
 from   Guìyáng   come
 coming from Guìyáng

Peripheral, vocative, and parenthetical phrases. Peripheral, vocative, and parenthetical phrases are all independent elements of a sentence. They frequently drift away from the main stream of a sentence via a pause, but they are semantically related to the rest of the sentence.

Peripheral phrases occur outside a sentence and are coreferential with the subject or object of the sentence. The peripheral phrase usually comes before the sentence it relates to. There is an obligatory pause between the peripheral phrase and the sentence. (In contrast, an appositional phrase need not have a pause between the phrase and the rest of the sentence.)

(308)   **ɕaŋ^{55}ljaŋ^{212}**   **tɐŋ^{33}**   **ɕaŋ^{55}mui^{53}**   **ja^{212}**   **ȶai^{31}**
Zhāng^Liáng   and   Zhāng^Mèi   two   older^sibling

  noŋ^{31}   **ȶit^{323}sən^{35}**   **ȶi^{53}**   **tən^{323}**   **ȵən^{212}**
younger^sibling   marry   create   root   person

Zhāng Liáng and Zhāng Mèi, older brother and younger sister, married and perpetuated mankind.

  pjiŋ^{212}pan^{31}   **jau^{212}**   **wu^{212}ɕən^{33}ɕo^{212}**   **mau^{33}**   **ȶaŋ^{323}**
friend   1s   Wú^Xīngxué (吴兴学)   3s   be

  saŋ^{33}   **mɐi^{31}**
craftsman   wood

My friend Wú Xīngxué, he's a carpenter.

Vocative phrases are also structurally independent of the sentence. They mostly consist of exclamations or nouns plus auxiliaries.

(309)   **ʔoi^{55}**   **ɕau^{35}**   **ka^{323}**   **jau^{212}**   **tɐŋ^{31}**
INT   2p   wait   1s   little

Hey! (you all) wait for me a moment.

  nɐi^{31}   **ʔa^{31}**   **ȵɐm^{53}**   **nai^{33}**   **ȵa^{212}**   **pi^{31}**   **ɕu^{13}**   **jau^{212}**
mother   INT   evening   this   2s   do^not   wait   1s

  ȶi^{55}   **ʔɐu^{31}**
eat   rice

Mum! This evening, don't wait for me to (come home and) eat.

Parenthetical phrases are normally used to express the speaker's attitude towards, or explanation of, a given state of affairs. Most occur in the middle of a sentence. Some are separated from the rest of the sentence by a pause, but some are not.

(310) $ti^{33}waŋ^{35}$ tiu^{55} nai^{33} li^{212} $çai^{33}$ tiu^{55} $nɐŋ^{55}$ li^{323}
place 1p this from village 1p still have

$çəp^{21}$ ta^{33} lji^{31} $khwən^{35}$ li^{323} $çoŋ^{212}$
ten more 0.5^kilometer road have CLF

$tən^{212}$ $phaŋ^{35}$ $phaŋ^{35}$
mountain high high

In our area here, more than five kilometers from our village, there is a very high mountain.

mau^{33} $ʔi^{212}tən^{55}$ $çi^{55}$ $tɐu^{33}$ sui^{212} $ʔit^{31}$ $ljeu^{31}$
3s certainly be PASS snake bite PAST

He was certainly bitten by a snake.

4.4 Sentence structure

Sentences in Dong fall structurally into two classes, simple and compound.

Simple sentences. Simple sentences have only one clause. They can be classified as either full sentences or minor sentences.

Full sentences have both subject and predicate.

(311) jau^{212} $ljaŋ^{35}$ $to^{323}ʔa^{55}$
1s like (v) sing

I like singing.

Minor sentences do not have both subject and predicate. They are made up of single words or phrases other than subject-predicate phrases.

There are two kinds of minor sentences. One is called 'subjectless', with the subject unspecified, as in (312). The other consists of a single word or phrase, as in (313).

(312) tok^{55} $pjən^{55}$ la^{31}
fall rain STM

It's raining.

(313) $mən^{55}$ ti^{33} $ʔe$
sky earth EX

Good heavens!

pui⁵⁵
fire
Fire!

Compound sentences. Compound sentences are composed of more than one clause. These clauses may or may not be linked by a conjunction or adverb. The clauses of most compound sentences are separated by some sort of pause or change of intonation. There are two basic types: coordinate and subordinate.

Coordinate sentences. The clauses in coordinate sentences can stand alone and are of equal status. Some coordinate sentences require the use of conjunctions or connecting adverbs to link clauses, but some do not. They can be divided into three types, according to relations between clauses in the coordinate compound: progression, juxtaposition, and alternation.

1. Progression. These describe a series of events and often have only a single subject.

(314) mau³³   tuŋ⁵⁵   ʔɐu³¹   lai⁵⁵   la³⁵   ʔeŋ⁵⁵ŋu⁴⁵³   wen³⁵
      3s   boil   rice   good   feed (v)   pigˆfeed   finish

      su³³   pai⁵⁵   lɐm³⁵   ja⁵³   pai⁵⁵   la³¹
      atˆonce   go   plantˆseedlings   field   go   STM

When he had finished boiling the rice and feeding the pigs, he went immediately to plant seedlings.

2. Juxtaposition. These list similar items or actions.

(315) mau³³   we³¹   ʔoŋ⁵⁵   ja³³   lai⁵⁵   tok²¹   le²¹²   ja³³   lai⁵⁵
      he   do   work   also   good   read   book   also   good

He both works well and studies well.

3. Alternation. These list a choice between different alternatives.

(316) mɐn⁵⁵   nai³³   khɐi³⁵   ja⁵³   ni⁵⁵   ɕi³³   te⁵³   ti³³
      day   this   plow   field   PTC   or   dig   land

Today (shall we) plow or dig the land?

Subordinate sentences. Normally the subordinate clause comes first, followed by the main clause, with emphasis being laid on the latter. The two clauses are usually linked by a subordinate conjunction or by an adverb, though sometimes no conjunction or adverb is needed. There are various semantic relations between subordinate and main clauses: transition, conditional, cause and effect, and comparative.

1. Transition. These clauses generally use linking phrases.

(317) saŋ³³ mɐi³¹ nai³³ tin⁵⁵ mja²¹² ɕɐi³⁵ pən³²³
craftsman wood this foot hand skillful but

ɕeŋ⁵³ wen⁵³ kuŋ²¹²
arrogant arrogant much

This carpenter is skillful, but very arrogant.

mau³³ sɐi³³lan²¹² ɲin²¹² ȶi³²³ ʈha¹³ pu³³ haŋ²¹²
3s although year age light but kind

haŋ²¹² tu⁵⁵ wo³¹
kind all know

Although he's young, he understands many things.

2. Conditional. The subordinate clause states a condition and the main clause states its result.

(318) pən³²³ ju⁵³ ɳa²¹² sin¹³ ȶiu⁵⁵ su³³leŋ³¹ ma³⁵
only need 2s call (v) 1p immediately come

You only need to call, and we'll come immediately.

ma³⁵ʔɐi³²³ thɐu⁴⁵³ kau³²³ nɐm³¹ ʔɐi³²³ wo³¹
not reach head water not know

ʈən²¹² phaŋ³⁵
mountain high

If you don't reach the (river) source, you'll not know how high the mountain is.

nu⁵³ ɳa²¹² ju⁵³ ʔi⁵⁵ nai³³ we³¹ ta³³lən²¹² ʔi⁵⁵nu³⁵
if 2s want way this do after how

haŋ²¹² jau²¹² su³³ kwe²¹² kwan³²³ la³¹
what 1s just not mind STM

If you want to do things this way, no matter what happens, I'll just not be bothered.

$nu^{53}pau^{53}$	na^{212}	kwe^{212}	$sən^{453}$	na^{212}	su^{33}	$ʔak^{323}$
if	2s	not	believe	2s	then	self

pai^{55}	nu^{53}	pa^{31}
go	see	IMP

If you don't believe, then go and see for yourself!

3. **Cause and effect.** The subordinate clause states a cause and the main clause states its effect.

(319)
wi^{33}	mau^{33}	kwe^{212}	san^{31}	$tən^{55}$	$ɕo^{212}ɕi^{212}$	mau^{33}
because	3s	not	use	strength	study (v)	3s

$ʔi^{55}$	$mɐn^{55}$	$ʔi^{55}$	$mɐn^{55}$	ta^{33}	tok^{55}	$lən^{212}$
one	day	one	day	PTC	fall (v)	behind

pai^{55}	la^{31}
go	STM

Because he didn't study diligently, day by day he fell further behind.

4. **Comparative.** The subordinate clause states one choice, the main clause compares another.

(320)
nu^{53}	$ʔaŋ^{323}$	to^{323}	ma^{55}	kwe^{212}	ta^{33}
if	speak	plant (v)	vegetable	not	compare

to^{323}	$pɐk^{21}$
plant (v)	radish

Rather than planting cabbage, it would be better to plant radish.

to^{323}	$ʔi^{55}$	$ɕon^{33}$	mau^{212}	$ʔɐi^{323}$	ta^{33}	$khɐi^{453}$
use	one	time	fertilizer	not	compare	rake (v)

$ʔi^{55}$	$ɕon^{33}$
one	time

Applying fertilizer once does not compare with raking the field once.

Compact compound sentences. Some compound sentences have a part that is omitted, resulting in something that looks like a simple sentence. Note that the compact sentence in (321) only has one subject and no pause between the clauses.

(321) ɲa²¹²   ɲon³³   pai⁵⁵   su³³   pai⁵⁵
       2s   be^willing   go   then   go
       If you want to go then go. (compact compound)

       ɲa²¹²   ɲon³³   pai⁵⁵   ɲa²¹²   su³³   pai⁵⁵
       2s   be^willing   go   2s   then   go
       If you want to go then go. (full compound)

A compound sentence may contain several compound sentences. The example in (322) is a subordinate compound sentence, but the main clause is preceded by two subordinate (compact) clauses, not just one.

(322) li³²³   sin²¹²   su³³   ʔuk³²³   sin²¹²   li³²³   mɐi³¹
       have   money   then   give   money   have   timber

       su³³   ʔuk³²³   mɐi³¹   kwe²¹²   sin²¹²   kwe²¹²
       then   give   timber   not^have money   not^have

       mɐi³¹   su³³   ʔuk³²³   ɲən²¹²   toŋ²¹²   so³³   ʈim⁵⁵
       timber   then   give   person   together   strength   build

       ku²¹²   lɐu²¹²
       drum   tower

If you have money give money, if you have timber give timber, if you have no money or timber then give manpower, and we'll unite our efforts to build the drum tower.

4.5 Sentence types

Sentences all have their own particular moods. There are four basic sentence mood types in Dong: declarative, interrogative, imperative, and exclamatory.

Declarative sentences. Declarative sentences state something, usually in a flat intonation, possibly with a modal auxiliary such as *jaŋ³¹* or *la³¹* (cf. (260)). Sometimes directional verbs acting as adverbs are used to mark the sentence as declarative.

(323) ʔɐu³¹   jan²¹²   li³²³   ɲən²¹²
       in   house   have   person
       There is someone at home.

tok⁵⁵   pjən⁵⁵   jaŋ³¹
fall (v) rain   STM
It's raining.

ȵa²¹²   ṭa⁵³   ʔe³²³   pai⁵⁵
2s   that   stupid   go
You're that stupid!

Negative statements are marked in the same way as positive ones with respect to intonation and auxiliaries, except that there is a negation word in the statements.

(324) ʔɐu³¹   jan²¹²   kwe²¹²   li³²³   ȵən²¹²
       in   house   not   have   person
       There's nobody at home.

       kwe²¹²   tok⁵⁵   pjən⁵⁵   jaŋ³¹
       not   fall (v) rain   STM
       It's not raining.

Interrogative sentences. Interrogative sentences may be formed in various ways: using interrogative pronouns; through rising intonation; using the A-not-A frame, where A is a predicate; using the conjunction ɕi³³ ('or', cf. (246) and (247)); and using question auxiliaries (cf. (264)). If interrogative pronouns are not used, interrogative sentences are characterized by rising intonation; if they are used, intonation is then relatively flat. Parallel with the division above, interrogative sentences are divided into the following six types: special, yes or no, A-not-A, alternative, conjectural, and rhetorical.

Special. The sentence contains interrogative pronouns nu³⁵ 'which', nɐu²¹² 'who', maŋ²¹² 'what', ṭi³²³ 'how many', and so on, or contains compound words made up of these interrogative pronouns.

(325) mɐn⁵⁵mu³²³   ȵa²¹²   pai⁵⁵   nu³⁵
       tomorrow   2s   go   where
       Where are you going tomorrow?

       le²¹²   nɐu²¹²   tɐu⁵³   ȵau³³   ki⁵⁵   nai³³   ʔa⁵⁵
       book   who   lose   at   place   this   Q
       Whose book has been left here?

In some cases, because of a given context, the interrogative pronoun goes without saying.

(326) ȵei³¹   ȵau³³   ʔa²¹²   nu³⁵   ni⁵⁵   →   ȵei³¹   ni⁵⁵
      mother at   place   where PTC   mother PTC
      Where's Mum?

Yes or no. These sentences normally use rising intonation and the question auxiliary *ʔa⁵⁵* at the end of the sentence. Otherwise, their sentence structure is just like that of a declarative sentence.

(327) ȵa²¹²   wo³¹me⁵⁵   mau³³   ʔa⁵⁵
      2s   know   3s   Q
      Do you know him?

A-not-A. These sentences have two forms according to whether the predicate has an object or not. When the predicate has no object, it consists of the positive and negative forms of a verb or adjective placed side by side.

(328) ȵa²¹²   wo³¹   kwe²¹²   wo³¹
      2s   know   not   know
      Do you know or not?

      tui⁵⁵   nai³³   khwan³⁵   kwe²¹²   khwan³⁵
      plum   this   sweet   not   sweet
      Is this plum sweet or not?

When the predicate has an object, it is possible for the object to appear after either the negative or the positive verb form.

(329) ȵa²¹²   wo³¹   kwe²¹²   wo³¹   wa³³   kɐm⁵⁵
      2s   know   not   know   speak   Dong
      Do you speak Dong or not?

      ȵa²¹²   wo³¹   wa³³   kɐm⁵⁵   kwe²¹²   wo³¹
      2s   know   speak   Dong   not   know
      Do you speak Dong or not?

      ʔɐu³¹   jan²¹²   li³²³   kwe²¹²   li³²³   ȵən²¹²
      in   house   have   not   have   person
      Is there anyone at home or not?

ʔɐu³¹   jan²¹²   li³²³   ɲən²¹²   kwe²¹²   li³²³
in   house   have   person   not   have
Is there anyone at home or not?

Alternatively, when the object appears after the positive verb form, the negative verb form can be abridged to *kwe²¹²* 'not' or *mi³¹* 'have not'.

(330) ɲa²¹²   li³²³   thɐu⁴⁵³   ɕaŋ⁵⁵hai³¹   kwe²¹²
       2s   have   reach   Shànghǎi (上海)   not
       Have you been to Shànghǎi or not?

       ȶi⁵⁵   ʔɐu³¹   mi³¹
       eat   rice   have^not
       Have you eaten or not?

Alternative. In these sentences, the word *ɕi³³* 'or' normally links the two parts.

(331) ɲa²¹²   pai⁵⁵   ɕi³³   jau²¹²   pai⁵⁵
       2s   go   or   1s   go
       Will you go or shall I?

Conjectural. These sentences generally add the question auxiliary *pa³¹* (cf. (264)) at the end.

(332) mau³³   mɐn⁵⁵   nai³³   nan²¹²   ma³⁵   pa³¹
       3s   day   this   difficult come   Q
       He can't come today, can he?

       ɲa²¹²   mi³¹   ȶi⁵⁵   ʔɐu³¹   pa³¹
       2s   not^have   eat   rice   Q
       You haven't eaten yet, have you?

Rhetorical. These sentences frequently adopt the same form as special or yes-or-no, interrogative sentences. They are used for emphasis and do not really anticipate a reply from the listeners. Thus they have the form of interrogative sentences, but the import of exclamatory sentences (cf. (335)).

(333) nu³⁵haŋ²¹²   ʔɐi³²³   pai⁵⁵   li³²³
       why   not   go   PTC
       Why (are you) not able to go!? (said when, in fact, it is possible to go)

Imperative sentences. Imperative sentences express commands, prohibitions, urgent requests, and so on. If the subject is second person, it is often not expressed. Imperative sentences often have a sharp falling intonation and often use modal auxiliaries pa^{31}, ma^{31}, $ʔa^{31}$, li^{31}, and lo^{31} at the end.

(334) pi^{31} pai^{55}
      do^not   go
      Do not go!

      sai^{35} jau^{212} pa^{31}
      give   1s   IMP
      Give (it) to me!

      $ɲa^{212}$ hoi^{453} $tham^{13}$ ma^{31}
      2s   quick   walk   IMP
      Walk faster!

Exclamatory sentences. Exclamatory sentences express strong feelings. They generally place stress on the part to be given prominence and often use the falling tone exclamation auxiliaries lo^{31}, la^{31}, $ʔo^{31}$, $ʔa^{31}$, and li^{31} (cf. (266)). Interjections appearing before exclamatory sentences serve to increase the intensity of the exclamations.

(335) ku^{212} leu^{212} nai^{33} $ɲɐŋ^{212}$ $phaŋ^{35}$ $ɲɐŋ^{212}$ $ʔo^{31}$
      drum   tower   this   really   tall   really   EX
      This drum tower is really very tall!

      $ʔo^{31}$ tiu^{212} $khwən^{35}$ nai^{33} $ʔi^{55}$ ta^{53} mak^{323} $ʔa^{31}$
      INT   CLF   road   this   way   that   big   EX
      Wow! This road is so wide!

      hai^{31} tek^{21} ta^{53} $ʔe^{323}$ li^{31}
      INT   CLF   that   stupid   EX
      Aaagh! That's so stupid!

      $ʔa^{33}ja^{31}$ pui^{55} nu^{35} mak^{323} $ʔa^{31}$
      INT   fire   which   big   EX
      Oh look! The fire is so big!

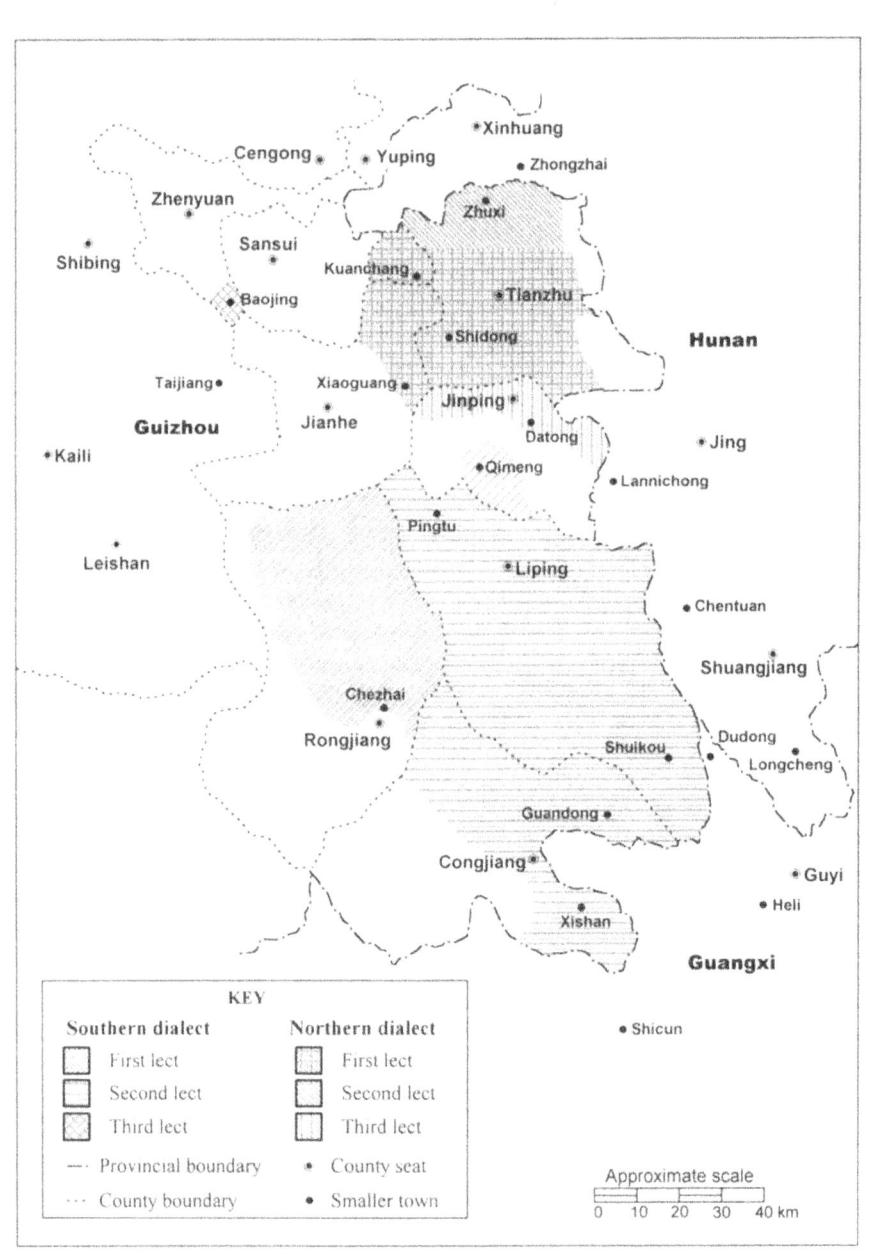

5
Dialects

5.1 Differentiation and distribution of dialects

Dialects in Dong are characterized mainly by differences in vocabulary and certain features of grammar and pronunciation. Lects within the dialects are mainly classified according to differences in pronunciation.

There are two dialects in Dong, southern and northern. The border between southern and northern dialects is taken as the southern region of Jǐnpíng (锦屏) County in Guìzhōu (贵州), where Dong, Miáo (苗) and Hàn (汉) nationalities live together. The southern dialect is divided into four lects, while the northern dialect is divided into three. Apart from the fourth lect of the southern dialect, which is found in the Róngshuǐ (融水) Miáo Autonomous County in the Guǎngxī (广西) Autonomous Region, the lects all occur in Guìzhōu province. Their distribution in Guìzhōu is shown on the map on the facing page.

The first lect area of the southern dialect includes Róngjiāng Zhānglǔ[17] (榕江章鲁), Lípíng Hóngzhōu (黎平洪州), and Jǐnpíng Qǐméng (锦屏启蒙); the second includes Lípíng Shuǐkǒu (黎平水口), Cóngjiāng Guàndòng (从江贯洞), and Róngjiāng Píngjiāng (榕江平江); and the third includes Zhènyuǎn Bàojīng (镇远报京).

Some material in this chapter has appeared in "Developmental Tendencies in Kam Phonology" in *Comparative Kadai: Linguistic Studies Beyond Tai*, edited by Jerold A. Edmondson and David B. Solnit, 1988.

[17]The lect areas and the county administrative areas do not exactly coincide. Within a given county, there are not only different lects, but in some cases, even different dialects. Thus, after a given county name, the name of a village in that county which is representative of a given lect appears. Places where the Dong spoken is the same as in one of these villages are thus identified with the corresponding lect.

The fourth lect of the southern dialect is hardly discussed here because it occurs only in Guǎngxī province (but see paragraphs above and below (343)).

The first lect area of the northern dialect includes Tiānzhù Shídòng (天柱石洞), Sānsuì Kuǎnchǎng (三穗款场), and Jiànhé Xiǎoguǎng (剑河小广); the second includes Tiānzhù Zhùxī (天柱注溪); and the third includes Jǐnpíng Dàtóng (锦屏大同).

The number of Dong people living in the southern and northern dialect areas of Guìzhōu is around 750,000 and 650,000, respectively, according to statistics from 1990. Over ninety percent of those in the southern area, and nearly fifty percent of those in the northern area, speak the Dong language.

5.2 Differences in pronunciation between lects

Main characteristics of dialect and lect pronunciations. The most notable differences in pronunciation between the southern and northern dialects are in differentiation of vowel length, in the velar coda *k*, and in tones 8 and 9'.

Vowels in the northern dialect are not differentiated by length. In the southern dialect (apart from the third lect exemplified by Zhènyuǎn Bàojīng), the vowel *a* has long and short forms.

The velar stop coda *k* of the southern dialect changes in all the northern lects: either it drops out altogether or it changes to the alveolar stop *t* or the glottal stop *ʔ*.

In the southern dialect, the tones 8 (short Yáng Rù) and 9' (long Cì Yīn Rù) are always different. In the northern dialect, apart from the third lect (where tones 9 and 10 merge), tones 8 and 9' merge.

Every lect has its own special features with regard to pronunciation. In the southern dialect, the first lect has nine tones in unchecked syllables. Except for stops, which come in aspirated and unaspirated pairs, syllable initials are unaspirated. In the vowel system, only *ə* is short, and only *a* has long and short forms. The second lect has six tones.[18] Syllable initials, except for some voiceless fricatives, all have aspirated and unaspirated counterparts. In the vowel system, *a* and some other vowels have long and short forms. The third lect also has six tones. Except for aspirated stops, there are no aspirated syllable initials.

The first lect of the northern dialect has nine tones. It preserves its bilabial syllable codas, and coronal and palatalized alveolar syllable initials are not in contrast. The second lect also has nine tones. Except when following *ə*, bilabial codas in the second lect are pronounced as alveolars, e.g., sam^{35} 'three' is pronounced san^{35}, and tap^{33} 'carry on a pole' is pronounced tat^{33}. Coronal and palatalized alveolar syllable initials are in contrast, e.g.,

---

[18]Number of tones quoted here, and subsequently in chapter 5, is number of tones in unchecked syllables.

ɳa⁵⁵ 'sticky' and nja⁵⁵ 'river'. The third lect has seven tones. This lect pronounces coronal sounds from the other lects as alveolar sounds, e.g., 'ask' in Dàtóng is sai²³ and in other lects ɕai³³ or ȶai³³.

Local variations in pronunciation of syllable initials. Tones and syllable initials are very closely related: with more tones, there are fewer initials; with fewer tones, there are more initials. In this section, syllable initial dialect variations arising from tone conditioning are briefly introduced, together with certain local variations in syllable initial pronunciation.

Tone conditioning. In Dong, syllable initials and tones condition one another. Tones divide according to whether syllable initials are aspirated or unaspirated, and because tones divide, syllable initials simplify and combine. Since this kind of conditioning has developed differently in different lects, great differences have arisen in the various systems of syllable initials, though the lects have similar rules governing relationships between initials and tones. Analysis of these relationships for the Dong spoken in Guìzhōu and for tones in unchecked syllables results in five types. Characteristics of the five types are summarized in the tables in (336).[19]

1. *Nine tones.* Syllable initials are unaspirated. The main distinctions in the language are in the tones and not in the initials. Shídòng speech in Tiānzhù (N1)[20] exemplifies this type.

2. *Nine tones.* Among the syllable initials, only the stops have aspirated and unaspirated counterparts. The language of this type sounds very similar to that of Type 1. It is exemplified by Zhānglǔ speech in Róngjiāng (S1).

3. *Seven tones.* Only the Yīn Píng (1, 1') tone divides into Quán Yīn (1) and Cì Yīn (1'); the other Yīn tones (3 and 5) do not split up. Among the syllable initials, only the stops divide into aspirated and unaspirated sets. That is to say, the Yīn Píng tone for syllables with stop initials divides into high and low tones, corresponding to nonaspiration and aspiration, respectively. The Yīn Píng tone for syllables with nonstop initials also divides into high and low, but the syllable initials are exactly the same. This also gives rise to two different syllables. With Yīn Shàng (3, 3') and Yīn Qù (5, 5') tones, there is no difference between syllable initials of these two types of syllable and no difference in tones, so they become homophones. This type is exemplified by Dàtóng speech in Jǐnpíng (N3).

---

[19]Place name abbreviations used in (336) and throughout this chapter: CG–Cóngjiāng Guàndòng, JD–Jǐnpíng Dàtóng, JG–Jǐnpíng Gāobà, JQ–Jǐnpíng Qíméng, JX–Jiǎnhé Xiǎoguǎng, LH–Lípíng Hóngzhōu, LP–Lípíng Píngtú, LS–Lípíng Shuǐkǒu, LZ–Lípíng Zhúpíng, RZ–Róngjiāng Zhānglǔ, SK–Sānsuì Kuǎnchǎng, TS–Tiānzhù Shídòng, TZ–Tiānzhù Zhùxī, ZB–Zhēnyuǎn Bàojīng

[20]Here, and throughout this chapter, abbreviations are used to indicate the dialects and lects of Dong. Thus, for example, '(N1)' refers to the first lect of the northern dialect, '(S2)' refers to the second lect of the southern dialect, and so on.

4. *Six tones.* There is no difference between Quán Yīn (1, 3, 5) and Cì Yīn (1', 3', 5') tones. Syllable initials split into aspirated and unaspirated sets. Thus the difference between these two sets of syllables lies in the syllable initials and not in the tones. Guàndòng speech in Cóngjiāng (S2) exemplifies this type.

5. *Six tones.* Among the syllable initials, only the stops divide into aspirated and unaspirated sets. That is to say, there are syllable initial differences between syllables with stop initials but none for syllables with nonstop initials. With the aspirated tone categories, however, voiced fricative initials are pronounced as voiceless fricatives and are therefore differentiated from unaspirated categories by different initials. This type is exemplified by Bàojīng speech in Zhènyuǎn (S3).

(336)   Stop initials

Type	1 TS (N1)	2 RZ (S1)	3 JD (N3)	4 CG (S2)	5 ZB (S3)	
Tone						
1	pa^{35}	pa^{55}	pa^{22}	pa^{55}	pa^{11}	leg
1'	pa^{11}	pha^{35}	pha^{11}	pha^{55}	pha^{11}	gray
3	pja^{33}	pja^{323}	pja^{23}	pja^{35}	pja^{23}	thunder
3'	pja^{13}	$phja^{13}$	$phja^{23}$	$phja^{35}$	$phja^{23}$	turn over
5	pa^{55}	pa^{53}	pa^{35}	pa^{42}	pa^{35}	leaf
5'	pa^{25}	pha^{453}	pha^{35}	pha^{42}	pha^{35}	scarf

Nonstop initials

Type	1 TS (N1)	2 RZ (S1)	3 JD (N3)	4 CG (S2)	5 ZB (S3)	
Tone						
1	ma^{35}	ma^{55}	ma^{22}	ma^{55}	ma^{11}	vegetable
1'	ma^{11}	ma^{35}	ma^{11}	mha^{55}	ma^{11}	come
3	na^{33}	na^{323}	na^{23}	na^{35}	na^{23}	face (n)
3'	na^{13}	na^{13}	na^{23}	nha^{35}	na^{23}	bow (n)
5	ja^{55}	ja^{53}	ja^{35}	ja^{42}	γa^{35}	field
5'	ja^{25}	ja^{453}	ja^{35}	jha^{42}	xa^{35}	red

Dialects 185

The uvular q. Most places where the southern dialect is spoken—most Dong villages in Lípíng, Cóngjiāng, and Róngjiāng; Qíméng in Jǐnpíng (S1) and Bàojīng in Zhènyuǎn (S3)—have the uvular stop *q* as a syllable initial. In places without the uvular stop, *k* or *ʔ* is used. In Tiānzhù Shídòng (N1), sometimes *k* is used and sometimes *ʔ*.

(337)
	CG (S2)	RZ (S1)	TS (N1)	TZ (N2)	Chinese	
	qa⁵⁵	ʔa⁵⁵	ʔa³⁵	ka⁵⁵	歌 gē	song
	qai⁴²	ʔai⁵³	ʔai⁵⁵	kai⁵³	鸡 jī	chicken
	qit³⁵	ʔit³²³	kit³³	kit³³	病 bìng	be ill
	qhin⁵⁵	ʔin³⁵	kin¹¹	kin³⁵	手臂 shǒu bì	arm (n)

The voiced velar fricative ɣ. The voiced velar fricative *ɣ* occurs in the northern dialect in Jiànhé Xiǎoguǎng (N1), Sānsuì Kuǎnchǎng (N1), and Tiānzhù Zhùxī (N2), and in the southern dialect in Lípíng Píngtú (平途, S2), Cóngjiāng Guàndòng (S2), and Róngjiāng Chēzhài (车寨, S1). In most areas it merges with the voiced palatal approximant *j*. Since a variety of different pronunciations occur with Cì Yīn tones, local variations in sound category are fairly complicated. Main variations in pronunciation are presented in (338) where the sound category from the language family is given in the first column, with examples in (339).

(338)
	Sound category	Tone conditions	RZ (S1)	CG (S2)	LP (S2)	ZB (S3)	TZ (N2)
	j	Yáng and Quán Yīn	j	j	j	j	j
	j	Cì Yīn	j	jh	ɕ	ɕ	j
	ɣ	Yáng and Quán Yīn	j	x	x	ɕ	ɣ
	ɣ	Cì Yīn	j	ɣ	ɣ	j	ɣ

(339)
	RZ (S1)	CG (S2)	LP (S2)	ZB (S3)	TZ (N2)	Chinese	
	jam⁵⁵	jam⁵⁵	jam³⁵	jam¹¹	jam⁵⁵	借	borrow
	jan³⁵	jhan⁵⁵	ɕan³⁵	ɕen¹¹	jen³⁵	园子	garden
	ja⁴⁵³	xa⁴²	xa⁵³	ɕa³⁵	ɣa³⁴²	红	red
	jan²¹²	ɣan³⁴	ɣan¹¹³	jan³¹	ɣan²¹³	家	home

The palatalized alveolar sounds tj, thj, *and* nj. Palatalized alveolar sounds occur in Cóngjiāng Guàndòng (S2) and in Jǐnpíng Qíméng (S1), and in the northern dialect in Tiānzhù Zhùxī (N2). In the southern dialect they mainly correspond to coronal sounds, while in the northern dialect some correspond to coronal sounds while others come from changes to palatalized bilabial sounds. Some examples are given in (340).

(340)
RZ (S1)	CG (S2)	JQ (S1)	TZ (N2)	Chinese	
ţeŋ^{53}	tjeŋ^{42}	ţeŋ^{53}	tjaŋ^{53}	饱 bǎo	full
ţhim^{35}	thjim^{55}	thjim^{24}	tjin^{35}	添 tiān	add
ņa^{55}	nja^{55}	nja^{55}	nja^{55}	河 hé	river
pja^{323}	pja^{35}	pja^{33}	tja^{33}	雷 léi	thunder
phjin^{35}	phjin^{55}	phjin^{24}	tjen^{35}	偏 piān	askew
mjeŋ^{55}	mjeŋ^{55}	mjaŋ^{55}	njeŋ^{55}	沟 gōu	ditch

The affricates ts *and* tš. The Dong of most areas does not have any affricate initials. In Guìzhōu, only Sānsuì Kuǎnchǎng (N1), Tiānzhù Zhùxī (N2), and Lípíng Píngtú (S2) have the voiceless affricate *ts*, and only Lípíng Píngtú has the sound *tš*. This latter sound is a cross between alveolar and coronal, with teeth and gums obstructing at the same time, and it is in contrast with *ts*. For example: tso^{42} 'physical strength' and tšo^{42} 'chopsticks', tsin^{113} 'money' and tšin^{113} 'cloth for wrapping around lower legs', tsot^{23} 'breathe' and tšot^{23} 'hair worn in a bun or coil'. The two sounds are in contrast, just as in other places the voiceless alveolar fricative *s* and voiceless coronal fricative *ɕ* (or voiceless coronal stop *ţ*) are contrastive. Basic correspondence is seen in (341) with examples in (342).

(341)
Sound category	Tone conditions	RZ (S1)	LP (S2)	SK (N1)	TZ (N2)
s	Yáng and Quán Yīn	s	ts	ts	ts
s	Cì Yīn	s	s	s	s
ɕ	Yáng and Quán Yīn	ɕ	tš	ɕ	ţ
ɕ	Cì Yīn	ɕ	ɕ	ɕ	ɕ

(342)
RZ (S1)	LP (S2)	SK (N1)	TZ (N2)	Chinese	
sai^{323}	tsai^{23}	tsai^{33}	tsai^{33}	肠子 cháng zi	intestines
sau^{453}	sau^{53}	sau^{35}	sau^{35}	白鹭 bái lù	egret
ɕok^{55}	tšok^{45}	ɕo^{55}	ţok^{55}	捶 chuí	beat (v)
ɕa^{13}	ɕa^{23}	ɕa^{23}	ɕa^{22}	纺 fǎng	spin

Dialects 187

The voiceless lateral fricative ɬ. This initial occurs only in the Dong of Zhènyuǎn Bàojīng (S3) and Guǎngxī Róngshuǐ (S4). It usually corresponds to *kw* in other places. Examples are given in (343).

(343) ZB(S3)   RZ (S1)   Chinese

    ɬa²³   kwa³²³   硬 *yìng*   hard
    ɬe³¹   kwe²¹²   水牛 *shuǐ niú*   water buffalo
    ɬiu³⁵   kwiu⁵³   秤 *chèng*   balance (n)
    ɬan¹¹   kwan⁵⁵   斧头 *fǔ tou*   ax
    ɬən³¹   kwɐn²¹²   烟 *yān*   smoke (n)
    ɬo²³   khwau¹³   酒 *jiǔ*   alcohol
    ɬan¹¹   khwan³⁵   甜 *tián*   sweet
    ɬe¹¹   kwe⁵⁵   黄瓜 *huáng guā* cucumber
    ɬaŋ¹¹   kwaŋ⁵⁵   光亮 *guāng liàng* bright
    ɬo³⁵   kwau⁵³   膝盖 *qī gài*   knee

Miscellaneous variations. Compared with other related languages, the system of syllable initials in modern Dong has gone through a process of simplification. There are no compound-consonant initials and no voiced stop initials, except in certain villages in Guǎngxī Róngshuǐ (S4). In the course of this simplification process, development in most areas has been basically uniform. There are some unusual correspondences, however, though relatively few words are affected. Four such correspondences are illustrated in (344)–(347).

(344) ŋw~m~khw (qh)

    RZ (S1)   TS (N1)   LS (S2)   Chinese

    ŋwɐt³⁵   mət³⁵   khwɐt²⁴   跳蚤 *tiào zao*   flea
    ŋu⁴⁵³   mu²⁵   qhu⁵³   猪 *zhū*   pig

(345) p (ph)~k (kh)~t~ɬ~pj (phj)

    RZ   JD   TS   ZB   SK   Chinese
    (S1)   (N3)   (N1)   (S3)   (N1)

    pa⁵⁵   ka²²   ta³⁵   ɬa¹¹   pja⁵⁵   鱼 *yú*   fish (n)
    phat¹³ kat²³   tat¹³   ɬat²³   pjat²³ 血 *xiě* blood

(346) *l*~*q*

RZ (S1)	LP (S2)	CG (S2)	Chinese	
la²¹²	*la¹¹³*	*qa³⁴*	菌子 *jùn zi*	mushroom
lan²¹²	*lan¹¹³*	*qan³⁴*	扁担 *biǎn dan*	shoulder pole
laŋ²¹²	*laŋ¹¹³*	*qaŋ³⁴*	下巴 *xià ba*	chin

(347) *kw* (*khw*)~*q* (*qh*)~*t*

RZ (S1)	JQ (S1)	TS (N1)	Chinese	
kwe³²³	*qe³³*	*te³³*	梯子 *tī zi*	ladder
kwa³²³	*qa³³*	*ta³³*	硬 *yìng*	hard
khwau¹³	*qhau²³*	*tau¹³*	酒 *jiǔ*	liquor

Local variations in pronunciation of syllable rhymes. Differences in the syllable rhyme systems of the various Dong areas are marked: some areas have fifty or more rhymes, others have only thirty or so. Variations, however, are well regulated. The main variations in syllable rhymes in the different Dong areas of Guìzhōu are divided into vowel variations and syllable coda variations.

Vowels. Compared with other languages in the Dòng-Tái (侗台) language family, the vowel system in Dong is fairly straightforward. A general trend in the pronunciation of Dong has been for contrasts between long and short vowels to disappear, leading to merging and simplification of syllable rhymes. Within the dialects, however, development has not been uniform: in some areas there are only six vowels, in others eight.

There are four basic vowel systems for Dong spoken in Guìzhōu. (1) Six vowels *a*, *e*, *i*, *o*, *u*, and *ə*, without any contrast in length. Basically the whole northern dialect belongs to this system. (2) Seven vowels *a*, *e*, *i*, *o*, *u*, *ə*, and *ɐ*. Only the vowel *a* has a long-short contrast. Most of the first and third lect areas of the southern dialect have a vowel system like this, including the standard dialect chosen for the Dong writing system. (3) Eight vowels *a*, *e*, *i*, *o*, *u*, *ə*, *ɐ*, and *ŏ*. The vowel *a* has a long-short contrast, as does the vowel *o* when it is followed by a velar consonant coda. Some places where the second lect of the southern dialect is spoken, including Lípíng Shuǐkǒu, for example, have vowel systems like this. (4) Eight vowels *a*, *i*, *o*, *e*, *u*, *ɐ*, *ĭ*, and *ŭ*. Apart from *o* and *e*, the vowels are all contrastive in length, but there is no central vowel *ə*. Most places where the second lect of the southern dialect is spoken have a vowel system like this.

Dialects

The long vowels are relatively stable and do not vary much in pronunciation from place to place. Variations in pronunciation of the short vowels are summarized in the following paragraphs.

1. ă *(also written as ɐ)*. Basically all areas of the southern dialect have a contrast between long and short *a*. In the northern dialect, there is no ɐ; it changes and merges with the ə or *a* rhyme. The rules for the changes are usually as follows: with nasal consonant codas, ɐ becomes ə, though in some places, with the coda ŋ, it becomes *a*; with stop consonant codas, it becomes ə in some places, *a* in others, or perhaps both ə and *a* according to different places of articulation. Correspondences appear in (348) with examples in (349).

(348)
Coda	RZ (S1)	ZB (S3)	JQ (S1)	TS (N1)	TZ (N2)	JD (N3)
m	ɐ	ə	ɐ	ə	ə	ə
n	ɐ	ə	ɐ	ə	ə	ə
ŋ	ɐ	ə	ɐ	a	a	ə
p	ɐ	ə	a	a	ə	ə
t	ɐ	ə	a	a	ə	ə
k	ɐ	ə	a	a	a	a

(349)
RZ (S1)	ZB (S3)	JQ (S1)	TS (N1)	TZ (N2)	JD (N3)	Chinese	
sɐm^{35}	səm^{11}	sɐm^{24}	səm^{11}	səm^{35}	səm^{22}	早	early
mɐn^{55}	pən^{11}	mɐn^{55}	mən^{35}	pən^{55}	pən^{22}	日子	day
tɐŋ^{53}	təŋ^{35}	tɐŋ^{53}	taŋ^{55}	taŋ^{53}	təŋ^{55}	凳子	stool
sɐp^{35}	—	sap^{55}	sap^{55}	səp^{55}	səp^{55}	捉	catch
tɐt^{55}	tət^{55}	tat^{55}	tat^{55}	tət^{55}	kət^{55}	砍	chop
tɐk^{55}	tək^{55}	tak^{55}	taʔ^{55}	taʔ^{55}	taʔ^{55}	胸	chest

Variations in ɐ are mainly due to conditioning of syllable codas, but some are also influenced by syllable initials. For example, in speech from Jǐnpíng Qǐméng (S1), after palatalized sounds the rhyme ɐŋ changes to əŋ and ɐp changes to ep, e.g., tjəŋ^{55} 'for a long time', tjəŋ^{53} 'be full', njep^{23} 'blink'; and between two bilabial sounds ɐ in Cóngjiāng Guàndòng (S2) changes to ŭ, e.g., pŭm^{35} 'cut down', pjŭm^{55} 'hair', wŭp^{55} 'shrivelled'; in Tiānzhù Shídòng (N1), the rhyme ɐt changes to *et* after coronal or palatal initials or after palatalization, e.g., ȶet^{13} 'scratch', jet^{55} 'squeeze'; and in Jiànhé Xiǎoguǎng (N1), ɐn and ɐt change to *en* and *et*, respectively, after palatalization or after palatal or velar initials, e.g., *ljen⁵⁵* 'untie', *jen³⁵* 'ridge at edge of field for walking on', *ket¹¹* 'small broken pieces of rice'.

2. *ĭ and ŭ*. Where the second lect of the southern dialect is spoken, the vowels *i* and *u* divide into long and short vowels in most places; for example, in Cóngjiāng Guàndòng, Lípíng Píngtú, and Róngjiāng Zhàihāo (寨蒿). The long vowels *i* and *u* come in rhymes with all kinds of syllable codas. Rhymes associated with *ĭ* and *ŭ* are mostly rhymes with bilabial or alveolar consonant codas. Syllables with these short vowels and velar consonant codas are rare. At the time of the general survey of Dong in the 1950s only two syllables with the *ĭŋ* rhyme were discovered, *tĭŋ⁵³* 'black' and *lĭŋ³³* 'ice'; and only two syllables with the *ĭk* rhyme were discovered, *lĭk²¹* 'physical strength' and *tĭk²¹* 'worth the money', both of which were loan words from Chinese. Not a single syllable was found with a *ŭ* rhyme and a velar consonant coda.

The general trend in the extinction of this kind of short vowel rhyme is for *ĭ* and *ŭ* to merge into *ə*. There are, however, individual exceptions to this rule. For example, in the speech of Zhènyuǎn Bàojīng (S3), with the two alveolar consonant syllable codas *n* and *t*, what used to be *ĭ* and *ŭ* are now long *i* and long *u*, respectively; while with the two bilabial consonant codas *m* and *p*, *ĭ* and *ŭ* have become an *ə* rhyme, but syllables which originally had an *ĭ* rhyme can freely be pronounced with long *i*, whereas syllables which originally had a *ŭ* rhyme cannot freely vary. In the speech of Jǐnpíng Qíméng (S1), there are analogous local variations in pronunciation. With codas *m* or *n*, *ĭ* and *ŭ* become *ə*; with coda *p*, *ĭ* and *ŭ* become *i* and *ə*, respectively; with coda *t*, *ĭ* and *ŭ* become *i* and *u*, respectively. Correspondences are presented in (350) with examples in (351).

(350)	Rhyme class	CG (S2)	LP (S2)	ZB (S3)	JQ (S1)	RZ (S1)
	ĭm	ĭm	ĭm	im/əm	əm	əm
	ŭm	ŭm	ŭm	əm	əm	əm
	ĭn	ĭn	ĭn	in	ən	ən
	ŭn	ŭn	ŭn	un	ən	ən
	ĭp	ĭp	ip	ip/əp	ip	əp
	ŭp	ŭp	up	əp	əp	əp
	ĭt	ĭt	it	it	it	ət
	ŭt	ŭt	ut	ut	ut	ət

Dialects

(351)

	CG (S2)	LP (S2)	ZB (S3)	JQ (S1)	RZ (S1)	Chinese	
	hǐm⁴²	tsǐm⁵³	sim³⁵/səm³⁵	səm⁵³	səm⁵³	浸泡	soak
	tǐm⁵⁵	tǐm³⁵	tim¹¹/təm¹¹	təm⁵⁵	təm⁵⁵	斗笠	bamboo hat
	lǔm³⁴	lǔm¹¹³	ləm³¹	ləm²¹²	ləm²¹²	风	wind (n)
	mǔm¹²	mǔm³¹	məm⁵⁵	məm³¹	məm³¹	老虎	tiger
	thǐn³⁵	thǐn²³	thin²³	thən²³	thən¹³	短	brief
	ɲǐn⁵⁵	ɲǐn³⁵	ɲin¹¹	ɲən⁵⁵	ɲən⁵⁵	臭	smelly
	whǔn³⁵	whǔn²³	hun²³	wən²³	wən¹³	裙子	skirt (n)
	thǔn⁴²	thǔn⁵³	sun³⁵	sən³⁴²	sən⁴⁵³	寸	0.033 meter
	ɕǐp³³	ɕip¹¹	—	ɕip³³¹	ɕəp²¹	十	ten
	ȶǐp⁵⁵	ȶip⁴⁵	ȶip⁵⁵/ȶəp⁵⁵	ȶip⁵⁵	ȶəp⁵⁵	捡	pick up
	hǔp³³	tsup¹¹	səp³¹	səp¹¹	səp²¹	吹	blow
	tǔp⁵⁵	tup⁴⁵	təp⁵⁵	təp⁵⁵	təp⁵⁵	折	break, snap
	tjǐt⁵⁵	ȶit⁴⁵	ȶit⁵⁵	tjit⁵⁵	ȶət⁵⁵	柴	firewood
	lǐt³³	lit¹¹	lit³¹	lit³³	lət²¹	栗子	chestnut
	qǔt³⁵	—	qut³³	qut³³	tət³²³	打结	tie a knot
	hǔt⁵⁵	tsut⁴⁵	sut⁵⁵	sut⁵⁵	sət⁵⁵	尾巴	tail

3. ŏ. In some locations associated with the second lect of the southern dialect, such as Lípíng Shuǐkǒu, there is a long-short distinction for the vowel o. This distinction only occurs before velar codas, namely as oŋ versus ŏŋ, or ok versus ŏk. When o appears before other codas it only occurs as long o. Since the coda ok is subject to tone conditioning (long ok only occurs with tones 9 and 10, short ŏk only occurs with tones 7 and 8), phonemically it does not need to divide into long and short. In fact, only oŋ and ŏŋ are in contrast. For example: whoŋ⁵³ 'pail', ȶoŋ⁴⁴ 'dress up', ȶŏŋ⁴⁴ 'clock', lŏŋ³⁵ 'winnowing fan'.

Rules for local pronunciations of long and short o are fairly clear: either the long and short oŋ combine, as in Róngjiāng Zhānglǔ (S1) and Tiānzhù Shídòng (N1), or the short ŏŋ becomes əŋ, as in Jǐnpíng Dàtóng (N3) and Tiānzhù Bènchù (坌处, N3).

The areas which have long and short vowels i and u, such as Cóngjiāng Guàndòng (S2) and Lípíng Píngtú (S2), also have short rhymes ŏŋ and ŏk. Since these areas do not have short rhymes ŭŋ or ŭk, these 'missing rhymes' are just compensated for by the rhymes ŏŋ and ŏk. It is very likely then that in early Dong the vowel *o*, like *e*, did not have long and short contrastive forms, and the rhymes *ŏŋ* and *ŏk* came originally from *ŭŋ* and *ŭk*.

Syllable codas. The Dong language has eight syllable codas: two high vowels *i* and *u*, three nasals *m*, *n*, and *ŋ*, and three stops *p*, *t*, and *k*. Variations in local pronunciation of syllable codas are relatively straightforward. In the southern dialect area in particular, there is comparatively little variation. Only in some parts of the northern dialect area are there major variations. At present, there is no variation to be found in the codas *i*, *u*, *n*, *ŋ*, and *t*, except that in rare instances the codas *n* and *ŋ* are interchanged. There is only variation in the velar and bilabial stop codas, *k* and *p*, and in the bilabial nasal coda *m*.

1. *Loss and change of the velar coda* k. There are four situations relating to the loss and change of the coda *k*. (1) The coda is completely lost and becomes a monophthong rhyme, as in the speech of Sānsuì Kuǎnchǎng (N1). (2) The coda is lost after mid or back vowels, and after front vowels it changes to *t*, as in the speech of Jiànhé Xiǎoguǎng (N1). (3) The coda is lost with even-numbered tones and retained with odd-numbered tones, as in the speech of Jǐnpíng Qǐméng (S1). (4) The coda is pronounced as a glottal stop *ʔ*. Speech of most places in the northern dialect area is like this. The glottal is still written as *k*.

Some example words are given in (352). Note that tone categories are given for the Jǐnpíng Qǐméng column (see (3) above).

(352)

RZ (S1)	SK (N1)	JX (N1)	JQ (S1)	TS (N1)	Chinese	
tok^{55}	to^{53}	to^{55}	tok^{7}	$toʔ^{55}$	落	fall (v)
$phuk^{13}$	pu^{23}	pu^{23}	$phuk^{9}$	$puʔ^{13}$	灰烬	ash
$tɐk^{55}$	ta^{55}	ta^{55}	tak^{7}	$taʔ^{55}$	胸	chest
pek^{323}	pe^{31}	pet^{33}	pek^{9}	$peʔ^{31}$	百	100
$ȶhik^{13}$	$ȶi^{31}$	$ȶit^{13}$	$thjik^{9}$	$ȶiʔ^{13}$	踢	kick (v)
$ljok^{21}$	ljo^{23}	ljo^{23}	ljo^{8}	$ljoʔ^{13}$	六	six
suk^{31}	su^{31}	su^{31}	su^{10}	$suʔ^{31}$	捆	tie (v)
lak^{31}	la^{31}	la^{31}	la^{10}	$laʔ^{31}$	儿子	son
$mɐk^{21}$	ma^{23}	ma^{23}	ma^{8}	$maʔ^{13}$	墨	ink
mek^{31}	me^{31}	met^{31}	me^{10}	$meʔ^{31}$	麦子	wheat
$ȶik^{31}$	$ȶi^{31}$	$ȶit^{31}$	tji^{10}	$ȶiʔ^{31}$	笛子	flute

2. *Variations in the bilabial codas* m *and* p. In the second lect of the northern dialect, the bilabial consonant codas *m* and *p*, except after the vowel *ə*, change to alveolar consonant codas *n* and *t*, respectively.

(353) RZ (S1)   TZ (N2)   Chinese

  ȶim³³   tjin⁴¹   垫 diàn   cushion (n, v)
  sip³²³   tsit³³   接 jiē   meet (v)
  sam³⁵   san³⁵   三 sān   three
  sap³²³   sat³³   连接 lián jiē   connect
  sɐm³⁵   səm³⁵   早 zǎo   early
  sɐp⁵⁵   səp⁵⁵   捉 zhuō   catch (v)
  məm³¹   məm¹¹   老虎 lǎo hǔ   tiger
  ɕəp²¹   ɕəp²³   十 shí   ten

Local variations in pronunciation of tones. Dong can be divided into three types according to number of tones (referring to tones in unchecked syllables): nine-toned, seven-toned, and six-toned. The differences between the three types are very closely related to aspiration and nonaspiration of syllable initials. In areas with six tones, the tone values for Quán Yīn (1, 3, 5) and Cì Yīn (1', 3', 5') tones are the same. In areas with nine tones, these tone values are different. In areas with seven tones, only the Píng tones (1) split into different Quán Yīn (1) and Cì Yīn (1') values; other Yīn tones do not split. In other words, in areas with six tones, two syllables with the same tones (but aspirated and unaspirated initials) have different tones in areas with nine tones, and may or may not have different tones in areas with seven tones. For example, consider three pairs of words written using the Dong script: *mal* 'vegetable' and *map* 'come', *nas* 'face' and *nat* 'arrow', and *wav* 'trousers' and *wak* 'draw'. In areas with six tones, the tones within each pair of words are the same; in areas with nine tones, the tones are all different; and in areas with seven tones, the tones of *mal* and *map* are different, but *nas* and *nat* have the same tones, as do *wav* and *wak*. This illustrates the main variation in pronunciation of tones in Dong.

There is great variation in the Rù Shēng (7, 7', 8, 9, 9', 10) tones of the northern dialect. The most general trend is for tones 8 and 9' to merge. In addition, in some areas the tones in checked syllables transform into tones of unchecked syllables, because of the disappearance of the consonant coda *k*. The typical situation is that after the *k* coda disappears, the syllable takes on the tone of the corresponding unchecked syllable, as in the speech of Jiànhé Xiǎoguǎng (N1) in (354).

(354)

Checked syllable		Unchecked syllable			
Tone categories	Tone values	Tone categories	Tone values		
7	55	5	55	to^{55}	fall (v)
7'	25	5'	25	lja^{25}	cold (adj)
9	33	3	33	$ȶa^{33}$	straw sandal
9'	23	3'	23	ljo^{23}	six
10	31	4	31	ta^{31}	measure (v)

In some places, after the syllable coda k is lost, the tone of a checked syllable may split into two tones in unchecked syllables, or alternatively, two tones in checked syllables may merge into a single tone in unchecked syllables. The speech in Sānsuì Kuǎnchǎng (N1) illustrates both splitting and merging of tones. After the syllable coda k disappeared, tone 7 in Kuǎnchǎng speech became tone 5 when the main vowel was o, and tone 1 when the main vowel was a; and tones 9 and 10 merged into tone 4. Note that tone categories, and not values, are given in (355).

(355)

RZ (S1)	SK (N1)	Chinese	
$çok^7$	$ço^5$	捣 dǎo	pound (v)
tok^7	to^5	落 luò	fall (v)
mok^7	mo^5	埋 mái	bury
$tɐk^7$	ta^1	胞 bāo	afterbirth
$tɐk^7$	$ȶa^1$	胸 xiōng	chest
$sɐk^7$	sa^1	洗 xǐ	wash (clothes)
pak^9	pa^4	外 wài	outside
pak^{10}	pa^4	白 bái	white

In some places, an independent tone value is retained even after the syllable coda k is lost. Speech in Jǐnpíng Qíméng (S1) follows this pattern. After the coda k dropped out of Yáng Rù rhymes (8 and 10) in Qíméng, long Yáng Rù (10) syllables took on tone 4 but short Yáng Rù (8) syllables did not merge with any tone in unchecked syllables but retained the original tone value, and the corresponding syllable initials remained voiced and aspirated.

Dialects 195

(356) RZ (S1)   JQ (S1)   Chinese

  pɐk⁸   pha³³¹   萝卜 luó bo   radish
  mɐk⁸   mha³³¹   墨 mò   ink
  tɐk⁸   tha³³¹   公牛 gōng niú   bull

A summary of Dong tone values in various places, corresponding to different tone categories, is presented in (357).

(357)

Tone	RZ (S1)	JQ (S1)	LS (S2)	LP (S2)	CG (S2)	ZB (S3)	TS (N1)	JX (N1)	SK (N1)	TZ (N2)	JD (N3)
1	55	55	44	35	55	11	35	35	55	55	22
1'	35	24	44	35	55	11	11	11	11	35	11
2	212	212	12	113	34	31	22	22	22	213	31
3	323	33	35	23	35	23	33	33	33	33	23
3'	13	23	35	23	35	23	13	23	23	22	23
4	31	31	11	31	12	55	31	31	31	11	33
5	53	53	53	53	42	35	55	55	53	53	35
5'	453	342	53	53	42	35	25	25	35	342	35
6	33	42	21	42	22	33	44	44	231	41	42
7	55	55	44	45	55	55	55	55	55	55	55
7'	35	24	44	45	55	55	25	25	25	35	55
8	21	331	32	11	33	31	13	23	23	23	31
9	323	33	35	23	35	33	33	33	33	33	33
9'	13	23	35	23	35	33	13	23	23	23	23
10	31	31	11	31	12	55	31	31	31	11	33

5.3 Differences in vocabulary between lects

There is a fairly broad base of vocabulary in Dong which is the same across all lects. According to statistics from *The Dong Nationality's Language Situation and Orthography Issue* (侗族的语言情况和文字问题, a report of the Conference on questions about the Dong language and script, convened in August 1958, after the first minority language survey of the Chinese Academy of Sciences), the average percentage of cognate words between northern and southern Dong is 71.7 percent. Among different points in the southern dialect area the average percentage of cognate words is ninety-two percent and among different points in the northern dialect area the average is eighty percent. Many words and phrases which differ between dialects are very similar in different lects of a given dialect, as seen in (358).

(358) RZ   LS   CG   TS   JD   Chinese
       (S1)   (S2)   (S2)   (N1)   (N3)

       tuŋ³³   tuŋ²¹   tuŋ²²   sau²⁵   sau³⁵   柱子   pillar
       ʔəm³²³ ʔəm³⁵   ʔum³⁵   sa²²   sa³¹   药   medicine
       n̪ip¹³   n̪hep³⁵ n̪hep³⁵ t̪iŋ²²   t̪iŋ³¹   火钳   fire tongs
       muŋ³¹   muŋ¹¹   muŋ¹²   pu³⁵   pu²²   个(人)   a classifier
       t̪əm³³   t̪əm²¹   t̪ŭm²²   hau¹¹   hau¹¹   山冲   valley
       ʔu³¹   qu¹¹   qu¹²   poŋ³³   ɕoŋ⁴²   雹子   hail (n)

Some of the vocabulary differences in Dong reflect different societal structures, modes of production, and local conventions in different places. For example, the phrases we³¹khwan¹³ 'a kind of social gathering for enjoyment', we³¹je⁴⁵³ 'a custom of collective visiting', and sip³²³sa³¹ 'a religious ceremony in honor of the goddess Sà (萨)' are peculiar to the southern dialect, and t̪e³⁵waʔ³¹ 'a kind of festival' is peculiar to the northern dialect.

For the most part, divergence in dialect vocabulary falls into one of seven categories.

One area uses native Dong words, another uses Chinese loan words. All the lects of the Dong language have assimilated a very substantial number of Chinese loan words, but the degree of assimilation is not uniform across different lects. So, in some areas a Chinese loan word is used where in others a native Dong word is used. In comparisons between the northern and southern dialects this phenomenon is often evident.

(359) RZ   LS   TS   JD   Chinese
       (S1)   (S2)   (N1)   (N3)

       me⁵⁵   me⁴⁴   ɕoŋ²²   ɕəŋ³¹   熊 xióng   bear (n)
       sət⁵⁵   sət⁴⁴   sau¹³   sau²³   扫 sǎo   sweep (v)
       lɐk⁵⁵   lɐk⁴⁴   loŋ³⁵   ləŋ²²   聋 lóng   deaf
       kwam³²³ kwam³⁵ pa³⁵   pa²²   疤 bā   scar (n)
       wom⁵³   wom⁵³   jən³⁵   jən²²   阴 yīn   overcast
       ɕiŋ³⁵   ɕiŋ⁴⁴   t̪aŋ³⁵   t̪aŋ²²   姜 jiāng   ginger

All areas use Chinese loan words, but the loan words have different origin. There are some words which, although they all come from Chinese and have the same meaning, are different in form, either because they were borrowed at different times, early or modern, or because they come from different synonyms in Chinese.

Dialects

(360) speak
    wa³³   RZ (S1)   话 *huà*   word
    ɕot³¹   TS (N1)   说 *shuō*   speak
    qaŋ²³   LH (S1)   讲 *jiǎng*   speak

earthen jar
    ʔoŋ⁵³   RZ (S1)   瓮 *wèng*   earthen jar
    kaŋ⁵⁵   TZ (N2)   缸 *gāng*   big jar or crock
    tam²²   SK (N1)   坛 *tán*   earthen jar

candle
    lap³¹   RZ (S1)   蜡 *là*   wax
    ɕo⁵⁵   JX (N3)   烛 *zhú*   candle

beginning of Spring
    ljəp²¹ɕən³⁵   RZ (S1)   an early loan   beginning of Spring
    lji²²tsən³³   TS (N1)   立春 *lì chūn*   beginning of Spring

flag
    ȶi²¹²   RZ (S1)   an early loan   flag
    ȶhi²¹²   JQ (S1)   旗 *qí*   flag

All areas use words made up of morphemes which are intrinsically Dong (including early Chinese loan words). Differences arise because the ways of creating the words, or the morphemes used in the words, are different from place to place. There are at least five identifiable situations.

Different areas use different characteristics of things. For example, in Róngjiāng Zhānglǔ (S1) the word for 'polished glutinous rice' is variously *ʔɐu³¹lai⁵⁵* 'good rice', *ʔɐu³¹kɐm⁵⁵* 'Dong rice', *ʔɐu³¹sau³²³* 'steamed rice', or *ʔɐu³¹tui⁵⁵* 'rice dished out on a plate' (*tui⁵⁵* is a kind of plate specially used for dishing out glutinous rice); and in most other areas it is known as *ʔɐu³¹to³³* 'sticky rice'.

Different areas use different synonyms

(361)   stone   stone bench
     pja⁵⁵   *tɐŋ⁵³pja⁵⁵*   RZ (S1)
     ȶin³⁵   *taŋ⁵⁵ȶin³⁵*   TS (N1)

lean (adj)	lean meat	
nau⁵⁵	nan³¹nau⁵⁵	RZ (S1)
jəm³⁵	nan³¹jəm³⁵	TS (N1)
big	father's elder brother	
lau³¹	pu³¹lau³¹	RZ (S1)
mak³⁵	pu¹¹mak³⁵	LS (S2)

Different areas use the same morphemes to make words, but combine them in a different order

(362) a species of pig
    ŋu⁴⁵³laŋ²¹²   RZ (S1)
    laŋ²²mu²⁵   TS (N1)

    rascally behavior
    kha³⁵na⁵⁵   RZ (S1)
    na³⁵ka¹¹   TS (N1)

    bean sprouts
    to³³ŋe²¹²   RZ (S1)
    ŋe²²to⁴⁴   TS (N1)

One area uses a monosyllabic word, another uses a polysyllabic word

(363) chin
    qaŋ³⁴   CG (S2)
    ʨi⁵⁵ʔaŋ²²   TS (N1)

    swallow (n)
    kin⁵⁵   TS (N1)
    ʔin⁵³si³²³   RZ (S1)
    ʔa²²ʔen³⁵   JD (N3)

    knee
    kwau⁵³   RZ (S1)
    kuŋ³⁵kwau⁵³   LS (S2)
    ŋau¹³ŋəu³⁵   TS (N1)

Dialects

One area uses a special term, another uses an analytical compound

(364) remote mountains
    $loŋ^{55}$ RZ (S1)
    $ta^{33}lau^{31}$ mountain/big   TS (N1)
    $ta^{33}jəm^{35}$ mountain/deep   JD (N3)

straw sandal
    tak^{323} RZ (S1)
    $γai^{22}waŋ^{55}$ shoe/grass   SK (N1)

bathe
    $ʔap^{323}$ RZ (S1)
    $ɕuk^{31}ɕən^{11}$ wash/body   TS (N1)

pheasant
    meu^{212} RZ (S1)
    $ʔai^{35}ta^{23}$ chicken/mountain   JD (N3)

Words from different areas have the same origin, but meanings have undergone change. In this case the words are the same, but the meanings are different. Tone categories are used in (365).

(365) $nən^{6}$
    neck   RZ (S1)
    neck of water buffalo   TS (N1)

$ʔo^{5}$
    father's younger brother   RZ (S1)
    man who accompanies groom to meet the new bride   TS (N1)

jun^{1}
    stand (v)   RZ (S1)
    squat   LZ (S2)

$ŋe^{2}$
    tooth   LP (S2)
    animal's tooth   LZ (S2)
    molar tooth   JG (N1)

$mɐn^{2}$
    sweet potato   RZ (S1)
    a kind of potato   JG (N1)

ʔoŋ³
    paternal grandfather   RZ (S1)
    paternal grandfather's father   LP (S2)

Some words have essentially the same meaning, but the emotional connotation of the words is different. For example: the word *pu³³* 'praise' in Róngjiāng Zhānglǔ (S1) and in other places has positive connotations, but in Lípíng Zhúpíng (竹坪, S2) it is essentially derogatory.

With some words, the part of speech varies. For example: the word *ɕem³³* in the southern dialect is a noun meaning 'wooden partition or wall', but in Tiānzhù Shídòng (N1) and some other northern dialect areas it is a verb meaning 'to erect a wooden partition'.

One area has several synonyms, while another has fewer synonyms or just one word. Differences arise because of differences in precision.

(366) cloth   cotton
        ja⁵⁵   *mjin²⁴*   CG (S2)
        mjin²¹²   *mjin²¹²*   RZ (S1)

        cut, chop   cut (a tree with an ax)
        te⁵³   *pem³²³*   RZ (S1)
        te⁵⁵   *te⁵⁵*   TS (N1)

        steam glutinous rice   steam foods other than glutinous rice
        sau³²³   *mei³⁵*   RZ (S1)
        sau³³   *sau³³*   TS (N1)

Another example is the word for tooth. In Lípíng Zhúpíng (S2) there are two words, *pjen⁵⁵* meaning human teeth and *ŋe¹²* meaning animal teeth. In southern areas of Cóngjiāng (and Jǐnpíng) there are also two words, *pjen⁵⁵* (or *pjən³⁵*) meaning front teeth and *ŋe¹²* meaning molars. In some other areas there is only one word—either *pjen⁵⁵* or *ŋe¹²*.

Words from all areas have basically the same meanings, but extrapolated meanings are different. In Róngjiāng Zhānglǔ (S1) and Tiānzhù Shídòng (N1) the word for arm is *ʔin³⁵* and *ʔin¹¹*, respectively. These words both also have the meaning 'sleeve'. In Róngjiāng the same word also means 'bracelet', but not in Tiānzhù.

In Zhānglǔ and Shídòng the word for 'bone' is *lak³²³* and *laʔ³¹*, respectively. In Zhānglǔ the same word can also be used to mean 'seam (in clothing)', but not in Shídòng.

Words from different areas are noncognate. An example is given in (367).

(367) bat (the mammal)
        $ʔo^{212}$ RZ (S1)
        $tu^{212}qoŋ^{212}$ JQ (S1)
        $ko^{55}li^{23}$ ZB (S3)
        $ṇa^{31}ŋu^{22}$ SK (N1)
        $ʔo^{22}ljo^{33}ljem^{33}$ JX (N1)
        $nok^{13}ni^{22}$ TS (N1)
        $ʔa^{31}lja^{31}pau^{31}$ JD (N3)

5.4 Differences in grammar between dialects

Differences in word order, phonetic changes of words in the northern dialect, and use of different function words clearly distinguish and characterize the two Dong dialects (for more details, see chapter 4).

Differences in word order. The southern dialect still preserves Dong's intrinsic word order in head-modifier phrases with noun as head: the modifier is usually placed after the head (cf. (269)). In most places in the northern dialect area, the modifier can be placed either before or after the head, but in structures where personal pronouns 'possess' the nouns they modify, the personal pronouns can only come before the nouns (cf. (270)), as illustrated in (368).

(368)   **$ṭai^{31}$**   **mau^{33}** pai^{55} $kui^{55}jaŋ^{212}$ $jaŋ^{31}$
      older^brother   3s   go   Guìyáng   STM
      His older brother went to Guìyáng. (southern)

      mau^{44}   **ko^{33}** pai^{35} $kui^{35}jaŋ^{212}$ $ljeu^{31}$
      3s   older^brother   go   Guìyáng   PAST
      His older brother went to Guìyáng. (northern)

      $pjət^{55}$ nai^{33} $ṭaŋ^{33}$ $pjət^{55}$ jau^{212}
      pen   this   be   pen   1s
      This is my pen. (southern)

      $pjet^{55}$ nai^{44} $ɕi^{55}$ jau^{22} ti^{33} $pjet^{55}$
      pen   this   be   1s   REL   pen
      This is my pen. (northern)

nuk³²³   ja⁴⁵³
flower   red
red flower (southern)

wa¹¹   ja²⁵   =   ja²⁵   ti³³   wa¹¹
flower   red   red   REL   flower
red flower (northern)

Differences in phonetic detail. In the northern dialect, classifiers and some numerals, nouns, and verbs are subject to phonetic change. Under certain conditions, syllable initials change to voiced fricatives or approximants at the same place of articulation as original initials. This phenomenon doesn't exist in the southern dialect.

Phonetic change in the northern dialect takes one of the following five forms.

1. When a classifier comes after the number ji^{35} 'one' or $ɕi^{33}$ 'ten' to form a numeral-classifier phrase, the classifier's syllable initial undergoes phonetic change (cf. (140)–(146)). It is not even necessary for the number ji^{35} to stand with the classifier; the classifier can stand alone in its changed form meaning 'a single one'. Thus this is a grammatical feature.

(369) a. jau²²   me²²   ja²²   pa³³   kwan³⁵
           1s   have   two   CLF   ax
           I have two axes.

       b. jau²²   me²²   ji³⁵   wa³³   kwan³⁵   =
           1s   have   one   CLF   ax
           I have one ax.

           jau²²   me²²   wa³³   kwan³⁵
           1s   have   CLF   ax
           I have one ax.

2. The numbers three to nine (apart from five in some areas), when they come after the number $ɕi^{33}$ 'ten' to form a two-digit number, are subject to phonetic change (cf. (165)). This can be viewed as continuous phonetic change, without any grammatical implications.

3. There are certain nouns which change phonetically when they are preceded by other words to form compound words (cf. (108)).

4. When certain nouns change and function as verbs, they undergo phonetic change (cf. (109)).

(370) **ţin³⁵** 'stone':   nəm³⁵   ţin³⁵   **jin³⁵**   mən²²
grab   stone   'stone'   3s
Grab the stone and hit it.

5. Certain verbs expressing the idea of swift action, when they have the connotation of 'to a strong degree, prompt and resolute', are subject to phonetic change (cf. (205)).

(371) **sun¹¹** 'pierce':   **ʐun¹¹**   mən²²   təi³⁵
pierce   3s   die
Pierce it to death.

Use of different function words. For example, the preposition indicating the passive is *tɐu³³* in the southern dialect (cf. (251)) and *ţaŋ³³* in the northern dialect.

(372) le²¹²   jau²¹²   **tɐu³³**   mau³³   tɐi²¹²   pai⁵⁵   la³¹
book   1s   PASS   3s   take   go   STM
My book was taken away by him. (southern)

       jau²²   ti³³   le²²   **ţaŋ³³**   mau⁴⁴   ʔau³⁵   pai³⁵   ljeu³¹
1s   REL   book   PASS   3s   take   go   PAST
My book was taken away by him. (northern)

6
Orthography

6.1 Language survey and the Dong orthography

Language survey and the emergence of a draft *Dong Orthography*. In 1951, the Government Affairs Office of the Central People's Government, in the document *Some Resolutions on Minority Affairs*, suggested the idea of helping minority peoples to create their own orthographies.

In 1954, the Government Affairs Office signed and responded to the *Report on the Question of Helping Nationalities Still Without Orthographies to Create Their Own Scripts*. This report was compiled by the Steering Committee for Research on Nationality Language Writing Systems of the Culture and Education Commission and by the Minority Affairs Commission, both of the Central People's Government. The official response gave the responsibility of careful research and drafting of plans to the Language Research Institute of the Chinese Academy of Sciences and the Government's Minority Affairs Commission.

The first ever nationwide scientific conference on nationality languages was convened in Běijīng (北京) in December 1955. The conference stipulated that within two years a general survey of minority languages should be conducted to help those nationalities needing to create, improve, or reform writing systems to carry out the work of designing suitable systems. After the conference, nationwide surveys of minority languages were launched.

The survey of the Dong language and the planning of an orthography for Dong were taken on by the Dong Section of the First Working Group of the Chinese Academy of Science's Minority Language Survey Team. The Working Group was mainly made up of fifteen personnel—staff and students—from the Language Department of the Central Institute of Nationalities in Běijīng, and ten comrades from the Central Southern Institute of Nationalities in Wǔhàn (武汉) and the Guìzhōu (贵州) Institute of Nationalities. These twenty-five people had all attended the National Training Seminar on Minority Language Survey. (The Seminar was jointly run by the Chinese Academy of Science's Minority Language Research Institute and the Central Institute of Nationalities' Language Department.)

The entire Dong Working Group first took part in the Dialect Survey for the Bùyī (布依) language, thus obtaining hands-on survey experience. Afterwards, in September 1956, work began on compiling the *Outline Survey of Dong Dialects and Lects*. At the beginning of December 1956, after the outline had been drafted, the members of the Working Group set off in three directions.

The middle area included Jìng (靖) County (now Jìngzhōu Miáo Dòng Autonomous County) and Tōngdào (通道) Dòng Autonomous County in Húnán (湖南) Province and Lóngshèng (龙胜) Minorities Autonomous County and Róngshuǐ (融水) Autonomous County in the Guǎngxī (广西) Zhuàng (壮) Autonomous Region.

The northern area included Tiānzhù (天柱), Jǐnpíng (锦屏), Jiànhé (剑河), Sānsuì (三穗), and Zhènyuǎn (镇远) Counties in Guìzhōu (贵州) Province and Xīnhuàng (新晃) Dòng Autonomous County in Húnán Province.

The southern area included Lípíng (黎平), Róngjiāng (榕江), and Cóngjiāng (从江) Counties in Guìzhōu and Sānjiāng (三江) Dòng Autonomous County in Guǎngxī's Zhuàng Autonomous Region.

Altogether twenty-two points where Dong is spoken were surveyed, covering fourteen counties. The survey was completed in February 1957.

After more than half a year of examining the results of the survey, the language was divided into dialects and lects, and tentative ideas were put forward for choosing a basic dialect, standard pronunciation, and writing system to be used in Dong literature. In September 1957, a planning conference was convened in Guìyáng to discuss problems related to a Dong orthography. As the conference delegates unanimously expressed the need for creating an orthography, participants immediately began sharing ideas about principles and questions pertinent to the task. After the conference, in keeping with delegates' suggestions, the Working Group and members of Guìzhōu's Nationality Language Steering Committee returned to Róngjiāng and other areas to do supplementary survey work. They gathered more data, carried out further analysis and research, and revised the draft orthography for Dong.

In Guìyáng, in August 1958, a scientific conference was convened by leaders of the Communist Party in Guìzhōu Province and attended by Dong nationality delegates from three provinces to discuss the Dong orthography. A basic dialect and standard pronunciation for Dong were decided upon, and a draft orthography was adopted. The draft *Dong Orthography* was endorsed for trial implementation by the Central Minorities Commission in October 1958.

Orthography 207

The standard dialect for the Dong orthography. The newly formulated Dong orthography used a script which combined sounds into syllables, i.e., a pīnyīn script. This meant choosing speech from a particular area to serve as a basis for designing the script, to provide both a unified standard for reading and a common set of letters for writing. The Dong script takes the southern dialect as basic and uses pronunciation from Róngjiāng County in Guìzhōu as the standard. Within Róngjiāng County, however, there is considerable variation in pronunciation, with areas where the first lect of the southern dialect is spoken and areas where the second lect is spoken. The Dong orthography was designed according to the pronunciation found in villages near the town of Róngjiāng, villages such as Zhānglǔ (章鲁) and Chēzhài (车寨), where pronunciation is basically the same. In Chēzhài, it should be noted, there are two extra sounds that Zhānglǔ Dong does not have: the uvular stop initial *q* and the velar fricative initial *y*. In order to facilitate study of Dong for people from the northern dialect area and to make the writing scheme simple and clear, these two letters are not used in the script, but the script is designed using speech from Zhānglǔ. In reading the script, either Zhānglǔ or Chēzhài pronunciation is permissible.

The population of speakers of the southern dialect is about two times that of the northern dialect (according to statistics from 1990) and covers a correspondingly wider area. In the southern dialect area, Dong is more generally spoken and the Dong script is likely to be more readily used than in the northern dialect area where a greater proportion of people speak a high level of Chinese. The speech in the neighborhood of Róngjiāng's Zhānglǔ represents well the speech of the southern dialect. The Dong villages there were not far from the town, which made communication easier and was advantageous in the development of Dong writing.

Design of the Dong orthography. Dong is written entirely in roman letters. In line with the *Five Principles for Designing Letters for Minority Nationality Language Writing Schemes* endorsed by the State Council, when a sound in Dong is the same as or very close to a sound in Chinese, as far as possible the same pīnyīn is used to represent the sound as is used for Chinese. For sounds which are peculiar to Dong and do not occur in Chinese, two letters are used. For example: the letters *i* and *u* are used to represent palatalized and labialized components, respectively, of syllable initials; and the letter *a* represents 'long *a*', while *ae* represents 'short *a*'. The merit in this scheme is that it both provides accuracy in representing pronunciation of Dong and also complements the Chinese system of pīnyīn.

Since a second thrust in implementing the Dong script in the 1980s, there has been a change in attitude towards articles 9 and 10 of the original orthography, at least for the time being. The ninth article stipulates that "new words and terminology should be written in Dong in the same way as in Chinese pīnyīn." In practice, however, it is very difficult to make this work. At present, Modern loan words from Chinese are being written in accordance with local borrowed pronunciation together with a letter representing the tone. The question affects the long-term development of the Dong script and relates to the question of its cooperation in teaching the system of Chinese pīnyīn. Clearly it needs to be handled with discretion.

The tenth article of the original scheme for writing stipulates that "the Dong script should use words as the basic units for writing and if a word includes two or more syllables, these syllables should be written joined together." Teachers and students of the orthography all felt that this was impracticable: firstly, because it is not easy to differentiate compound words and phrases in Dong, and it is therefore difficult to lay down precise rules for joining words together; and secondly, because each syllable in Dong marks the tone with the last letter of the syllable and after joining syllables it is often difficult to differentiate them while reading. This being so, current textbooks and publications all adopt the approach of separating syllables. From the practical angle, this approach facilitates study of the script. It has been warmly received.

6.2 Implementation and use of the Dong orthography

Implementation of the Dong orthography. In October 1958 the Central Minorities Commission endorsed the trial implementation of the draft *Dong Orthography*. The first test implementation of the new script was undertaken in Róngjiāng's Chējiāng (车江), an area with standard pronunciation. After three months of teaching, the script was enthusiastically received by the Dong people there. In May 1963, a group of people began the second test implementation in the district of Máogòng (茅贡) in Lípíng County. The Party and government at the time encouraged the implementation of the orthography. Morale among the students was high and the results of their studies were very good. The Province and the Autonomous Region both set up Minority Language Steering Committees and allocated a number of expert cadres to the work. In Kǎilǐ (凯里), the capital of the Qián Dōng Nán (黔东南) Miáo Dòng Autonomous Region, a minority language school was set up and a group of Dong language teachers was trained. The Guìzhōu Province Minority Language Steering Committee and related bodies published various reference books and reading materials, including *Dong Chinese Dictionary*, *Chinese Dong Dictionary*, and *Dong Language Textbook*. After 1966, the work of experimental implementation of the Dong script was compulsorily suspended.

In 1978, after the third meeting of the eleventh General Assembly of the Party, interest in promoting the Dong script was renewed. In 1981, a Working Conference on Experimental Implementation of Nationality Scripts was convened in Qián Dōng Nán, covering the whole Miáo Dòng

Autonomous Region. The Regional Government authorized a summary of the Conference to be released as its fifteenth official document in 1981. The work of experimental implementation of the Dong script was to adhere to the spirit of this summary, following well-established principles.

From 1981 to 1982, the first new batch of pilot projects implementing the Dong script was launched in Róngjiāng's Chēzhài of the southern dialect and in Tiānzhù's Shuǐdòng (水洞) of the northern dialect. In these two villages there were altogether eighty-two students.

In 1983 there were two more periods running experimental classes. This time the scope of the classes was greatly extended. Classes were given in Róngjiāng's Chējiāng, Jiālì (加利), and Duānlǐ (端里), in Cóngjiāng's Luóxiāng (洛香), Pílín (皮林), Xīnān (新安), Lóngtú (龙图), Guàndòng (贯洞), Xīshān (西山), Zēngchōng (增冲), and Gāozēng (高增), and in Lípíng's Yándòng (岩洞), Sìzhài (四寨), Tóngguān (铜关), Kǒujiāng (口江), and Bàzhài (坝寨). The above are all southern dialect points. In the northern dialect area, classes were given in Tiānzhù's Shuǐdòng, Shídòng (石洞), Zhùxī (注溪), Xīkǒu (溪口), and Sānhé (三合), in Jǐnpíng's Huángmén (黄门), Qǐméng (启蒙), and Dàtóng (大同), in Jiànhé's Dàguǎng (大广) and Xiǎoguǎng (小广), in Zhènyuǎn's Bàojīng (报京), and in Sānsuì's Kuǎnchǎng (款场). Altogether the teaching encompassed thirty-five Dong villages and more than 10,000 people participated in the studies.

In August 1983 the Guìzhōu Minority Affairs Commission and Guìzhōu Education Commission jointly signed and made public a document entitled *Circular Concerning Promotion of Pilot Nationality Language Teaching in Nationality Schools*. After this, experimental teaching of the Dong script moved from the countryside into the schools. In the same year, various classes in different kinds of schools began experimental teaching of the script; for example, classes in the Middle School in Róngjiāng's Chējiāng, in Fēngmíng (凤鸣) Elementary School in Tiānzhù, and in Hóngmén (红门) Elementary School in Jǐnpíng. By 1985, there were 118 classes in Dong elementary schools teaching the script, with about 3,230 children involved. At the same time 174 classes had been set up in Dong rural areas for teaching the script and somewhere around 18,300 people had participated in these classes.

While these trial implementations of the orthography were underway, the number of qualified teachers of the orthography was growing. From August 6–30, 1982, the Qián Dōng Nán Region ran the first ever training class for teachers of the Miáo and Dong orthographies. There were thirty-seven people in the Dong class. Soon afterwards, Róngjiāng, Tiānzhù, Lípíng, Cóngjiāng, and Jǐnpíng Counties each held four consecutive classes for training teachers of the Dong orthography. The number of qualified teachers of the orthography rose from 66 in 1983 to 428 in 1985. This brigade of teachers was scattered widely throughout the Dong countryside. It was the main force behind the implementation of the orthography and played a decisive role in the work, helping bilingual education to make its debut in the schools.

Use of the Dong orthography. The Dong orthography adopts the roman alphabet for combining sounds into syllables. It is easy to understand. The original students in the rural areas, after about 100 hours of study over a period of three months, had basically mastered the script, its initials, rhymes, and tones, and its spelling system. Moreover, they were able to produce fairly proficiently all kinds of simple written compositions. Those students who had a high level of Dong and Chinese were able to translate articles of general scientific interest from Chinese into Dong, and they were able to set out in writing some popular Dong literature and translate it into Chinese.

After the Dong script had been promoted in Róngjiāng Chējiāng, those who had studied it returned home. They were then able to put the songs that their mothers and sisters had been singing into writing. When the parents saw how their children had quickly mastered the script and were using it with ease, they considered it to be very useful; and in the Zhōngbǎo (中宝) area, for example, many people requested that courses teaching the script be set up.

By 1985, more than 3,000 people in Lípíng County had mastered the script. They were able to use it to write letters, invitation cards, and *duì lián* (对联 'antithetical couplets') and to record Dong poems, songs, and stories. Some of them even used it to write reports or applications. Articles in Dong in publications such as Guìzhōu's *Miáo Dòng Journal* were accessible to them and enabled them to study some popular science. Some people submitted articles for publication. For example, the book *Selected Writings from Dong Traditional Literature*, published by the Guìzhōu Province Nationalities Commission, includes the collected works of more than ten people who had studied and learned the Dong script. Not a few people, having mastered the script, subscribed to newspapers and periodicals using the script, such as *Miáo Dòng Journal*, *Nationality Work*, and *Southern Wind*. They were thus able to broaden their horizons and read some articles useful for everyday living.

In Tiānzhù Shuǐdòng, students of the script finished their study of initials, rhymes, and tones in something over 120 hours of study. Most of them could use the script to write ordinary sentences, and some could use it to record poems and songs or write official documents and letters. For example, one female student, Lóng Qīnghuā (龙青花), described a good deed in the article "Ans xangc", 'Going to buy and sell (once a week)'. The whole article was only 140 syllables long, but it was written in easy, natural, and understandable language. Lóng Dì (龙弟), a student from Gāodàn (高旦), wrote the Spring Festival couplet in (373).

(373) *Nyinc aov bail mags nyeeus bul bul lail,*
Eip xenp map jeel dens songl songl meec.
The old year has gone and old and young alike all did well,
In the new year there will be plenty of food to eat and clothes to wear.

Studying Chinese after studying Dong can make progress in Chinese extremely fast. Take for example the young lady Wú Liángměi (吴良美) from Lípíng's Yándòng. She had never before studied in school and was illiterate in Chinese. In 1983 she studied the Dong script for three months in the village evening class and was able to master it. Then she was able to use the script to annotate the sounds and meanings of Chinese characters, using Dong to study Chinese. By 1985, she was able to recognize the Chinese characters in the first volume of the Dong textbook, more than 1,000 characters. Since her study methods were good and her progress fast, the Lípíng Nationalities Commission made an exception to its normal rules and enrolled her as a teacher of Dong.

Numerous students, speaking from first-hand experience, were saying: "In the past we studied Chinese for many years and still were not able to record songs, write letters, or do anything else with Chinese. Now we've studied the Dong script for two or three months and already we can write songs. The gains from studying Chinese for several years do not match the gains from studying Dong for several months." The Dong script helps to further the use of the mother tongue in the everyday lives of the Dong people.

6.3 Using Chinese characters to record Dong

The Dong nationality has always had its own language but formerly never had a suitable orthography for the language. For many generations it was common to use Chinese characters to record Dong. This was the natural consequence of living side by side with Hàn (汉) Chinese neighbors. The specific ways of using Chinese characters to record Dong were many and varied, and there was no accepted standard. Basically, however, the methods all fell into one of the following three categories.

Use Chinese characters with identical or similar pronunciations to Dong words. For example: use Chinese 高锦 *gāo jǐn* (literally 'tall/brocade') to record Dong $kau^{323} tən^{212}$ 'the top of a mountain'; or use 万万凶卡赛要报 *wàn wàn xiōng kǎ sài yào bào* (literally '10,000/10,000/fierce/block/match/ want/announce') to record $wan^{35} wan^{35} ɕoŋ^{55} kha^{35} sai^{35} jau^{212} pau^{53}$ 'quietly listen and let me speak'.

Use Chinese characters with identical meanings to Dong words. Usually a sign is made beside or beneath the Chinese character to indicate that the meaning of the character should be joined with Dong pronunciation. For example: use 风ₓ *fēng* 'wind' to record the Dong *ləm²¹²* 'wind'; or use 挑ₓ *tiāo* 'carry on a pole' to record the Dong *tap³²³* 'carry on a pole'.

In some cases, a Chinese character does not directly correspond to the Dong word with the same meaning, but instead to another Dong word which has the same sound as that word. For example, the words for 'rain' (雨 *yǔ*) and 'feather' (羽毛 *yǔ máo*) in Dong are the same, *pjən⁵⁵*, and 雨ₓ is used to represent the word for 'feather'.

Use the method of *fǎn qiè*²¹ (反切). Usually this involves using two Chinese characters to record one Dong syllable.

In one system the first character gives the syllable initial and the second character gives the syllable rhyme. For example, use 九无 *jiǔ wú* 'nine/nothing' to write the Dong word *ʝu³²³* 'nine'; or use 尼亚 *ní yà* 'Buddhist nun/inferior' to write *ɲa⁵⁵* 'river'.

Alternatively, the first character gives the syllable initial and vowel, while the second gives the coda. For example, use 达姆 *dá mǔ* 'reach/nurse' to write *tam⁵⁵* 'handle (e.g., of a knife)'; or use 得克 *dé kè* 'get/restrain' to write *tek³²³* 'make a noise'.

Sometimes three Chinese characters are used to write one Dong syllable, though this is less common. In such cases, the first character gives the syllable initial, the middle one gives the vowel or the nuclear vowel in case there is a compound vowel, and the last gives the syllable coda. For example, 其阿母 *qí ā mǔ* 'it/breathe out/mother' is used to write *tham¹³* 'walk, go'.

The writing of some words is put together not according to the pronunciations of the Chinese characters, but from pronunciations of Dong words which have meanings equivalent to those of the Chinese characters. For example, use 身洞 *shēn dòng* 'body/hole' to write *ɕəm²¹²* 'drooping appearance'; this takes the syllable initial from pronunciation of the Dong word *ɕən³⁵* 'body' and the rhyme from pronunciation of the Dong word *ʈəm²¹²* 'cave'.

Using Chinese characters to record the sounds of Dong was prevalent for a long time. It was not, however, a scientific way of writing the language. There was no given standard. Every person used his own scheme for writing. Thus it turned out that the different ways of writing were frequently inconsistent: the same Chinese characters were used to write different Dong sounds and the same Dong sounds were written using different Chinese characters. People other than the authors would have great difficulty

---

²¹For explanation of *fǎn qiè*, see footnote 4 in §1.1.

identifying clearly the intended meanings. So for a long time, the writings which were handed down were confined to attempts by individuals to guard against forgetfulness. They were nevertheless effective in their own way as scripts serving to promote Dong culture and to create, propagate, and preserve Dong folk literature.

Many writings still survive which use Chinese characters to represent Dong. These include volumes of songs, almanacs, agricultural books, medical books, family trees, and genealogical tables of whole clans. There are even some hand-copied books dating from the beginning of the Qīng dynasty (1616–1911). The first ever Dong play in the history of Dong literature, *Méi Liángyù* (梅良玉), used Chinese characters to write Dong.

After Liberation (1949) and before the creation of a Dong script, the use of Chinese characters for recording Dong was even more widespread than before. Collectors of folk songs in the Dong countryside used Chinese characters for recording on-the-spot data and the organization for local propaganda also used Chinese characters to write Dong. The songs in the books *Dong Nationality Choral Songs* (侗族大歌, published in August 1958 by the Guìzhōu People's Publishing House) and *Dong Nationality Folk Songs* (侗族民歌, published in May 1960, written by members of the Planning Committee of the Guìyáng Branch of the Chinese Association of Musicians and edited by the Guìzhōu University Art Department) were entirely written with Chinese characters representing Dong words.

Appendix 1
Vocabulary of the Two Dong Dialects

	Róngjiāng Zhānglǔ (榕江章鲁) southern Dong	Tiānzhù Shídòng (天柱石洞) northern Dong	Chinese	
1.	mən⁵⁵	mən³⁵	天空	sky
2.	ta⁵⁵mɐn⁵⁵	tau³³wən³⁵	太阳	sun
3.	khaŋ³⁵	ɬaŋ¹¹	阳光	sunlight
4.	kwaŋ⁵⁵ȵan⁵⁵	mjan³⁵	月亮	moon
5.	ɕət⁵⁵	sət⁵⁵mjan³⁵	星	star (n)
6.	ma³²³	kwa³³	云	cloud (n)
7.	pja³²³	pja³³	雷	thunder (n)
8.	lap³²³	lap³¹	闪电	lightning
9.	ləm²¹²	ləm²²	风	wind
10.	pjən⁵⁵	mjən³⁵	雨	rain (n)
11.	nui⁵⁵	ni³⁵	雪	snow (n)
12.	mun²¹²	mon²²	雾	fog
13.	ʔu⁵³, ʔaŋ⁵³	ʔaŋ⁵⁵	冰	ice
14.	ʔu³¹	poŋ³³loŋ³³	冰雹	hail
15.	me⁵⁵	me³⁵	霜	frost
16.	nɐm³¹mun²¹²	nəm³¹sən³³	露水	dew
17.	ɬhi⁴⁵³	ɬi²⁵	空气	air
18.	phjuŋ³⁵, sən³²³	pjuŋ¹¹	蒸气	vapor
19.	pui⁵⁵	wi³⁵	火	fire
20.	kwɐn²¹²	ʔən²²	火烟	smoke (n)
21.	ti³³	ti⁴⁴	天地	the world
22.	ɬən²¹²	ɬən²², ta³³	山	mountain

23.	ljiŋ³¹	ʔiu³⁵	岭	mountain range
24.	ȶi³³	pja⁴⁴, ta³³	山坡	hillside
25.	ȶəm³³	ȶəm⁴⁴	山谷	valley
26.	nan³³, kan⁵³pja⁵⁵	ŋam³¹pja³⁵	悬岩	cliff
27.	ȶəm²¹², ʔam⁵⁵	toŋ⁴⁴, ȶəm²²pja³⁵	山洞	cave
28.	hʋi¹³	hai³¹	海	sea
29.	ȵa⁵⁵	ȵa³⁵	河	river
30.	kui³²³, hau³⁵	kui³³	溪	stream (n)
31.	mjiŋ⁵⁵	mjiŋ³⁵	沟	canal
32.	mʋŋ⁵⁵	taŋ²², taŋ²²ljoŋ²²	潭	deep pool
33.	sa³³	sa⁴⁴, tan¹¹	河滩	river rapids
34.	mən⁵³	mən⁵⁵	井	well (n)
35.	pi⁵⁵	pe³⁵	水坝	dam (n)
36.	pjan⁵³	wjan⁵⁵	平坝	level land
37.	pu⁵³	pjiŋ²²waŋ¹¹	荒坪	wasteland
38.	pjiŋ²¹²	pjiŋ²²	坪	level ground
39.	khwən³⁵	kən¹¹	路	road
40.	ja⁵³	ja⁵⁵	田	field
41.	ȶen⁵⁵ja⁵³	ȶən³⁵ja⁵⁵	田埂	ridge between fields
42.	ti³³	ti⁴⁴, ȶen³³	旱地	dry land
43.	pja⁵⁵, ȶin⁵⁵	pja³⁵, ȶin³⁵	石头	stone
44.	ɕe³⁵	sa¹¹	沙	sand
45.	puŋ⁵³, phən³⁵	pən¹¹	尘土	dust (n)
46.	nam³³, mak³¹	ʔən³³	泥土	soil, mud
47.	nʋm³¹	nəm³¹	水	water
48.	laŋ³³, pʋu⁵⁵	laŋ⁴⁴nəm³¹	水浪	wave (n)
49.	nʋm³¹mən⁵³	nəm³¹mən⁵⁵	泉水	spring (n)
50.	nʋm³¹lau³¹, nʋm³¹pjiŋ²¹lap³¹	nəm³¹lau³¹, ɕaŋ³³laŋ³⁵lau³¹	洪水	flood (n)
51.	ȶəm⁵⁵	jəm³⁵	金子	gold
52.	ȵʋn²¹²	ȵən²²	银子	silver
53.	toŋ²¹²	toŋ²²	铜	copper
54.	khwət³⁵, thje¹³	tət³⁵	铁	iron
55.	sik¹³	siʔ³¹	锡	tin
56.	jon²¹²	jen²²	铅	lead
57.	saŋ³⁵	ʔaŋ³⁵	钢	steel
58.	jim²¹², ko⁵⁵	pau²²	盐	salt
59.	ŋat³¹	ŋat³¹	碱	alkali
60.	phuk¹³	puʔ¹³	草木灰	ash

61.	than⁴⁵³	tan²⁵	炭	charcoal
62.	ţi³³waŋ³⁵, sən⁵⁵	ţi⁴⁴waŋ¹¹, sən³⁵	地方	place
63.	ʔai⁵⁵	ʔai³⁵	街	street
64.	ki³¹	ɕaŋ³³	场集	marketplace
65.	ɕai³³, sən⁵⁵	ɕai⁴⁴	村寨	village
66.	taŋ²¹²hak³¹, taŋ²¹²jo³²³	ʔo²²jo¹¹	学校	school
67.	lau²¹²	ʔo²²lau²²	监狱	prison
68.	ţiu²¹², lo³¹	ţiu²²	桥	bridge
69.	wən²¹², mu³³	mo¹³	坟	grave
70.	ka³¹	ţa³¹	汉族	Hàn
71.	kɐm⁵⁵	kəm³⁵	侗族	Dòng
72.	miu⁵⁵	miu³⁵	苗族	Miáo
73.	jiu²¹²	jau²²su²²	瑶族	Yáo
74.	ɕoŋ³³	saŋ³⁵su²²	壮族	Zhuàng
75.	sui¹³	sui³¹su²²	水族	Shuǐ
76.	ɳən²¹²	jən²²	人	person
77.	lak³¹ʔun³²³	laʔ³¹ʔun³³	小孩	child
78.	ɳən²¹²lau³¹	jən²²lau³¹	老人	old person
79.	ʔoŋ³²³, ʔau²¹²lau²¹²	ʔoŋ³³, kau³¹kau³¹, pu³¹lau³¹	老爷爷	old man
80.	sa³¹	nəi³¹lau³¹	老婆婆	old woman
81.	pan⁵⁵, lak³¹pan⁵⁵	lo³¹wan³⁵	男人	male (person)
82.	tu²¹²sa³¹, ɳən²¹²mjek³²³	lo³¹lje¹³, nəi³¹sa³¹, nəi³¹nəi³¹	妇女	female (person)
83.	lak³¹han⁴⁵³, lak³¹lji³¹	laʔ³¹ki³¹	小伙子	young fellow
84.	lak³¹mjek³²³	ku³⁵ɳaŋ³³	姑娘	girl
85.	pu³¹ʔaŋ³³	lo³¹wan³⁵	中年男子	middle-aged man
86.	nɐi³¹ʔaŋ³³	nəi³¹nəi³¹, nəi³¹sa³¹	中年妇女	middle-aged woman
87.	joŋ³¹	pjən³⁵	兵	soldier
88.	saŋ³³	su⁵⁵, ɕaŋ⁴⁴	师傅	master worker
89.	saŋ³³ʔa⁵⁵	su⁵⁵ʔa³⁵	歌师	song teacher
90.	saŋ³³mɐi³¹	moʔ¹¹ɕaŋ⁴⁴	木匠	carpenter
91.	sɐk²¹	saʔ¹³	盗贼	robber
92.	waŋ²¹²ţi⁵³	waŋ²²ţi⁵⁵	皇帝	emperor
93.	muŋ³¹	muŋ¹³	官	official

94.	$pji\eta^{212}pan^{31}$	$wo^{11}\mathcal{t}i^{35}$, $po\eta^{22}jau^{31}$	朋友	friend
95.	$wak^{31}\textcipa{\textctc}a\eta^{55}$	$\mathcal{t}\partial n^{22}\textcipa{\textctc}o\eta^{35}$	群众	the masses
96.	$ta^{55}pha^{35}$	$ta^{35}\mathcal{t}o^{31}$	瞎子	blind person
97.	$pa^{55}tet^{31}$	$pje^{35}s\textsubring{l}^{33}$	跛子	lame person
98.	$kha^{35}lvk^{55}$	$lo\eta^{35}s\textsubring{l}^{33}$	聋子	deaf person
99.	$\textipa{P}ek^{13}$	$\textipa{P}e\textipa{P}^{13}$	客人	guest
100.	$kwen^{53}$	$j\partial n^{22}kwen^{55}$	熟人	acquaintance
101.	$sau^{31}mvi^{453}$	$la\textipa{P}^{31}sau^{31}m\partial i^{25}$	新郎	bridegroom
102.	$mai^{31}mvi^{453}$	$mai^{31}m\partial i^{25}$	新娘	bride
103.	$\textipa{P}o\eta^{323}ma\eta^{33}$	$\textipa{P}o\eta^{33}pu^{31}$	祖宗	ancestry
104.	$ma\eta^{33}$	$tai^{25}, tai^{25}m\partial n^{35}$	曾祖	great-grandfather
105.	$\textipa{P}o\eta^{323}$	$\textipa{P}o\eta^{33}$	祖父	paternal grandfather
106.	sa^{31}	nai^{33}	祖母	paternal grandmother
107.	ta^{55}	ta^{35}	外祖父	maternal grandfather
108.	te^{55}	te^{35}	外祖母	maternal grandmother
109.	pu^{31}	$\mathcal{t}a^{33}, kau^{31}$	父亲	father
110.	nvi^{31}	$ma^{33}, n\partial i^{31}$	母亲	mother
111.	lak^{31}	$la\textipa{P}^{31}$	儿子	son
112.	lja^{13}	lja^{13}	儿媳妇	daughter-in-law
113.	$lak^{31}mjek^{323}$, $lak^{31}pvi^{31}$	$la\textipa{P}^{31}lo^{31}lje\textipa{P}^{11}$	女儿	daughter
114.	$lak^{31}sau^{31}$	$la\textipa{P}^{31}sau^{31}$	女婿	son-in-law
115.	$lak^{31}khwan^{35}$	$la\textipa{P}^{31}tan^{11}$	孙子, 外甥	grandson
116.	$\mathcal{t}ai^{31}$	$ko^{33}, \mathcal{t}ai^{31}$	哥哥	older brother
117.	$\mathcal{t}ai^{31}, pvi^{31}$	$\textcipa{\textctc}e^{31}$	姐姐	older sister
118.	$no\eta^{31}$	$nu\eta^{31}$	弟弟	younger brother
119.	$no\eta^{31}$	$nu\eta^{31}$	妹妹	younger sister
120.	$pu^{31}lau^{31}$	$\mathcal{t}a^{33}lau^{31}$	伯父	father's older brother
121.	$pu^{31}lau^{31}$	$ji^{11}\mathcal{t}e^{33}ma\textipa{P}^{31}$	姨父 (母姐之夫)	husband of mother's older sister
122.	$nvi^{31}lau^{31}$	$ma^{33}lao^{31}$	伯母	wife of father's older brother

123.	nei³¹lau³¹	ji¹¹ma³³	姨母	mother's older sister
124.	pu³¹ʔun³²³, ʔo⁵³	man³¹ta³³	叔父	father's younger brother
125.	pu³¹ʔun³²³	ji¹¹te³³ɲiu¹³	姨父 (母妹之夫)	husband of mother's younger sister
126.	nei³¹ʔun³²³, wei³³	man³¹ma³³, wəi⁴⁴	叔母	wife of father's younger brother
127.	nei³¹ʔun³²³, wei³³	ji¹¹ma³³	姨母 (母之妹)	mother's younger sister
128.	ljoŋ³³	tu²², tu³⁵	舅父 (母之兄)	mother's older brother
129.	ljoŋ³³	tu²²	姑父 (父姐之夫)	husband of father's older sister
130.	ljoŋ³³	tu²²	翁 (大于己父之夫父)	husband's father (older than own father)
131.	ljoŋ³³	tu²²	岳父 (大于己父之妻父)	wife's father (older than own father)
132.	tu²¹²	tu²²	舅父 (母之弟)	mother's younger brother
133.	tu²¹²	tu²²	姑父 (父妹之夫)	husband of father's younger sister
134.	tu²¹²	tu²²	翁 (小于己父之夫父)	husband's father (younger than own father)
135.	tu²¹²	tu²²	岳父 (小于己父之妻父)	wife's father (younger than own father)
136.	pa³²³	naŋ³³	舅母 (母兄之妻)	wife of mother's older brother
137.	pa³²³	naŋ³³	姑母 (父之姐)	father's older sister

#	Form 1	Form 2	Chinese	English
138.	pa^{323}	$ȵaŋ^{33}$	姑 (大于己母之夫母)	husband's mother (older than own mother)
139.	pa^{323}	$ȵaŋ^{33}$	岳母 (大于己母之妻母)	wife's mother (older than own mother)
140.	$ʔu^{55}$	$ȵaŋ^{33}$	舅母 (母弟之妻)	wife of mother's younger brother
141.	$ʔu^{55}$	$ȵaŋ^{33}$	姑母 (父之妹)	father's younger sister
142.	$ʔu^{55}$	$ȵaŋ^{33}$	姑 (小于己母之夫母)	husband's mother (younger than own mother)
143.	$ʔu^{55}$	$ȵaŋ^{33}$	岳母 (小于己母之妻母)	wife's mother (younger than own mother)
144.	mai^{31}	mai^{31}, sa^{31}	妻子	wife
145.	sau^{31}	sau^{31}	丈夫	husband
146.	$ʔo^{53}$	ta^{33}	继父	stepfather
147.	$nɐi^{31}wɐi^{33}$	$wəi^{44}$	继母	stepmother
148.	$han^{453}ljiŋ^{33}$	$tan^{35}ɕən^{11}$	单身汉	single man
149.	$ʈu^{33}, ʈu^{33}siŋ^{212}$	$ʈu^{44}$	情人	sweetheart
150.	$ɕən^{35}$	$ʔu^{35}jən^{11}$	身体	body
151.	kau^{323}	kau^{33}	头	head
152.	na^{212}	na^{22}	囟门	fontanel
153.	$pjɐm^{55}$	$pjəm^{35}kau^{33}$	头发	hair
154.	$sa^{35}pja^{55}$	$pjen^{35}sʅ^{33}$	辫子	plait
155.	$pai^{323}, ʈot^{323}$	$ʔəu^{33}$	发髻	hair in bun
156.	$pjak^{323}$	$pjaʔ^{31}$	额头	forehead
157.	$pjən^{55}ta^{55}$	$mji^{11}ta^{35}$	眉毛	eyebrow
158.	$ɕəp^{55}ta^{55}$	$pjən^{35}ta^{35}$	睫毛	eyelash
159.	ta^{55}	ta^{35}	眼睛	eye
160.	$nɐŋ^{55}$	$naŋ^{35}$	鼻子	nose
161.	kha^{35}	ka^{11}	耳朵	ear
162.	na^{323}	na^{33}	脸	face
163.	$ŋɐi^{33}$	$ŋaʔ^{11}, kən^{55}ʔaŋ^{22}$	腮	cheek
164.	$ʔəp^{55}$	mu^{55}	嘴	mouth
165.	$tin^{55}ʔəp^{55}$	$tin^{55}mu^{55}$	唇	lip

Vocabulary of the Two Dong Dialects

166.	mut^{31}	$mjut^{31}$	胡子	beard
167.	$laŋ^{212}$	$ȵi^{55}ʔaŋ^{22}$	下巴	chin
168.	$ȵən^{33}$	$toŋ^{22}ʔo^{22}$	脖子	neck
169.	sa^{35}	$sa^{11}, pja^{11}, pa^{11}la^{11}$	肩膀	shoulder
170.	lai^{212}	kom^{22}	背	back
171.	sak^{13}	$te^{33}laʔ^{13}$	腋窝	armpit
172.	$tɐk^{55}$	$taʔ^{55}$	胸	chest
173.	$mi^{212}, ȵo^{31}$	mi^{22}	乳房	breast
174.	mi^{212}	mi^{22}	奶汁	milk
175.	$loŋ^{212}$	tu^{33}	肚子	belly
176.	$po^{53}, pjo^{55}ljo^{55}$	$ȵi^{55}tu^{33}$	肚脐	navel
177.	$ʔui^{323}lai^{212}$	$jəu^{35}$	腰	waist
178.	$sən^{31}$	$ʔoŋ^{35}ʔe^{31}$	屁股	buttocks
179.	pa^{55}	$kwa^{35}lau^{31}, pa^{35}lau^{31}$	大腿	leg, thigh
180.	$kwau^{53}$	$ŋau^{13}ŋəu^{35}$	膝盖	knee
181.	$tət^{55}$	$peu^{35}mi^{31}$	小腿	lower leg
182.	tin^{55}	tin^{35}	脚	foot
183.	$ɕoŋ^{35}tin^{55}$	$təu^{31}lin^{35}$	脚后跟	heel
184.	$ʔin^{35}$	kin^{11}	胳膊	arm
185.	mja^{212}	mja^{22}	手	hand
186.	$lak^{31}tin^{55}$	$naŋ^{35}tin^{35}$	脚趾	toe
187.	$lak^{31}tɐŋ^{55}$	$naŋ^{35} mja^{22}$	手指	finger
188.	$ȵəp^{35}mja^{212}$	$ȵəp^{35}mja^{22}$	指甲	fingernail
189.	pi^{212}	$ʔa^{33}la^{35}, kja^{35}$	皮肤	skin
190.	$ȵiu^{323}$	$ȵiu^{33}, ȵəu^{55}$	皱纹	wrinkle
191.	$nuŋ^{212}$	$nuŋ^{22}pjəm^{35}$	汗毛	body hair
192.	$phui^{35}$	$ɕi^{55}$	痣	mole, nevus
193.	$lja^{55}, kwam^{323}$	pa^{35}	疤	scar (n)
194.	tum^{53}	$sin^{25}, kət^{55}$	疮	sore (n)
195.	nan^{31}	nan^{31}	肌肉	muscle
196.	$phat^{13}$	tat^{13}	血	blood
197.	$ʔən^{55}$	$ʔən^{35}$	筋	tendon, vein
198.	$ȵui^{33}kau^{323}$	$ȵi^{22}kau^{33}$	脑髓	brain
199.	lak^{323}	$laʔ^{33}$	骨头	bone
200.	$pjɐn^{55}, pjɐn^{55}ta^{53}na^{323}$	$pjən^{35}to^{35}, pjən^{35}$	牙齿 (门)	front tooth
201.	$pjɐn^{55}, pjɐn^{55}tən^{323}$	$pjən^{35}ŋe^{22}, ŋe^{22}$	牙齿 (臼)	back tooth
202.	ma^{212}	ma^{22}	舌头	tongue
203.	$leu^{53}ʔu^{212}$	$ma^{22}ȵəu^{33}$	小舌	uvula

204.	*laŋ²¹²*	*poŋ²²mu⁵⁵*	腭	palate
205.	*ʔu²¹²*	*ʔau³¹ʔo²²*	喉咙	throat
206.	*pup³²³*	*wi²⁵*	肺	lung
207.	*səm³⁵*	*səm¹¹təu²²*	心	heart
208.	*tɐp⁵⁵*	*səm¹¹*	肝	liver
209.	*loŋ²¹²*	*tu³³*	胃	stomach
210.	*po⁵³*	*tam³³*	苦胆	gallbladder
211.	*sai³²³*	*sai³³*	肠子	intestines
212.	*ʔe³¹*	*ʔe³¹*	屎	excrement
213.	*ɲeu⁵³*	*ɲiu⁵⁵*	尿	urine
214.	*tət⁵⁵*	*soŋ⁵⁵ʔe³¹*	屁	flatulence
215.	*pən⁵³*	*pən⁵⁵*	汗	sweat
216.	*ɕen²¹²*	*ŋo¹³*	痰	phlegm
217.	*ŋwe²¹²*	*nəm³¹mje²²*	口水	saliva
218.	*muk³¹*	*muʔ³¹*	鼻涕	nasal mucus
219.	*nɐm³¹ta⁵⁵*	*nəm³¹ta³⁵*	眼泪	tears
220.	*kwe²¹²*	*tu²²wi²²*	水牛	water buffalo
221.	*sən²¹²*	*tu²²ljou¹³*	黄牛	cow
222.	*ma³¹*	*ma³¹*	马	horse
223.	*lje³²³*	*lje³³, pje⁵⁵*	羊	sheep, goat
224.	*ŋu⁴⁵³*	*mu²⁵*	猪	pig
225.	*ŋwa³⁵*	*kwa¹¹*	狗	dog
226.	*meu³¹*	*meu³¹*	猫	cat
227.	*tɐk²¹*	*taʔ¹³*	公 (牛)	male (animal)
228.	*mɐi³¹*	*nəi³¹*	母 (牛)	female (animal)
229.	*sɐi⁵³*	*səi⁵⁵*	母 (未下崽的牛)	as 228, but not yet given birth
230.	*pau⁵⁵*	*ŋau³⁵*	角	horn
231.	*pjən⁵⁵*	*pjəm³⁵*	毛, 羽毛	fur, feather
232.	*sət⁵⁵*	*sət⁵⁵*	尾巴	tail
233.	*kha³⁵ko⁵³*	*ka¹¹loŋ²²*	兔子	rabbit
234.	*ʔai⁵³*	*ʔai⁵⁵*	鸡	chicken
235.	*ʈən⁵³ʔai⁵³*	*ʈən⁵⁵ʔai⁵⁵*	鸡冠	cockscomb
236.	*pət⁵⁵*	*pət⁵⁵*	鸭	duck
237.	*ŋan³³*	*ŋan⁴⁴*	鹅	goose
238.	*sɐi¹³*	*səi¹³*	公 (鸡)	male (bird)
239.	*mɐi³¹*	*nəi³¹*	母 (鸡)	female (bird)
240.	*ʔaŋ³³*	*ʔaŋ⁴⁴*	母 (未下蛋)	as 239, but not yet laid eggs
241.	*pa⁵³*	*pa⁵⁵*	翅膀	wing
242.	*ljoŋ²¹²*	*ljoŋ²²*	龙	dragon

243.	məm³¹	məm³¹	老虎	tiger
244.	məm³¹peu⁵³	məm³¹peu⁵⁵	豹子	leopard
245.	me⁵⁵	ɕoŋ²²	熊	bear
246.	lai⁵³	lai⁵⁵	野猪	wild boar
247.	ȵɐn³⁵	ȵən¹¹	野猫	wildcat
248.	ȵɐn³⁵min³²³	pe¹¹mjen³³	豪猪	porcupine
249.	mun³³	lei²⁵	猴子	monkey
250.	lən³³, ləŋ³³	to²²loŋ⁴⁴	穿山甲	pangolin
251.	mjan³²³	mjan³³	水獭	otter
252.	no¹³	no¹³	老鼠	mouse
253.	no¹³nən¹³	no¹³ȶin³³	松鼠	squirrel
254.	pjuŋ⁵⁵	laŋ²²	狼	wolf
255.	ʔo²¹², je³³ju²¹²	noʔ¹³ni²²	蝙蝠	bat
256.	mok²¹	noʔ¹³	鸟	bird
257.	pɐu²¹²	ko²²	鸽子	pigeon
258.	ʔam⁵⁵	ʔam³⁵	老鹰	eagle
259.	ʔɐu³⁵, ʔɐu³⁵kha³⁵	ʔau³⁵wa³¹	猫头鹰	owl
260.	ʔin⁵³si³²³	kin⁵⁵	燕子	swallow (n)
261.	sau⁴⁵³	sau²⁵, lu²²su²²	白鹭	egret
262.	ljai¹³	ljai¹³	麻雀	sparrow
263.	ʔa⁵⁵ɕak¹³	ʔa³⁵jaʔ³¹	喜鹊	magpie
264.	ʔa⁵⁵	ʔa³⁵nəm³⁵	乌鸦	crow (n)
265.	meu²¹²	ɕi⁴⁴	雉	pheasant
266.	ȵa³⁵	ȵa³⁵	啄木鸟	woodpecker
267.	tok⁵⁵ʔuk⁵⁵	toʔ³⁵ʔuʔ³³	布谷鸟	cuckoo
268.	pjin³²³	wu³³kiu³³	乌龟	tortoise
269.	sui²¹²	si²²	蛇	snake
270.	je⁵⁵	ji³⁵	青蛙	frog
271.	mɐu⁵³	lut¹³	蝌蚪	tadpole
272.	ȶɐi³³	ʔaŋ³⁵ʔei⁵⁵	螃蟹	crab
273.	pa⁵⁵	ta³⁵	鱼	fish (n)
274.	kwən⁵³pa⁵⁵	tən⁵⁵ta³⁵	鳞	scale (n)
275.	mjɐi³¹	ta³⁵mjei³¹	鲤鱼	carp
276.	pik³¹	ta³⁵piʔ³¹	鲫鱼	crucian carp
277.	ŋo³³	ȵo⁴⁴	黄鳝	eel
278.	ŋwat²¹	mjət¹³	泥鳅	loach
279.	ȶoŋ³³	ȵo²²	虾	shrimp
280.	ȵo²¹²	ȵo²²	虾米	dried shrimp
281.	nui²¹²	ni²²	虫	insect
282.	ʔiŋ⁵⁵	kiŋ³⁵	臭虫	bedbug

283.	ŋwɐt³⁵	mət³⁵	跳蚤	flea
284.	tau⁵⁵, nɐn⁵⁵	tau³⁵, nəi²²	虱子	louse
285.	mjuŋ³¹	ɲuŋ³¹	蚊蝇	fly (n)
286.	nun⁵⁵	nun³⁵	蛆	maggot
287.	ŋo²¹²	si¹¹ŋo²²	蜘蛛	spider
288.	sɐn³¹	sən³¹	蚯蚓	earthworm
289.	mjiŋ²¹²	ma³¹mjiŋ²²	蚂蟥	leech
290.	kwap³²³	lap³³	蟑螂	cockroach
291.	mət²¹	mət¹³	蚂蚁	ant
292.	tɐk⁵⁵	taʔ⁵⁵	蚱蜢	grasshopper
293.	ma³²³mən³²³	maŋ³⁵mit³¹	蝴蝶	butterfly
294.	lɐu⁵³	kei³⁵ləu⁵⁵	螺蛳	snail
295.	mɐi³¹	məi³¹	树	tree
296.	saŋ³⁵	saŋ¹¹məi³¹	树根	root of tree
297.	pa⁵³	pa⁵⁵	树叶	leaf
298.	jau³⁵	məi³¹jau¹¹	枫树	maple
299.	phak¹³	məi³¹pen³³	杉树	China fir
300.	soŋ²¹², soŋ²¹²pek³²³	məi³¹soŋ²²	松树	pine
301.	phak¹³no¹³	soŋ¹¹peʔ³³	柏树	cypress
302.	jin¹³	məi³¹jin¹³	青杠树	a type of tree
303.	ʔau²¹²	məi³¹saŋ¹¹	桑树	mulberry
304.	ju²¹²	məi³¹ju²²	茶油树	tea-oil tree
305.	pɐn⁵⁵	məi³¹kwən³⁵	竹子	bamboo
306.	naŋ²¹²	naŋ²²	竹笋	bamboo shoot
307.	ʔan⁵⁵	ʔan³⁵	苎麻	flax (ramie)
308.	tau⁵⁵	taŋ⁴⁴tau³⁵	藤子	vine
309.	sun⁵⁵	sun³⁵	刺	thorn
310.	tui⁵⁵, təm³³	nən³⁵ti³⁵, nən³⁵təm⁴⁴	果子	fruit
311.	liu²¹²	liu²²	桔子	tangerine
312.	tui⁵⁵jɐi²¹²	ti³⁵	梨	pear
313.	tui⁵⁵pɐŋ⁵⁵	ti³⁵lau¹³	桃子	peach
314.	tui⁵⁵	ti³⁵	李子	plum
315.	min³¹	min³¹	柿子	persimmon
316.	ʔit³²³	ʔit³¹	葡萄	grape
317.	lət²¹	lət¹³	栗子	chestnut
318.	jaŋ²¹²mui²¹², lak³¹sai⁵³	jaŋ²²mi²²	杨梅	red bayberry
319.	wa³⁵, nuk³²³	wa¹¹	花	flower (n)

320.	$ʔɐu^{31}$	$ʔəu^{31}$	稻子	rice (plant)
321.	$ʔɐu^{31}tim^{55}$	$ʔəu^{31}ɕin^{35}$	梗稻	ordinary rice
322.	$ʔɐu^{31}to^{323}$, $ʔɐu^{31}lai^{55}$	$ʔəu^{31}to^{33}$	糯稻	glutinous rice
323.	$pɐn^{55}, wɐn^{212}$	$ɕoŋ^{33}, pən^{35}$	种籽	seed
324.	ka^{323}	ka^{33}	秧	seedling
325.	$mjeŋ^{212}$	$mjaŋ^{22}$	稻穗	ear of grain
326.	ta^{55}	ta^{35}	谷芒	beard of grain
327.	$paŋ^{55}$	$paŋ^{35}$	稻草	rice straw
328.	$ʔɐu^{31}mek^{31}$	$meʔ^{31}$	麦子	wheat
329.	$ʔɐu^{31}ɕu^{55}$	$pau^{35}ku^{22}$	玉米	maize
330.	$waŋ^{212}ŋa^{212}$	$ʔa^{35}ljaŋ^{22}$	高粱	Chinese sorghum
331.	$ʔɐu^{31}pjaŋ^{323}$	$ʔəu^{31}wjiŋ^{22}$	小米	millet
332.	$mjin^{212}$	$mjin^{22}wa^{11}$	棉花	cotton
333.	ma^{55}	ma^{35}	菜	vegetable
334.	$ma^{55}pak^{31}$	$ma^{35}pe^{33}sai^{25}$	白菜	Chinese cabbage
335.	$ma^{55}ʔat^{323}$	$ma^{35}ʔat^{33}$, $ma^{35}ŋu^{11}$	青菜	greens; a type of cabbage
336.	$ŋɐm^{212}$	$ma^{35}tu^{44}sai^{25}$	韭菜	Chinese chive
337.	$ma^{55}ŋəm^{212}$	$ma^{35}ŋəm^{22}$	苋菜	amaranth
338.	$pɐk^{21}$	$lo^{31}waʔ^{13}$	萝卜	radish
339.	ta^{212}	ta^{33}	茄子	eggplant
340.	jak^{323}	$wi^{35}təu^{11}$	芋头	taro
341.	$ljan^{33}siu^{55}$	$ljan^{44}$	辣椒	red pepper
342.	$toŋ^{212}phu^{35}$	$ma^{35}soŋ^{11}$	葱	onion
343.	son^{453}	son^{25}	蒜	garlic
344.	$ɕiŋ^{35}$	$taŋ^{35}$	姜	ginger
345.	$mɐn^{212}$	$hoŋ^{22}ɕau^{22}$	红薯	sweet potato
346.	pu^{212}	pu^{22}	瓜	gourd
347.	tup^{323}	$tut^{33}, toŋ^{35}ka^{35}$	冬瓜	white gourd
348.	kwe^{55}	kwe^{35}	黄瓜	cucumber
349.	$lak^{31}jan^{453}$	$mau^{22}lin^{11}$	丝瓜	towel gourd
350.	to^{33}	to^{44}	豆子	bean
351.	$to^{33}soŋ^{212}$	$to^{44}loŋ^{22}$	黄豆	soya bean
352.	$to^{33}pɐk^{55}$	$to^{44}pje^{33}, to^{44}mja^{31}$	扁豆	hyacinth bean
353.	$to^{33}ʔeŋ^{55}$	$to^{44}ɕaŋ^{22}ʔaŋ^{35}$	豇豆	string bean
354.	$to^{33}set^{13}$	$to^{44}tau^{35}$	绿豆	mung bean
355.	$to^{33}mak^{31}$	$wa^{11}sən^{33}$	花生	peanut
356.	$ju^{212}me^{212}, ŋa^{55}$	$ju^{22}we^{22}$	芝麻	sesame

357.	ȵaŋ¹³	ȵaŋ¹³	草 grass
358.	ȵaŋ¹³ta⁵⁵, ta⁵⁵	ȵaŋ¹³tau¹³	茅草 cogongrass
359.	ʔiu³²³	ma³⁵ʔiu³³	蕨菜 brake (young)
360.	khau⁴⁵³	ȵaŋ¹³kau²⁵	蕨菜 brake (when fully grown)
361.	la²¹²	ʔa²²	菌子 mushroom
362.	la²¹²kha³⁵ȵo¹³	ʔa²²mu¹¹ʔe³¹	木耳 edible fungus
363.	tɐu⁵⁵, ȵo⁵³	tɔu³⁵	青苔 moss
364.	nɐi¹³, ŋɐi¹³	ŋɔi¹³	浮萍 duckweed
365.	ʔɐu³¹	ʔɔu³¹	米, 饭 cooked rice
366.	ʔɐu³¹san³⁵	ʔɔu³¹san¹¹	白米 (polished) rice
367.	ʔɐu³¹ɕe²¹², ʔɐu³¹hət³⁵	ʔɔu³¹jət³⁵	早饭 breakfast
368.	ʔɐu³¹hət³⁵, ʔɐu³¹mɐn⁵⁵	ʔɔu³¹wən³⁵	午饭 lunch
369.	ʔɐu³¹ȵɐm⁵³	ʔɔu³¹ȵəm⁵⁵	晚饭 supper, dinner
370.	ʔɐu³¹ʔeŋ⁵⁵	ʔɔu³¹lan³³	粥 porridge
371.	ʔɐu³¹siu⁵³, kiŋ³²³	ʔɔu³¹liu⁵⁵, ʔa²²liu⁵⁵	锅巴 crust of cooked rice
372.	si²¹², ʔɐu³¹si²¹²	si²²tɔŋ³³	糍粑 glutinous rice cake
373.	pe⁵³, ʔɐu³¹si²¹²pau⁵⁵	si²²ŋɔu³³ŋɔu³⁵, si²²pa⁵⁵pe⁵⁵	粽子 glutinous rice wrapped in leaf
374.	nan³¹	nan³¹	肉 meat
375.	nan³¹wət⁵⁵, nan³¹səm¹³	nan³¹wət⁵⁵	腌肉 salted pork
376.	nan³¹pui²¹²	nan³¹pi²²	肥肉 fat meat
377.	nan³¹nau⁵⁵	nan³¹jəm³⁵	瘦肉 lean meat
378.	nan³¹ɕaŋ³¹	nan³¹ɕaŋ³¹	腊肉 bacon
379.	pa⁵⁵səm¹³, pa⁵⁵wət⁵⁵	ta³⁵wət⁵⁵	腌鱼 salted fish
380.	pa⁵⁵ɕik³²³	ta³⁵ɕiʔ³¹	烤鱼 barbecued fish
381.	ju²¹²	ju²²	油 oil (n)
382.	to³³ŋe²¹²	ŋe²²to⁴⁴, tɔu³⁵ja³³	豆芽 bean sprouts
383.	to³³hu³³	to⁴⁴hu²⁵	豆腐 beancurd
384.	ma⁵⁵səm¹³	ma³⁵səm¹³	酸菜 pickled vegetable
385.	sɐu³²³	su²⁵	醋 vinegar
386.	taŋ²¹²	taŋ²²	糖 sugar, candy
387.	kɐi⁵³	kəi⁵⁵	蛋 egg
388.	nun⁵⁵kɐi⁵³man¹³	kəi⁵⁵waŋ³³	蛋黄 egg yolk

389.	nun⁵⁵kɐi⁵³pak³¹	kəi⁵⁵ɕim³³, kəi⁵⁵paʔ³¹	蛋清	egg white
390.	khwau¹³	tau¹³	酒	alcohol
391.	tau²¹²khwan³⁵	tau¹³pan¹¹	甜酒	sweet alcohol
392.	ɕe²¹²	ɕe²²	茶	tea
393.	pa⁵³ɕe²¹², ɕe²¹²	pa⁵⁵ɕe²²	茶叶	tea leaves
394.	jen⁵⁵, jin⁵⁵	jen³⁵	烟	smoke (n)
395.	jen⁵⁵sɿ³⁵	sɿ¹¹jen³⁵	烟丝	cut tobacco (n)
396.	ʔəm³²³	sa³³	药	medicine
397.	pa³³	pa⁴⁴	糠	chaff
398.	nɐm³¹ʔam⁵⁵	nəm³¹mu²⁵	泔水	swill
399.	ʔeŋ⁵⁵ŋu⁴⁵³	ʔeŋ³⁵mu²⁵	猪食	pig feed
400.	mje²¹²	mje²²	纱	yarn
401.	sin⁴⁵³, san⁵³	sin⁵⁵, san⁵⁵	线	thread
402.	sɿ³⁵	sɿ¹¹	丝	silk
403.	ja⁵⁵, mjin²¹²	ȶa³⁵	布	cloth
404.	ɕu²¹²	ɕu²²	绸	silk fabric
405.	ʔuk³²³	tuʔ³¹	衣服	clothing
406.	ʔin³⁵ʔuk³²³	kin¹¹tuʔ³¹	衣袖	sleeve
407.	tɐi³³	təi⁴⁴tuʔ³¹	衣袋	pocket
408.	khɐu³⁵	ʔau²⁵	纽扣	button
409.	ʔu⁴⁵³, so⁵³	ku²⁵	裤子	trousers
410.	wən¹³	wən¹³	裙子	skirt
411.	pha⁴⁵³, ja¹³kau³²³	pa²⁵kau³³	头帕	scarf
412.	meu³³, ʔəm³¹tɐu²¹²	meu¹³	帽子	cap
413.	ɕin²¹²	ɕin²²	裹腿	shank wrapper
414.	thau⁴⁵³, wa³²³	wa³³	袜子	sock
415.	hai²¹²	hai²²	鞋	shoe
416.	ȶak³²³, hai²¹²paŋ⁵⁵	ȶaʔ³¹	草鞋	straw sandal
417.	pji³³	pji⁴⁴	篦子	bamboo comb
418.	ȶɐp⁵⁵	ton¹¹ka¹¹	耳环	earring
419.	ljəm³³hu²¹²	ton¹¹ʔo²²	项圈	necklace
420.	ʔin³⁵, ȶok³¹	ɕin⁴⁴	手镯	bracelet
421.	tan³²³, jaŋ³³	jaŋ⁴⁴	被子	quilt (n)
422.	pun⁵⁵	mun⁵⁵kau³³	枕头	pillow
423.	min³²³	min³³	席子	straw mat
424.	sun¹³	ȶam⁵⁵	蚊帐	mosquito net
425.	sɿ³⁵	sɿ¹¹	蓑衣	rain cape
426.	təm⁵⁵	təm³⁵	斗笠	bamboo hat
427.	jan²¹²	jan²²	房子	house

428.	lɐu²¹², koŋ²¹²	ləu²²	楼	building
429.	sa²¹²pui⁵⁵	sau¹¹wi³⁵, sa²²wi³⁵	火塘	wood or charcoal fire
430.	so³¹	so³¹	谷仓	barn
431.	ton³³, taŋ⁵⁵	ton⁴⁴	牲畜圈	livestock pen
432.	tɐu³²³	təu³³	窝	nest
433.	çon⁵⁵	çon³⁵	砖	brick
434.	ŋwe³¹	ŋe³¹	瓦	tile
435.	phjin⁴⁵³	pjin²⁵	木板	wood board
436.	tuŋ³³	sau²⁵	柱子	pillar
437.	to⁵⁵	to³⁵	门	door
438.	to⁵⁵siŋ³²³	to³⁵ke¹³	窗子	window
439.	ljaŋ²¹²	ljaŋ²²	梁	beam
440.	ʔak³²³	ʔat³¹	椽子	rafter
441.	jak³¹	ki¹¹jen¹¹	篱笆	fence (n)
442.	çiŋ²¹², khai⁴⁵³	ʈai²⁵	墙壁	wall
443.	jan³⁵	jen¹¹	园子	garden
444.	pi²¹²pan²¹², çoŋ²¹²	tai²²	桌子	table
445.	tɐŋ⁵³	taŋ⁵⁵	凳子	bench, stool
446.	tɐŋ⁵³tɐu³³, tɐu³³	tɐu⁴⁴, ji³¹	椅子	chair
447.	çaŋ²¹²	toi⁵⁵	床	bed
448.	loŋ³¹	çaŋ¹¹	箱子	box
449.	ʈui³³	kui⁵⁵	柜子	wardrobe
450.	kwe³²³	te³³, ʔe³³	梯子	ladder
451.	pən²¹²	pən²²	盆	basin
452.	çiu⁵³mjin³³	çiu⁵⁵mjin⁴⁴	镜子	mirror
453.	kwaŋ⁵⁵sət⁵⁵	sət³⁵ʈi³³	扫帚	broom
454.	khat¹³	sa¹¹pa³¹	刷子	brush (n)
455.	pui⁵⁵, pui⁵⁵ju²¹²	wi³⁵ju²²	灯	light (n)
456.	pui⁵⁵ku³³	ten³⁵loŋ²²	灯笼	lantern
457.	lap³¹	lap³¹	蜡烛	candle
458.	ʈət⁵⁵	ʈət⁵⁵	柴	firewood
459.	lam³³	lam⁴⁴, tau³⁵	绳子	rope
460.	jaŋ³⁵	jaŋ¹¹	香(烛)	joss stick
461.	sət³⁵	sət³⁵	漆	paint
462.	jak³¹	jaʔ³¹	锈	rust
463.	pui⁵⁵lu²¹², sau⁵³	sau⁵⁵	灶	cooking stove
464.	tau⁵⁵	tau³⁵, kiʔ¹³	锅	pot
465.	tɐu⁵³	təu⁵⁵	蒸笼	food steamer
466.	mja³¹, mit³¹	mja³¹, mit³¹	刀	knife

Vocabulary of the Two Dong Dialects

467.	mja³¹	mja³¹ʔəu¹³	柴刀	chopper
468.	kwaŋ³²³, tui³¹	tui³¹, po³³	碗	bowl
469.	pan²¹²	pon²²	盘子	plate
470.	ȶip³¹	pon²²	碟子	small dish
471.	ɕo³³	ɕo⁴⁴	筷子	chopsticks
472.	pi⁵⁵, ʈen³²³	ɕen³³	杯子	cup
473.	hu²¹², pjiŋ²¹²	wu¹¹	壶	kettle
474.	ʔoŋ⁵³, soŋ⁵⁵	təm²²	坛子	earthen jar
475.	ʔaŋ⁵⁵	ʔaŋ³⁵	缸	vat, big jar
476.	woŋ⁴⁵³	woŋ²⁵	木桶	wooden pail
477.	ʔu⁵⁵, muk³¹, ljap³¹	ʔu³⁵	箍儿	hoop
478.	ȶhak¹³	ʔaŋ¹¹ȶiu³³	三脚架	tripod
479.	mjai⁵³	ɕa¹¹	瓢	gourd ladle
480.	ɲip¹³	ljaŋ²²ȶiŋ²²	火钳	fire tongs
481.	muŋ⁵⁵, ʈau²¹²	muŋ³⁵	篮子	basket
482.	wai²¹²	ɕen⁵⁵	扇子	fan (n)
483.	kwiu⁵³	tiu⁵⁵, ʔiu⁵⁵	秤	balance (n)
484.	ɕik¹³	ɕiʔ¹³	尺子	ruler
485.	ȶhəm³⁵	ȶəm¹¹	针	needle
486.	son⁵³	ɕi²²son⁵⁵	锥子	awl
487.	miu²¹²	sen³³tau³⁵	剪刀	scissors
488.	ȶiŋ⁵⁵	ȶiŋ³⁵	钉子	nail (n)
489.	sin²¹²	sin²²	钱	money
490.	li³³	li⁴⁴	利息	interest
491.	khwa⁴⁵³, ho⁴⁵³	ho²⁵	货	goods
492.	san⁴⁵³	san²⁵	雨伞	umbrella
493.	pɐk⁵⁵so¹³	so¹³	锁	lock (n)
494.	ɕi²¹²so¹³	jo¹³ɕi²²	钥匙	key
495.	ɕa³⁵	ɕa¹¹	水车	waterwheel
496.	ȶeu³³	ȶeu⁴⁴	轿子	sedan (chair)
497.	lo⁵⁵	la³⁵	船	boat (n)
498.	pai²¹²	pai²²	木筏	raft (n)
499.	kwan⁵⁵	kwan³⁵	斧头	ax
500.	ʔui⁵³	waŋ²²ɕi²²	锤子	hammer (n)
501.	siu⁵³	siu⁵⁵	凿子	chisel (n)
502.	ʈo⁵³	ʈo⁵⁵	锯子	saw (n)
503.	thoi³⁵	toi¹¹	刨子	planer
504.	khɐi³⁵	ȶəi¹¹	犁	plow (n)
505.	pa²¹²	pa²²	耙	rake (n)
506.	ʔek³²³	kiʔ¹³	牛轭	yoke (n)

#				
507.	ɬhit^{13}, ɕu^{212}	kəu^{33}, ko^{55}ləu^{33}	锄头	hoe (n)
508.	lan^{212}	ʔan^{22}	扁担	shoulder pole
509.	ŋe^{35}	ʔaŋ^{55}ɕe^{11}	叉子	fork (n)
510.	lim^{31}	sit^{31}	楔子	wedge (n)
511.	lɐk^{55}	ʔa^{35}	桩子	stake (n)
512.	ɕeu^{53}, jin^{323}	jai^{33}mau^{33}	粪箕	basket for manure
513.	ljim^{212}	ko^{55}liŋ^{22}	镰刀	sickle
514.	tip^{323}	tip^{33}	摘禾刀	knife for cutting rice
515.	lu^{212}	woŋ^{11}ɕaŋ^{11}	风箱	bellows
516.	ɲen^{31}	ɕui^{31}ɲen^{31}	水碾	water-powered roller
517.	toi^{53}	ləi^{55}	碓	tilt hammer
518.	kəm^{55}	kəm^{35}	臼	mortar
519.	ʔan^{33}	ʔan^{44}kəm^{35}	杵	pestle
520.	ɕai^{35}	ɕai^{11}	筛子	sieve
521.	loŋ^{323}	loŋ^{33}	簸箕	winnowing fan
522.	mo^{33}	mo^{44}	磨子	millstone
523.	suŋ^{212}	suŋ^{22}	织布机	loom (n)
524.	mɐi^{31}tak^{323}, pau^{55}tak^{323}	məi^{31}taʔ^{31}	梭子	shuttle
525.	ɬi^{323}, ɕi^{323}	ɕi^{33}	纸	paper
526.	pjət^{55}	pjət^{55}	笔	pen
527.	mɐk^{21}	maʔ^{13}	墨	ink
528.	le^{212}	le^{22}	书本	book
529.	si^{33}	si^{44}	字	character
530.	kuŋ^{55}	kuŋ^{35}	鼓	drum (n)
531.	ɬoŋ^{55}, toŋ^{212}ɬoŋ^{55}	ɕoŋ^{35}	钟	bell
532.	jin^{35}	ke^{33}ɬin^{22}	二胡	èr hú, Chinese stringed instrument
533.	la^{212}, toŋ^{212}la^{212}	toŋ^{22}la^{22}	锣	gong
534.	ɬik^{31}	ɬiʔ^{31}	笛子	dí zi, Chinese flute
535.	seu^{55}	so^{31}na^{22}	唢呐	suǒ nà, Chinese cornet
536.	lən^{212}	lən^{22}	芦笙	lú shēng, Chinese wind pipe
537.	pheu^{453}pjat^{323}	pau^{25}pju^{55}	鞭炮	firecracker
538.	pheu^{453}	pau^{25}	炮	canon

539.	na^{13}	$ʈen^{55}, ɕen^{55}$	弓箭	bow (n)
540.	$ɕoŋ^{453}$	$ɕoŋ^{25}$	枪	gun
541.	$ʔəm^{323}ɕoŋ^{453}$	$sa^{22}pau^{25}$	火药	gunpowder
542.	je^{35}	je^{11}	网	net (n)
543.	sit^{13}	$ʔan^{33}ʈiu^{55}$	钓鱼竿	fishing rod
544.	$sən^{212}$	$sən^{22}$	神	god
545.	$ʈui^{323}$	$ʈui^{33}$	鬼	ghost
546.	$sa^{31}pja^{323}$	pja^{33}	雷霆	thunderclap
547.	$kwɐn^{55}$	$kwən^{35}$	魂魄	soul
548.	$miŋ^{33}$	$miŋ^{44}$	命	fate
549.	$lək^{21}, so^{33}$	so^{44}	力气	strength
550.	$jiŋ^{323}$	$niŋ^{33}$	影子	shadow
551.	$pjen^{55}$	$pjən^{35}ʔan^{35}$	梦	dream (n)
552.	$suŋ^{35}, li^{31}$	$suŋ^{11}$	话	word
553.	$ji^{453}, ɕi^{55}$	ji^{55}	戏	play (n)
554.	$ɲon^{212}, ku^{33}$	ku^{44}	故事	story
555.	$ɕɐm^{53}, ton^{53}$	$ton^{55}ku^{44}$	谜语	riddle
556.	$ɲin^{212}ʈi^{323}$	$ɲin^{22}ʈi^{33}$	年纪	age
557.	$siŋ^{453}$	$siŋ^{55}$	姓	(has) surname
558.	$kwan^{55}$	tan^{35}	名字	forename
559.	$lu^{33}, ɕɐi^{33}$	$lu^{44}, ɕei^{25}$	事情	matter
560.	tam^{323}	tam^{33}	胆量	courage
561.	$maŋ^{53}$	$waŋ^{11}jaŋ^{35}$	方向	direction
562.	$maŋ^{53}toŋ^{55}$	$toŋ^{35}waŋ^{11}$	东方	east
563.	$maŋ^{53}nam^{212}$	$nam^{22}waŋ^{11}$	南方	south
564.	$maŋ^{53}si^{35}$	$si^{11}waŋ^{11}$	西方	west
565.	$maŋ^{53}pɐk^{55}$	$pe^{33}waŋ^{11}$	北方	north
566.	$taŋ^{212}ta^{53}$	$taŋ^{35}ta^{55}$	中间	middle
567.	$maŋ^{53}ɕe^{323}$	$maŋ^{55}ɕe^{33}$	左边	left
568.	$maŋ^{53}wa^{35}$	$maŋ^{55}wa^{11}$	右边	right
569.	$maŋ^{53}ʔun^{53}$	$maŋ^{55}sun^{25}$	前边	in front
570.	$maŋ^{53}lən^{212}$	$maŋ^{55}sən^{22}$	后边	at the back
571.	$ljɐm^{13}lən^{212}$	$ljəm^{13}mən^{22}$	背后	behind
572.	$maŋ^{53}ʈɐu^{31}$	$maŋ^{55}ʔau^{31}$	里边	inside
573.	$maŋ^{53}nuk^{323}$	$maŋ^{55}wan^{31}$	外边	outside
574.	$maŋ^{53}ʔu^{55}$	$maŋ^{55}ʔu^{35}$	上边	above
575.	$maŋ^{53}te^{323}$	$maŋ^{55}te^{33}$	下边	below
576.	$tiŋ^{53}$	$tiŋ^{55}, maŋ^{55}te^{33}$	底下	under
577.	$ɕi^{212}$	$ɕi^{22}$	时间	time
578.	$mɐn^{55}nai^{33}$	$pən^{35}nai^{44}$	今天	today

579.	mɐn⁵⁵ɲuŋ⁵⁵	pən³⁵ɲuŋ³⁵	昨天	yesterday
580.	mɐn⁵⁵ʔun⁵³	pən³⁵kun⁵⁵	前天	the day before yesterday
581.	mɐn⁵⁵ʔun⁵³han⁵³	pən³⁵kun⁵⁵təu³³	大前天	three days ago
582.	mɐn⁵⁵mu³²³	pən³⁵mo⁴⁴	明天	tomorrow
583.	mɐn⁵⁵na³²³	pən³⁵na³³	后天	the day after tomorrow
584.	mɐn⁵⁵ʔa³²³	pən³⁵mo⁴⁴na³³, pən³⁵lən²¹²	大后天	three days from now
585.	ȵɐm⁵³, ʔɐn⁵⁵ȵɐm⁵³	kau³³ȵɐm⁵⁵	晚上	evening
586.	ʔɐn⁵⁵mɐn⁵⁵	kau³³wən³⁵	白天	daytime
587.	hət³⁵, ʔɐn⁵⁵ hət³⁵	kau³³jət³⁵	早上	morning
588.	ʔɐn⁵⁵ȶan⁵⁵	kau³³han³⁵	夜里	at night
589.	si³²³	si³¹	子	the 1st of the twelve Earthly Branches (EBs)
590.	ɕu¹³	ɕu³¹	丑	2nd of 12 EBs
591.	jən²¹²	jən²²	寅	3rd of 12 EBs
592.	meu³¹	mau³¹	卯	4th of 12 EBs
593.	ɕən²¹²	ɕən²²	辰	5th of 12 EBs
594.	si³¹	si³⁵	巳	6th of 12 EBs
595.	ŋo²¹²	wu³¹	午	7th of 12 EBs
596.	mi³³	wei³¹	未	8th of 12 EBs
597.	ɕən³⁵	ɕən⁴⁴	申	9th of 12 EBs
598.	ju³¹	ju³¹	酉	10th of 12 EBs
599.	ɕət³⁵	ɕi¹¹	戌	11th of 12 EBs
600.	hai⁵³	hai⁵⁵	亥	last of 12 EBs
601.	ɕu³⁵ʔət⁵⁵	ȶu¹¹jət⁵⁵	初一	first of month
602.	ɕu³⁵ȵi³³	ȶu¹¹ȵi⁴⁴	初二	second of month
603.	ɕiŋ⁵⁵ŋwet³¹	ɕiŋ³⁵wet³¹	一月	January
604.	ȵi³³ŋwet³¹	ȵi⁴⁴wet³¹	二月	February
605.	sam³⁵ŋwet³¹	sam¹¹wet³¹, san¹¹wet³¹	三月	March
606.	si⁴⁵³ŋwet³¹	si²⁵wet³¹	四月	April
607.	ŋo³¹ŋwet³¹	ŋo³¹wet³¹	五月	May
608.	ljok²¹ŋwet³¹	ljoʔ¹³wet³¹	六月	June
609.	sət³⁵ŋwet³¹	sət³⁵wet³¹	七月	July
610.	pet³²³ŋwet³¹	pet³³wet³¹	八月	August
611.	ȶu³²³ŋwet³¹	ȶu³³wet³¹	九月	September
612.	ɕap²¹ŋwet³¹	ɕəp³⁵wet³¹	十月	October

#				
613.	ȵan^{55}toŋ^{55}	ɕət^{35}wet^{31}	十一月	November
614.	ɕəp^{21}ȵi^{33}ŋwet^{31}, ȵan^{55}ȵin^{212}	ɕi^{33}ȵi^{33}wet^{31}, mjan^{35}ȵin^{22}	十二月	December
615.	ȵin^{212}nai^{33}	ȵin^{22}nai^{44}	今年	this year
616.	ȵin^{212}pe^{55}	ȵin^{22}we^{35}	去年	last year
617.	ȵin^{212}ʔun^{53}	ȵin^{22}kun^{55}	前年	the year before last
618.	ȵin^{212}sa^{212}	ȵin^{22}sa^{22}	明年	next year
619.	ȵin^{212}lən^{212}	ȵin^{22}lən^{22}	后年	the year after next
620.	ta^{33}ʔun^{53}	ɕi^{22}wun^{55}, ɕi^{22}lon^{55}	从前	formerly
621.	ɕi^{212}nai^{33}	ɕiŋ^{22}nai^{44}	现在	at present
622.	ta^{33}lən^{212}, pai^{55}lən^{212}	ta^{44}lən^{22}, ɕi^{22}lən^{22}, ta^{44}pai^{55}	以后	after
623.	ȵan^{55}tɐu^{212}	kəu^{33}mja^{35}	月初	beginning of month
624.	ta^{53}ȵan^{55}	ta^{55}mjan^{35}	月中	middle of month
625.	phe^{35}ȵan^{55}	sət^{35}mjan^{35}	月底	end of month
626.	ʔi^{55}, ʔət^{55}	ji^{35}, jət^{35}	一	one
627.	ja^{212}, ȵi^{33}	ja^{22}, ȵi^{44}	二	two
628.	sam^{35}	sam^{11}, san^{11}	三	three
629.	si^{453}	si^{25}	四	four
630.	ŋo^{31}	ŋo^{31}	五	five
631.	ljok^{21}	ljoʔ^{13}	六	six
632.	sət^{35}	sət^{35}	七	seven
633.	pet^{323}	pet^{33}	八	eight
634.	ʈu^{323}	ʈu^{33}	九	nine
635.	ɕəp^{21}, ɕi^{55}	ɕəp^{35}, ɕi^{33}	十	ten
636.	ɕəp^{21}ʔət^{55}	ɕi^{11}jət^{35}, ɕət^{35}	十一	eleven
637.	ɕəp^{21}ȵi^{33}	ɕi^{11}ȵi^{44}	十二	twelve
638.	pek^{323}	peʔ^{31}	百	one hundred
639.	sin^{35}	sin^{11}	千	one thousand
640.	wen^{33}	wan^{44}	万	ten thousand
641.	ʈi^{33}ʔət^{55}	ʈi^{44}ji^{33}	第一	the first
642.	ʈi^{33}ȵi^{33}	ʈi^{44}ȵi^{44}	第二	the second
643.	ʈi^{33}sam^{35}	ʈi^{44}sam^{11}, ʈi^{44}san^{11}	第三	the third
644.	pan^{53}, maŋ^{55}, tot^{31}	pan^{55}, wan^{55}, tot^{31}, ʐaŋ^{44}	半	half
645.	ʈi^{323}	ʈi^{33}	几	a few

646.	muŋ³¹	pu³⁵	个 (人)	classifier (CLF), people
647.	ȶek²¹, nɐn⁵⁵	nən³⁵, ta²²	个 (蛋)	CLF, eggs, etc.
648.	ȶiu²¹²	ȶiu²²	条 (河)	CLF, rivers, etc.
649.	tu²¹²	to²²	只, 头	CLF, animals
650.	nɐt⁵⁵	nən³⁵	粒 (米)	grain
651.	ȶiu²¹²	ȶiu²²	根 (担)	CLF, poles, etc.
652.	pak³²³	pa³³	把 (刀)	CLF, knives, etc.
653.	ʔoŋ⁵⁵	noŋ³⁵	棵	CLF, trees
654.	pu³³	pu⁴⁴	座 (桥)	CLF, bridges, etc.
655.	nɐm⁵⁵	nəm³⁵	把 (米)	handful (of rice, etc.)
656.	pən³²³	pən³³	本 (书)	CLF, books, etc.
657.	ȶiu²¹²	wei³¹	支 (笔)	CLF, pens, etc.
658.	poŋ³²³	toi³⁵	堆	heap, pile
659.	taŋ²¹²	ȶiu²²	丘 (田)	CLF, fields, etc.
660.	paŋ³²³	kwai³⁵	块 (石)	CLF, stones, etc.
661.	pak³²³	ȶui⁵⁵	句 (话)	CLF, words, etc.
662.	mɐi³¹	məi³¹	首 (歌)	CLF, songs, etc.
663.	mɐi³¹	məi³¹	件 (衣)	CLF, clothes
664.	tap³²³	tap³¹	担 (柴)	CLF, firewood, etc.
665.	ȶeu³³	ȶəu⁴⁴	双 (鞋)	pair (of shoes, etc.)
666.	tɐu³¹	təu³³	群	group
667.	toi⁵³, kɐu⁵³	ȶəu⁴⁴, lei⁵⁵	双, 队	pair, team
668.	ɕon⁵³, pjat³²³, kɐu³³	kau⁴⁴	串 (椒)	string, cluster
669.	ȶik³²³	ȶiʔ³¹	滴 (水)	drop (of water, etc.)
670.	ʔen⁵⁵	ʔen³⁵	间 (房)	CLF, rooms, etc.
671.	peu⁵⁵	pau³⁵	包 (糖)	bag
672.	ȶən⁵⁵	ȶən³⁵	斤	0.5 kilogram
673.	ljaŋ³¹	ljaŋ³¹	两	0.05 kilogram
674.	tam⁵³	tan⁵⁵	石 (谷)	100 liters
675.	tɐu³²³	təu³³	斗 (米)	10 liters
676.	ɕaŋ³⁵, toŋ²¹²	ɕoŋ¹¹	升	1 liter
677.	lji³¹	lji³¹	里	0.5 kilometer

678.	ɕaŋ³³	ɕaŋ⁴⁴	丈	3.125 meters
679.	phe⁴⁵³	ʔe²⁵	庹	arm spread
680.	ɕik¹³	ɕiʔ¹³	尺	0.333 meter
681.	ɕe³⁵	təp³¹	拃	handspan
682.	sən⁴⁵³	sən²⁵	寸	0.033 meter
683.	khwai⁴⁵³	kwai²⁵	元 (钱)	Rénmínbì (RMB)
684.	ʈo²¹²	ʈo²²	角 (钱)	0.1 RMB
685.	wən³⁵	wən¹¹	分 (钱)	0.01 RMB
686.	mɐu³¹	məu³¹	亩	0.067 hectare
687.	ʈim³²³, ɕoŋ²¹²	ʈin³¹	点 (钟)	CLF, for time
688.	ɕon³³	ton³³	次	time, occurrence
689.	tau⁵³	tau⁵⁵	回	time, occasion
690.	ȵi⁵⁵, mɐn⁵³	ki³⁵	些	some
691.	jau²¹²	jau²²	我	1s
692.	ʈiu⁵⁵	ʈau³⁵	我们	1p (exc)
693.	tau⁵⁵	ʈau³⁵	咱们	1p (inc)
694.	ȵa²¹²	ȵa²²	你	2s
695.	ɕau³⁵	ɕau¹¹	你们	2p
696.	mau³³, ʔe³⁵	mau⁴⁴	他	3s
697.	ʔe³⁵, ʈa³³mau³³	mau⁴⁴ʔe¹¹	他们	3p
698.	tɐŋ²¹²tɐu³¹	ləu³¹jən²²	大家	everyone
699.	ʔak³²³, si³³ʔa⁵⁵	ʔak³³, so³¹ʔa³⁵	自己	oneself
700.	ʔe³⁵, tən⁵⁵	ʔe¹¹	别人	other people
701.	nai³³	nai⁴⁴	这	this
702.	mɐn⁵³nai³³	ku¹¹nai⁴⁴	这些	these
703.	ki⁵⁵nai³³, ʔau³¹nai³³	ʔo²²nai⁴⁴	这里	here
704.	ʔi⁵⁵nai³³, nai³³, nai³³jaŋ³³	jaŋ⁴⁴ku³¹	这样	this way, like this
705.	ʈa³³	ka⁵⁵	那 (近)	that (near)
706.	ʈa⁵³	ka⁵⁵	那 (远)	that (far)
707.	mɐn⁵³ʈa⁵³	ku¹¹ka⁵⁵	那些	those
708.	ki⁵⁵ʈa⁵³, ʔau³¹ʈa⁵³	ʔo²²ka⁵⁵	那里	there
709.	ʔi⁵⁵ʈa⁵³, ʈa⁵³, haŋ²¹²ʈa⁵³	jaŋ⁴⁴ku³¹, ja⁵⁵jaŋ⁴⁴	那样	that way, like that
710.	nɐu²¹²	nəu²²	谁	who, whom
711.	nu³⁵	nəu¹¹	哪	which
712.	ki⁵⁵nu³⁵, ʔau³¹nu³⁵	ʔo²²nəu¹¹	哪里	where
713.	maŋ²¹²	məŋ²²	什么	what

714.	nu³⁵jaŋ³³, we³¹nu³⁵, ʔi⁵⁵nu³⁵	juŋ²²jaŋ⁴⁴	怎么	how
715.	nu³⁵kuŋ²¹²	tuŋ²²nun¹³	多少	how many, how much
716.	nu⁵³, nɐŋ²¹²	nu⁵⁵	看	look
717.	kwiŋ⁵³	ɕeu⁵⁵	遥望	look into the distance
718.	nɐp³⁵	ŋəp³⁵, nəp⁵⁵	闭 (眼)	close (eyes)
719.	thiŋ⁴⁵³, ɕoŋ⁵⁵kha³⁵	tiŋ²⁵, ɕaŋ³⁵ka¹¹	听	listen
720.	ti⁵⁵, tan⁵⁵	te³⁵	吃	eat
721.	ti⁵⁵, wum³¹	te³⁵, wum³¹	喝	drink
722.	ʔit³¹	kit³¹	咬	bite (v)
723.	lja²¹²	lja²²	舔	lick
724.	ŋɐm³¹	kəp⁵⁵	啃	gnaw
725.	ʔɐn³⁵	ʔən³⁵, tən¹¹	吞	swallow (v)
726.	phju⁴⁵³	pju²⁵	吐 (沫)	spit
727.	wen³⁵, ne⁵⁵	mje³⁵, wen¹¹wo³⁵	呕吐	vomit
728.	səp²¹	səp¹¹	吹	blow
729.	wa³³, ʔaŋ³²³, pau⁵³	ɕot³¹, ɕei³⁵, sei³⁵	说	talk (v)
730.	tok²¹, to³²³	toʔ¹³	读	read
731.	hem³¹, sin¹³	sin¹³	喊	call, shout
732.	ʔau⁵⁵, tɐi²¹²	ʔau³⁵, tai²²	拿 (持)	take
733.	nɐm⁵⁵	nəm³⁵	握	grasp
734.	sa³⁵	sa¹¹	搓	rub with hands
735.	jak³²³	ne³⁵	撕	tear (v)
736.	təp⁵⁵	təp³⁵	拾 (捡)	pick up
737.	tok⁵⁵	toʔ⁵⁵	掉落	fall, drop
738.	sɐp⁵⁵	sap⁵⁵	捉	arrest, catch
739.	tɐp²¹, liu⁵⁵	tiu³³, pe³¹	扔, 丢	throw away
740.	pjan³³, nan⁴⁵³	nan²⁵	撒	scatter
741.	peŋ⁵³	ta³³	掷	cast (v)
742.	jo³²³	jo³³	伸	stretch
743.	kai²¹², khɐŋ⁴⁵³	jai²², ne³⁵	拉	pull
744.	woŋ¹³, ljau³⁵	ljau¹¹, po²²	推	push
745.	ʔum³²³	ʔum³³	抱	hold, hug
746.	ŋau²¹²	ŋau²²	摇	shake
747.	thik¹³	tiʔ¹³	踢	kick (v)
748.	tok²¹	tui¹³	跪	kneel
749.	ɕai¹³	tai¹³	踩	step on
750.	pjiu⁵⁵	pjiu³⁵	跳	jump
751.	jap³²³	ta³³	跨	stride

Vocabulary of the Two Dong Dialects

#	Dialect 1	Dialect 2	Chinese	English
752.	jun^{55}	jun^{35}	站	stand
753.	$tham^{13}$	tam^{13}	走	walk
754.	$pjeu^{53}$	pit^{13}, tat^{31}	跑	run
755.	sui^{53}	sui^{55}, $ɲau^{44}$	坐	sit
756.	$ʔɐm^{53}$	poi^{55}	背	carry on back
757.	$lɐi^{31}$, pek^{31}	$tən^{31}pe^{31}$	跌	fall, tumble
758.	pa^{212}	pa^{22}, pja^{22}	爬	crawl
759.	$pɐŋ^{33}$	$pəŋ^{44}$	靠	lean on
760.	$ɲau^{33}$	$ɲau^{44}$	住	live (v)
761.	sa^{53}, $sa^{53}so^{33}$	$sa^{55}so^{44}$	休息	rest (v)
762.	nun^{212}, $nɐk^{35}$	$naʔ^{35}$	睡	sleep (v)
763.	ljo^{35}	ljo^{11}	醒	wake up
764.	we^{31}	we^{31}	做	do, make
765.	$ɕau^{453}$, pji^{55}	siu^{11}	修理	repair
766.	sap^{323}	sap^{13}	连接	connect
767.	tun^{53}	tun^{55}	打 (铁)	forge (iron)
768.	heu^{35}, $ʔui^{53}$	$ʔeu^{11}$	打 (人)	hit (v)
769.	$wən^{33}$	pun^{35}, wun^{22}	搬	take away
770.	$tuŋ^{55}$	$tuŋ^{35}$	抬	carry, lift, raise
771.	tap^{323}	tap^{33}	挑	carry on a pole
772.	$ʔun^{55}$	$ʔun^{35}$	扛	shoulder (v)
773.	$khɐi^{35}$	tai^{11}	犁	plow (v)
774.	$khɐi^{453}$	pa^{22}	耙	rake (v)
775.	te^{53}, $lɐu^{55}$, $ʔon^{55}$	weu^{35}	挖	dig
776.	mja^{212}, to^{323}	mja^{22}, to^{33}	种	plant (v)
777.	$ljəm^{212}$	$ljəm^{22}$	浇	pour liquid on
778.	$ʔat^{323}$	$ʔən^{33}$	割, 锯	cut (e.g., grass)
779.	$tɐt^{55}$, $pɐm^{323}$, la^{53}, te^{53}	tat^{55}, $maʔ^{55}$, te^{55}	砍	chop (e.g., tree)
780.	tu^{55}, ne^{55}	ne^{35}	扯	tear (v)
781.	$saŋ^{31}$	$saŋ^{31}$	养	keep, raise
782.	$phja^{35}$	pja^{11}, ma^{33}	喂	feed (v)
783.	jim^{55}	sen^{35}	阉	castrate or spay
784.	$tɐm^{323}$	$təm^{33}$	织 (布)	weave
785.	san^{35}	$ɕo^{55}$	编织	knit
786.	$tɐi^{323}$	tai^{33}	买	buy
787.	pe^{55}	pe^{35}	卖	sell
788.	$jɐi^{33}$	$ɕo^{25}$	数 (物)	count
789.	son^{453}	son^{25}	计算	calculate
790.	$kwiu^{53}$	$ʔiu^{55}$, tiu^{55}	称 (物)	weigh

791.	ʔeu³²³	ʔeu⁵⁵	教	teach
792.	ɕo²¹²	jo¹¹	学	learn
793.	ɕa³²³	ɕa³³	写	write
794.	mjat³²³	ma²²	擦	clean, erase
795.	phek¹³	pa³⁵	贴	paste, stick (v)
796.	tuŋ⁵⁵	tuŋ³⁵	煮	boil (e.g., rice)
797.	kwat³²³, ɕeu¹³	ɕeu¹³	炒	stir fry
798.	mɐi³⁵, sau³²³	sau³³	蒸	steam (v)
799.	phjeŋ³⁵	pjeŋ¹¹	烤 (衣)	dry (clothes)
800.	phjeu³⁵	pjau¹¹	烤 (火)	warm up (by fire)
801.	sa¹³	sa¹³	杀	kill
802.	ȵak⁵⁵	sit¹¹	切 (菜)	chop (vegetables)
803.	kwet³¹	kwet³¹	刮 (毛)	shave (hair)
804.	sit¹³	sen³³	剪	cut (with scissors)
805.	paŋ⁵⁵, ȶip³²³	paŋ³⁵	缝	sew
806.	ɕep¹³	ȵo¹³	插	stick in
807.	pən²¹²	pən²², mo²²	磨 (刀)	sharpen (knife)
808.	mo³³	mo⁴⁴	磨 (米)	grind (rice)
809.	wɐn⁴⁵³	wən²⁵	簸 (米)	winnow
810.	tui³²³	tui³³	舀 (米)	ladle (v)
811.	tən³²³	tən³³	穿, 戴	put on, wear
812.	thot¹³	tot¹³	脱	take off
813.	ɕuk³²³	ɕuʔ³¹	洗 (手)	wash (hands)
814.	sɐk⁵⁵	saʔ⁵⁵	洗 (衣)	wash (clothes)
815.	ʔap³²³	ɕuʔ³¹	洗澡	bathe
816.	jɐm³²³	jəm³³	染	dye (v)
817.	ʔam⁵³	ʔam⁵⁵	补	mend
818.	khe³⁵	ke¹¹	梳	comb (v, n)
819.	sət⁵⁵	sau¹³	扫	clean, sweep
820.	ʔɐi³⁵	ʔai¹¹	开	open (v)
821.	soŋ⁴⁵³, to³²³	soŋ⁵⁵, tu⁵⁵	放 (置)	lay, put
822.	ɕɐŋ³⁵, ȶeu⁵³	kwa⁵⁵	挂	hang
823.	ljɐn⁵³	ljoŋ⁵⁵	解开	untie
824.	suk³¹	suʔ³¹	捆	tie, bind
825.	han⁴⁵³, wət⁵⁵	han²⁵, jet⁵⁵	塞	stuff (v)
826.	ʔəm⁵³, mok⁵⁵	saŋ⁵⁵, moʔ⁵⁵	埋	bury
827.	ɕu³⁵, jin³¹	ɕu¹¹	收藏	store up
828.	lai³³, ʔen³²³	ʔen³³	挑选	choose

Vocabulary of the Two Dong Dialects

829.	ʈum⁵⁵	kun³⁵	积聚	accumulate
830.	ʈak³²³	taʔ³¹, ʈiŋ⁵⁵	钉 (钉)	hammer (v)
831.	ʈaŋ³²³	ʈim³³	点 (灯)	light (v)
832.	ʔau⁵⁵, ju⁵³	ju⁵⁵	要	want, need
833.	li³²³	li³³	得到	get
834.	tok⁵⁵, tɐu⁵³	toʔ⁵⁵, leu³¹	失落	lose (something)
835.	səm³³	lau¹¹	寻找	look for
836.	joŋ³³	joŋ⁴⁴	用	use (v)
837.	we³¹pjan³²³	we³¹jen³³	玩耍	have fun
838.	lam¹³	jeu²²	游玩	play (v)
839.	jiŋ²¹²	jiŋ²²	赢	win
840.	ɕui³⁵	ɕe¹¹	输	lose, fail
841.	to³²³ʔa⁵⁵	ɕaŋ⁵⁵ʔa³⁵	唱歌	sing
842.	peŋ⁵³	peŋ⁵⁵	射	shoot
843.	ham⁴⁵³, ɕai³²³	ɕai³³	问	ask
844.	ɕun³⁵, ɕan³⁵	jiŋ⁵⁵, ɕan¹¹	答	answer (v)
845.	jam⁵⁵	jam³⁵	借	borrow
846.	pɐi³²³	pəi³³	还	give back
847.	sai³⁵	sai¹¹	给	give
848.	pau⁵³, ləp²¹	pau⁵⁵	告诉	tell
849.	ʈu⁵³	ʈu⁵⁵	救	rescue (v)
850.	phje⁴⁵³	wən¹¹, pje²⁵	分	share
851.	ɕiu¹³	ʈim³⁵	欠	owe
852.	ka³²³	ʈa³³	等候	wait
853.	təm⁵⁵, tuŋ³²³	tuŋ³³	遇见	meet
854.	kwa⁵³, phjit¹³	kat¹³, ʈen¹¹	骂	scold (v)
855.	lɐŋ³³	ʈət³¹	逃	run away
856.	lɐm⁵⁵, ʈik³²³	wi¹¹, ʈiʔ³¹	追	chase
857.	ljɐk²¹	ljaʔ¹³	偷	steal
858.	tiŋ⁵³, lɐu³¹	ho³⁵, ləu³⁵, pjen²⁵	欺骗	deceive
859.	ko⁵⁵	ko³⁵	笑	laugh (v)
860.	ne³²³	ŋe³³	哭	cry (v)
861.	ʔɐi⁵³, ljaŋ³⁵, ɕok³⁵, pin²¹²	ʔei⁵⁵, ljaŋ¹¹	爱	love (v)
862.	ʔɐi⁵³, ljaŋ³⁵	ʔei⁵⁵	喜欢	like (v)
863.	pu³³, ʔɐn³³	pau⁴⁴	称赞	praise (v)
864.	sən⁴⁵³	sən²⁵	相信	believe, trust
865.	wo³¹	wo³¹	知道	know
866.	ton⁵³	ton⁵⁵	猜	guess (v)

867.	nən³³	nən⁴⁴	记得	remember
868.	lam²¹²	lam²²	忘记	forget
869.	mje³³, ɕaŋ⁴⁵³	saŋ¹³	想	think
870.	hɐn³¹, sɐŋ⁵⁵	hən²⁵, səŋ³⁵	恨	hate (v)
871.	jau¹³	ko¹³	怕	fear (v)
872.	ʔam³²³	kan³¹	敢	dare
873.	wo³¹	wo³¹	会	know, be able
874.	ȶaŋ³²³, ɕiŋ⁵³, ɕi⁵⁵	ɕi⁵⁵	是	be
875.	li³²³	me²²	有	have
876.	ma³⁵, tɐŋ⁵⁵	ma¹¹	来	come
877.	pai⁵⁵	pai³⁵	去	go
878.	ɕon⁵³	ɕon⁵⁵	转	turn (v)
879.	thɐu⁴⁵³	təu²⁵	到	reach, arrive
880.	ta³³	ta⁴⁴	过	cross, pass
881.	ȶha⁴⁵³	ȶa²⁵	上 (山)	go up
882.	lui³³	lui⁴⁴	下 (山)	go down
883.	ʔuk³²³	ʔuʔ³¹	出	go out
884.	lau³²³	lau³³	进	enter
885.	tən⁵⁵	toi³⁵lən²²	退后	fall back
886.	ȵau³³	ȵau⁴⁴	在	at, in, on
887.	ɕa⁴⁵³	ɕa²⁵	晒	dry in the sun
888.	tok⁵⁵	toʔ⁵⁵	下 (雨)	fall (rain)
889.	wet¹³, ɕui³⁵	wai³³, ɕi¹¹	刮 (风)	blow (wind)
890.	lap³²³	ti³³lap³³	打闪	flash (lightning)
891.	ʔuŋ¹³pja³²³	kuŋ¹³pja³³	打雷	thunder (v)
892.	ʔui³⁵	tui¹¹	流	flow
893.	pən³¹	wən¹¹	溢	overflow
894.	poŋ²¹²	poŋ²²	浮	float (v)
895.	jɐm⁵⁵	ɕiŋ³³	沉	sink (v)
896.	ȵe⁵³, ɕek¹³	je¹³	裂开	split open
897.	pɐŋ⁵⁵	pəŋ³⁵	倒塌	collapse
898.	piŋ⁵³	miŋ⁵⁵	缺口	breach (v)
899.	ɕon³³	ton⁴⁴, ɕon⁴⁴	旋转	revolve
900.	tu⁵³, tɐk⁵⁵	taŋ³¹, taʔ⁵⁵	断	snap (v)
901.	pha⁴⁵³, la⁵³	la⁵⁵	破 (开)	break (e.g., glass)
902.	səm⁵³	səm⁵⁵	浸 (衣)	soak (clothes)
903.	ma⁴⁵³	səm⁵⁵	浸 (米)	soak (rice)
904.	lɐu³³	ʔe³⁵	漏	leak (v)
905.	lət³⁵	lət³⁵	滴水	drip (v)

Vocabulary of the Two Dong Dialects 241

906.	lak^{13} tau^{33}		沸	boil (v)
907.	pjin^{53}	pjin^{55}	变	change
908.	pjiŋ^{33}, ʔit^{323}, ne^{53}	pjiŋ^{44}, kit^{33}, ne^{55}	病	be ill
909.	tan^{212}, tan^{212}ɕu^{13}	ʔan^{55}lan^{55}, tan^{22}	发抖	shiver
910.	pu^{55}	po^{55}	肿	swell
911.	saŋ^{31}	saŋ^{31}	生 (养)	give birth to
912.	tɐi^{55}	təi^{35}	死	die
913.	pən^{323}	pən^{31}	飞	fly (v)
914.	khɐu^{453}	kəu^{25}	吠	bark (v)
915.	jen^{55}	ʔən^{35}	啼	crow (v)
916.	ʔuk^{323}, soŋ^{453}	ʔuʔ^{31}	下 (蛋)	lay (eggs)
917.	pjɐm^{55}	pjəm^{35}	孵	hatch
918.	peu^{53}	toŋ^{35}ŋe^{33}	发 (芽)	sprout (v)
919.	ʔɐi^{35}	ʔəi^{11}	开 (花)	blossom (v)
920.	wən^{35}, ȶit^{323}	ȶit^{13}	结 (果)	bear (fruit)
921.	lui^{212}, lan^{33}	lan^{44}	烂	rotten
922.	mak^{323}, lau^{31}	maʔ^{33}, lau^{31}, lei^{22}	大	big
923.	ʔun^{323}, ni^{53}	ni^{55}, ȵeu^{33}, ʔun^{33}	小	small
924.	phaŋ^{35}	paŋ^{11}	高	tall, high
925.	thɐm^{453}	təm^{25}	低	short (of stature)
926.	jɐm^{55}	jəm^{35}	深	deep
927.	lin^{53}	nen^{55}	浅	shallow
928.	siu^{53}, ɕo^{453}	ka^{11}, ta^{11}	尖	pointed
929.	ton^{212}	ton^{22}	圆	round
930.	waŋ^{35}, si^{453}waŋ^{35}	waŋ^{11}	方	square
931.	jai^{323}	jai^{33}	长	long
932.	thən^{13}	ȶən^{13}	短	short, brief
933.	so^{35}	su^{11}	粗	coarse
934.	si^{453}	si^{25}	细	thin, slender
935.	na^{55}	na^{35}	厚	thick (e.g., book)
936.	maŋ^{55}	maŋ^{35}	薄	thin, flimsy
937.	khwaŋ^{13}	kwət^{13}	宽	wide
938.	sok^{35}	ɕe^{31}	窄	narrow
939.	kai^{55}	ȶai^{35}	远	far
940.	ȶən^{31}	pei^{35}	近	near
941.	kuŋ^{212}, ʔoi^{55}	ȶuŋ^{22}	多	much, many
942.	jun^{323}	ȵun^{13}	少	little, few
943.	sɐŋ^{212}	tiu^{22}	直	straight
944.	ȶoŋ^{53}	ȶoŋ^{55}	弯	curved

945.	weŋ²¹²	wiŋ²²	横	horizontal
946.	pjiŋ²¹²	pjiŋ²²	平	flat, level
947.	sɐk⁵⁵	tau³³	陡	steep
948.	ɕiŋ⁵³	ɕiŋ⁵⁵	正	straight, upright
949.	phjin³⁵, je³⁵	ɕa³³, pjen¹¹	歪	askew, inclined
950.	ţha¹³	ţa¹³	轻	light (adj)
951.	ţhɐn³⁵	ţən¹¹	重	heavy
952.	kwa³²³	ta³³, ŋən¹³	硬	hard
953.	ma³²³	ma³³	软	soft
954.	ţo⁵³	ţo⁵⁵	韧	pliable but strong
955.	kwaŋ⁵⁵, lik¹³	taŋ³⁵	亮	bright
956.	təŋ⁵³	toŋ⁵⁵	暗	dark (adj)
957.	khaŋ³⁵	lai³⁵ţaŋ¹¹	晴	fine
958.	wom⁵³	jom³¹, mən³⁵jən³⁵	阴	overcast
959.	liŋ³¹	liŋ³¹	旱	drought
960.	lau³³	lau³³, mən³⁵nəm³¹	涝	waterlogging
961.	ja⁴⁵³	ja²⁵	红	red
962.	man¹³	man¹³	黄	yellow
963.	pha³⁵	lan³³	蓝	blue, gray
964.	pak³¹	paʔ³¹	白	white
965.	nɐm⁵⁵	nəm³⁵	黑	black
966.	su³⁵	ŋu¹¹	绿	green
967.	ʔɐm⁵³	mai⁵⁵	紫	purple
968.	wa³⁵, ʔen⁵³	wa¹¹	花	colorful
969.	nɐk⁵⁵	ţo³³	稠	thick, dense
970.	sik¹³	man³³	稀	thin (e.g., soup)
971.	tik³²³	mun³¹	满	full
972.	lai⁵⁵jɐk²¹, pjaŋ⁵³	lje²², lai³⁵jaʔ¹³	美丽	beautiful, pretty
973.	pui²¹²	pi²²	胖	fat (adj)
974.	wum⁵⁵	ţiu³³, wum³⁵	瘦	thin, lean
975.	wo³⁵, sin³⁵	sən¹¹	干净	clean (adj)
976.	wa⁵³, wok²¹	wa⁵⁵	脏	dirty
977.	lau³¹	lau³¹	老	tough, old
978.	lji³¹	ki³¹, ɲaʔ³⁵	嫩	tender, delicate
979.	lai⁵⁵	lai³⁵	好	good
980.	ja³¹, wai³³	wai⁴⁴, ja³¹	坏	bad
981.	hoi⁴⁵³	woi²⁵	快	fast, quickly
982.	ʔɐn⁵⁵, ɲam⁴⁵³	men¹³	慢	slow, slowly
983.	so³²³	so³³	干	dry (adj)

Vocabulary of the Two Dong Dialects

984.	jɐk^{55}	ja?^{55}	湿	wet (adj)
985.	mɐi^{453}	məi^{25}	新	new
986.	ʔau^{53}	ʔau^{55}	旧	old
987.	ɕeŋ^{35}	ɕeŋ^{11}	生 (的)	raw
988.	ɕok^{21}	ɕo?^{13}	熟 (的)	cooked
989.	jai^{33}	jai^{44}	锋利	sharp
990.	təp^{21}	ʔa^{22}	钝	blunt
991.	sɐm^{35}	səm^{11}	早	early
992.	ʔɐn^{55}, we^{35}	we^{11}	迟	late
993.	ȵɐŋ^{212}	ɕən^{55}	真	real, true
994.	ta^{31}, ʔa^{323}	ʔa^{33}, waŋ^{13}	假	fake, false
995.	ʈui^{53}	ʈui^{55}	贵	expensive
996.	phjen^{212}ji^{55}, pjin^{212}ȵi^{212}	pjen^{22}ȵi^{22}	便宜	cheap
997.	joŋ^{212}ji^{33}, ji^{55}li^{323}	joŋ^{22}ji^{44}	容易	easy
998.	nan^{212}	nan^{22}	难	difficult
999.	loŋ^{33}, ȵom^{33}	mo^{55}, soŋ^{22}	松	loose
1000.	ʈen^{323}	ʈən^{33}	紧	tight
1001.	tun^{55}, ljoŋ^{31}	tun^{35}, lai^{55}	热	hot
1002.	ljɐk^{35}, leŋ^{31}	lja?^{35}	冷	cold
1003.	sau^{323}	pjau^{33}	暖和	warm (adj)
1004.	jim^{453}	ljaŋ^{22}	凉快	cool (adj)
1005.	səm^{13}	səm^{13}	酸	sour
1006.	khwan^{35}	pan^{11}	甜	sweet
1007.	ʔɐm^{212}	ʔəm^{22}	苦	bitter
1008.	ljan^{33}	ljan^{13}	辣	peppery, hot
1009.	hɐt^{35}	hət^{35}	咸	salty
1010.	pat^{323}	pat^{31}	涩	tart (adj)
1011.	taŋ^{55}	taŋ^{35}	香	fragrant, delicious
1012.	ȵən^{55}	ȵən^{35}	臭	smelly, foul
1013.	siŋ^{35}	siŋ^{11}	腥	fishy (smell)
1014.	ʈəŋ^{53}	ʈəŋ^{55}	饱	full (of food)
1015.	jɐk^{323}	pe?^{33}	饿	hungry
1016.	jak^{323}nɐm^{31}	so^{44}ʔo^{22}, so^{13}ʔo^{22}	渴	thirsty
1017.	tɐi^{55}khwau^{13}	ʈəŋ^{55}tau^{13}	醉	intoxicated
1018.	tɐi^{55}hu^{13}, ne^{53}	ken^{35}, ne^{55}	累	tired
1019.	ʈhum^{35}, ȵan^{35}	ʈum^{11}	痒	itchy
1020.	ʔit^{323}	kit^{31}	痛	painful
1021.	tiu^{31}, ɕɐi^{35}	ɕɐi^{11}, ljai^{35}	聪明	clever, skillful

1022.	ʔe³²³	ɕau¹¹, wa³¹	愚笨	foolish, stupid
1023.	jɐk³⁵	ȶən²²ȶiŋ³³	勤	hard-working
1024.	soi²¹², khwət³⁵	tət⁵⁵	懒	lazy
1025.	mɐŋ³¹, khwan³⁵sai³²³	wan¹¹ȵi¹³	高兴	happy
1026.	sɐu²¹², ju⁵⁵	ȶəu³³, jo⁵⁵	忧愁	sad
1027.	hu¹³	ʔu¹³	穷	poor
1028.	kwa³³, hu⁴⁵³	me²²	富	rich
1029.	ʔen⁵⁵ȶɐu⁵⁵	ja⁵⁵ʔau²²	刚才	just now
1030.	ʔun⁵³	wun⁵⁵, sun³⁵	先	earlier, first
1031.	lən²¹²	lən²²	后	after, later
1032.	lɐŋ³¹	ɕu³¹	立刻	immediately
1033.	men³³, pən³²³	ȶən³³ɕaŋ²²	常常	often, always
1034.	sɐi⁴⁵³sɐi⁴⁵³	wan¹¹wan¹¹	慢慢	slowly
1035.	taŋ⁵³taŋ⁵³	taŋ⁵⁵taŋ⁵⁵	渐渐	gradually
1036.	ȵɐŋ²¹², hən³¹	hən³¹	很	really, very
1037.	lət³⁵, ɕet¹³, tu⁵⁵	hau³⁵,tu³⁵	都	all, both
1038.	pu³³, ja³³	ja⁴⁴, je³¹	也	also, too
1039.	si³⁵	sai⁵⁵	再	again, once more
1040.	ʔeŋ⁵³, ju³³	ju⁴⁴	又	again, also
1041.	su³³, lɐŋ³¹	su³¹, ɕu³¹	就	at once, right away
1042.	ʔɐi³²³, kwe²¹²	kwe²², ʔəi³³	不	no, not
1043.	mi³¹	me³¹	未	have not, not
1044.	pi³¹	pi³¹	别	do not
1045.	nɐŋ⁵⁵	han¹¹	还	still, yet
1046.	wan²¹²	ji³¹ȶən³³	已经	already
1047.	ȵim³⁵, tɐŋ³³, jin³⁵	ȵim³⁵, toŋ²², we³¹jin¹¹, to³³	和	and
1048.	ʔi²¹²ȶən⁵⁵	ji²²ȶən³³	一定	certainly
1049.	nu⁵³, nu⁵³pau⁵³, jaŋ³³	nu¹¹, nu¹¹pau⁵⁵, jaŋ⁴⁴	如果	if
1050.	kop³²³, ha³³, kop³²³kop³²³	ja⁵⁵ɕi²², ka¹³ka¹³	才	a moment ago, just
1051.	pen³³	ɕi²²ju³⁵	总是	so long as
1052.	pek³¹, ʔoŋ³⁵	ʔoŋ³⁵, ʔoŋ¹¹	空,白	empty, blank

Appendix 2
Co-occurrence of Dong Initials, Rhymes, and Tones

246 The Dong Language in Guizhou Province, China

Co-occurrence of Dong Initials, Rhymes, and Tones

Rhyme	Tone	Initial: p	ph	m	w	t	th	n	l	s	tˢ	tsh	ts	ɕ	j	k	kh	ŋ	ʔ	h	pj	phj	mj	lj	kw	khw	ŋw
ai	6	×		×	×	×		×	×					×	×	×		×		×							
	5'		×		×		×			×						×		×							×		
	5	×		×	×			×	×					×		×		×						×	×	×	
	4	×		×	×		×	×	×					×													
	3'		×			×				×			×			×		×					×				
	3	×		×	×		×	×				×	×	×			×										
	2	×		×		×								×	×	×											
	1'					×		×	×		×	×															
	1	×				×	×	×	×	×			×		×					×	×	×					
u	6	×		×	×	×				×	×	×	×	×	×	×	×		×					×			
	5'		×		×							×		×			×	×		×							
	5	×				×		×	×	×	×			×	×	×			×	×					×		
	4	×			×	×		×	×			×	×	×			×							×			
	3'						×		×				×				×										
	3	×		×	×	×				×	×			×	×			×		×							
	2	×		×	×	×	×	×	×	×		×	×	×	×		×								×		
	1'		×			×	×	×	×		×	×				×		×		×	×						
	1	×		×	×	×		×			×					×	×	×		×							
o	6	×		×	×	×			×	×			×	×			×	×							×		
	5'			×	×	×		×				×				×									×	×	×
	5	×							×	×		×			×			×									
	4				×	×			×			×	×	×	×		×	×	×							×	
	3'				×			×			×		×	×	×	×						×					
	3		×		×	×		×	×	×	×				×										×		
	2	×		×	×	×	×	×	×		×	×						×	×	×							
	1'		×		×	×		×	×	×	×							×			×			×			
	1	×		×	×	×			×	×					×	×	×		×								

248   The Dong Language in Guizhou Province, China

Co-occurrence of Dong Initials, Rhymes, and Tones

The Dong Language in Guizhou Province, China

Rhyme	Tone	Initial	p	ph	m	w	t	th	n	l	s	ț	șh	ȵ	c	j	k	kh	ŋ	ʔ	h	pj	phj	mj	lj	kw	khw	gw
an	1		×			×		×	×			×	×					×				×				×		
an	1'			×	×	×		×				×	×	×												×	×	
an	2		×	×	×	×		×	×	×	×		×		×			×		×			×			×	
an	3		×			×					×				×			×	×	×	×							
an	3'				×		×							×												×		
an	4		×	×	×		×	×	×								×								×	×	×	
an	5		×				×	×			×	×				×	×				×							
an	5'				×	×						×	×		×													
an	6		×		×		×	×	×	×		×			×	×			×			×	×					
am	1			×			×					×	×	×														
am	1'									×				×														
am	2						×	×		×			×						×									
am	3		×			×				×		×	×			×										×	×	
am	3'								×	×		×	×		×											×		
am	4		×						×				×				×					×						
am	5						×			×				×	×													
am	5'					×																						
am	6							×	×	×			×							×								
iu	1		×		×	×			×	×	×			×	×	×	×							×			×	×
iu	1'				×					×				×		×					×		×					
iu	2		×	×	×			×		×				×	×						×		×					
iu	3					×		×	×		×	×		×	×	×			×	×			×					
iu	3'					×			×			×			×	×			×	×								
iu	4					×	×		×			×		×	×	×												
iu	5					×			×			×	×		×											×	×	
iu	5'				×			×			×	×	×				×											
iu	6							×		×	×	×			×	×	×						×					

Co-occurrence of Dong Initials, Rhymes, and Tones

Rhyme	Tone	Initial	p	ph	m	w	t	th	n	l	s	t	sh	ts	c	j	k	kh	v	ʔ	h	pj	phj	mj	lj	kw	khw	ŋw
ua	6			×	×		×										×	×				×	×					
	5'			×	×			×	×			×	×	×											×			
	5		×	× ×			× ×	×								×			×									
	4		×	×	×			× ×					× ×	× ×					×									
	3'						×		×							×												
	3		×	×	×			× × ×				× ×	× ×	×					×									
	2		×	× ×				×	×	× ×					×			× ×										
	1'		×					× ×			×	× ×																
	1		×	×	×	×	× ×			× ×		×	×					×										
ua	6					×	× × × ×	× × ×																				
	5'					×		×	×		×																	
	5					× ×		× ×	×		×	×		×														
	4		×				× × × ×		×		× × ×		×															
	3'				×	×		×	×		×																	
	3		×		×		× × ×		× ×	× ×			×															
	2		×		×		× ×	×		× ×		× ×																
	1'			×		×	× ×			×																		
	1				×	× × × ×	× × × ×	× ×	×		×																	
aŋ	6		×	× × ×		× ×	× × ×	× ×	×		×																
	5'			×	×	×		×	× ×		×																	
	5			×	×		× ×	× × ×	× ×	×		×																
	4		×				× ×	× ×	×		× ×																	
	3'					×	× × ×		×		×																	
	3		×	× ×	× × × ×	×		× ×	×	× ×																		
	2		×	× × ×	× × × ×	× × × ×	×	×		×																	
	1'		×	×	×	× ×	×	× ×	×	×		×	×														
	1		×	×	×		× ×		× ×		× ×	×		×													

Rhyme	aa								em								en							
Tone	1	1'	2	3	3'	4	5	5'	6	1	1'	2	3	3'	4	5	5'	6	1	1'	2	3	3'	4	5	5'	6
Initial																											
p	×						×		×	×		×							×			×			×		×
ph	×		×			×	×										×		×								
m	×			×		×	×			×		×				×		×	×	×			×			×	×
w		×						×								×				×		×	×				×
t	×		×			×	×		×							×		×									
th			×				×																				
n	×			×				×								×								×		×	
l	×	×					×	×																	×		
s			×						×	×			×					×			×		×			×	
t			×				×	×	×			×								×	×						
sh			×				×													×	×						
ts												×			×												
c		×	×		×			×					×				×	×				×			×	×	×
j							×	×	×			×				×					×	×					×
k	×			×			×	×	×								×	×		×	×						
kh								×					×				×	×	×			×			×		
ŋ			×																								
ʔ	×			×													×								×		×
h									×												×					×	
pj																					×				×	×	×
phj																									×		
mj																			×							×	
lj		×																									
kw																			×			×					×
khw								×	×										×	×	×		×				×
ŋw																			×								×

Co-occurrence of Dong Initials, Rhymes, and Tones

The Dong Language in Guizhou Province, China

Rhyme					æ									im									in					
Tone	1	1'	2	3	3'	4	5	5'	6	1	1'	2	3	3'	4	5	5'	6	1	1'	2	3	3'	4	5	5'	6
Initial																												
p																			×		×	×			×		×
ph														×							×						
m														×								×			×		
w	×																										
t						×	×					×			×				×					×			
th						×						×			×												
n									×						×				×			×			×		
l											×								×			×			×		
s					×						×									×		×	×		×		×
t̠			×								×							×		×		×					
t̠h																							×				
ts															×	×		×			×		×				
c															×				×		×				×		×
j				×									×	×											×		
k																						×				×	
kh																								×	×		
ŋ																											
ʔ																			×			×			×		×
h																											
pj																				×		×					×
phj															×												×
mj																											
lj																											
kw																						×					
khw																											
ŋw																											

Co-occurrence of Dong Initials, Rhymes, and Tones

Rhyme	Tone	Initial: p	ph	m	w	t	th	n	l	s	ʈ	ʈh	ts	ɕ	j	k	kh	ŋ	ʔ	h	pj	phj	mj	lj	kw	khw	ŋw
oŋ	6	×		×	× ×		×		×			×	× × × ×		× ×				×								
oŋ	5'					×		×	×				×			×											
oŋ	5					×			× ×				× ×		×	×											
oŋ	4	×				×	×						×	×		×						×					
oŋ	3'													×					×								
oŋ	3					×	×	×							×												
oŋ	2	×	×									× × × × ×							×								
oŋ	1'		×										× ×		×												
oŋ	1	×	×	×				× × ×		× ×						×											
om	6				×			×		×							×										
om	5'																										
om	5	×	× ×					×								×											
om	4	×		×																							
om	3'																×										
om	3																										
om	2																										
om	1'																										
om	1	×		×												×											
iŋ	6		×	×		×														×		×					
iŋ	5'		×				×	×					×														
iŋ	5	×	×	×	×		×		× ×							×					× ×					
iŋ	4						× ×														×		× ×				
iŋ	3'		×		×	× ×		×							×												
iŋ	3	×	×			×	× ×		× ×												×		×				
iŋ	2				×		× ×	×													×		× ×				
iŋ	1'		×		×		×				× ×	×									×						
iŋ	1	×	×	×			× ×		×	×		×											× ×				

Rhyme: un

Initial \ Tone	1	1'	2	3	3'	4	5	5'	6
p				×					
ph			×						×
m									
w	×			×		×	×		×
t	×					×	×		
th			×	×					
n	×		×	×	×	×	×		×
l									
s									
ṭ							×		
ṭh									
ts									
c		×						×	
j		×	×	×	×	×			
k									
kh						×	×		
ŋ				×					
ʔ	×			×					×
h	×								
pj									×
phj								×	×
mj									
lj									
kw				×	×	×			
khw				×	×				
ŋw									

Rhyme: um

Initial \ Tone	1	1'	2	3	3'	4	5	5'	6
p									
ph									
m	×		×			×	×		×
w									
t									
th									
n				×		×			×
l									
s									
ṭ									
ṭh									
ts									
c			×			×			
j									
k									
kh									
ŋ									
ʔ				×					
h									

Rhyme: oŋ

Initial \ Tone	1	1'	2	3	3'	4	5	5'	6
p	×		×	×		×			×
ph			×	×				×	×
m		×	×					×	
w		×	×						
t	×		×		×		×		
th									
n	×	×		×	×	×	×		×
l	×	×	×	×	×		×		×
s	×								
ṭ									
ṭh									
ts	×	×	×			×	×	×	×
c	×	×	×	×		×	×	×	×
j		×	×			×	×	×	×
k	×			×	×	×	×	×	×
kh		×	×						
ŋ									
ʔ									
h	×								
pj			×						×
phj		×							
mj				×					
lj									
kw						×	×		×
khw									
ŋw									

Co-occurrence of Dong Initials, Rhymes, and Tones

Rhyme	ak				ap			at			ak				Tone
Tone	7	7'	8	9	9'	10	7	7'	8	7	7'	8	7	7'	8	9	9'	10	Initial
Initial																
p	×		×		×	×	×	×	×			×	×		×	p
ph			×	×	×	×	×	×	×	×	×	×	×	×	×	ph
m	×		×	×		×	×		×	×	×	×	×		×	m
w							×					×				w
t										×		×	×		×	t
th	×		×	×	×	×	×	×	×		×		×		×	th
n	×		×	×	×		×		×			×	×	×	×	n
l	×	×	×	×	×			×		×	×	×	×	×	×	l
s							×		×			×				s
t			×	×	×	×	×	×	×		×		×	×	×	t
th										×		×		×		th
ts							×						×			ts
c												×				c
j		×		×		×				×	×	×		×	×	j
k							×		×	×			×	×	×	k
kh				×		×	×	×	×			×	×	×	×	kh
ŋ	×		×		×	×					×					ŋ
ʔ			×					×		×	×		×			ʔ
h												×				h
pj	×			×												pj
phj														×		phj
mj									×							mj
lj				×						×	×	×		×	×	lj
kw	×	×	×			×				×	×	×			×	kw
khw	×		×	×						×			×	×		khw
ŋw			×					×		×				×		ŋw

Co-occurrence of Dong Initials, Rhymes, and Tones

Rhyme	ep						et						ek						ap					
Tone	7	7'	8	9	9'	10	7	7'	8	9	9'	10	7	7'	8	9	9'	10	7	7'	8	9	9'	10
Initial																								
p			x	x		x				x								x	x		x			
ph				x		x										x	x	x	x		x			
m			x	x						x							x		x		x			
w					x					x		x												
t			x	x	x	x											x		x		x			
th				x	x						x								x		x			
n				x		x				x						x								
l			x	x	x	x											x		x		x			
s				x															x		x			
ts			x	x	x													x			x			
tsh			x	x		x				x							x		x		x			
ȵ						x										x								
ɕ			x								x	x					x		x		x			
j			x	x	x					x	x					x	x		x		x			
k			x	x	x					x		x							x		x			
kh						x				x	x	x				x			x					
ŋ																	x				x			
ʔ																x								
h			x		x																x			
pj																								
phj				x						x	x													
mj										x														
lj			x													x	x		x					
kw					x							x												
khw			x																x					
ŋw												x												

Rhyme		at						ak						ip						it					
Tone	7	7'	8	9	9'	10	7	7'	8	9	9'	10	7	7'	8	9	9'	10	7	7'	8	9	9'	10
Initial																								
p	×																					×		×
ph		×	×																					×
m	×	×	×													×		×				×	×	
w																×								
t	×	×	×													×	×	×				×		×
th	×		×																					
n																						×		×
l	×	×	×													×	×	×				×	×	×
s	×		×													×	×	×						×
ts	×		×					×	×							×						×	×	×
tsh	×		×				×	×														×	×	
ȵ																×		×					×	
ɕ	×	×	×																					
j																								
k	×																							
kh			×																					
ŋ		×																						
ʔ	×		×																					×
h	×	×																						
pj																								
phj		×																	×					
mj																								
lj			×																					
kw																×								
khw																×								
ŋw																								

Co-occurrence of Dong Initials, Rhymes, and Tones

Rhyme	ik						op						ot						ok					
Tone	7	7'	8	9	9'	10	7	7'	8	9	9'	10	7	7'	8	9	9'	10	7	7'	8	9	9'	10
Initial																								
p					×	×					×	×						×	×	×	×	×	×	×
ph																			× × ×	× ×	× × × ×		×	×
m										× ×											×	×	×	
w																					×			
t				×								×						×						
th										×	× ×					× ×	×	×				×		
n				× ×	×	× × ×				×								×	× ×	×	× × ×	×		× ×
l						× × ×												×		×				
s										×								×	×		×			
ť				× × ×	×	× × ×				×	× ×	× ×									×			
th́					×					×							×	×						
ṇ				× ×	×													×	× ×	× × ×	×	×	× × ×	× ×
c						×												×	× ×					
j				×															×					
k				×	×					×	× ×											×	×	×
kh					×																× × ×			
ŋ						×													× ×					
ʔ				×								× ×					×	× ×						
h				×								× ×					×	× ×	×					
pj						×															× × ×	× ×		
phj					×							×						× ×						
mj																								
lj																								
kw																			×	×	×			
khw																								
ŋw																								

Rhyme	up						ut						uk					
Tone / Initial	7	7'	8	9	9'	10	7	7'	8	9	9'	10	7	7'	8	9	9'	10
p				×						×		×						×
ph				×							×	×					×	×
m											×							
w																		
t											×					×		
th											×	×				×		×
n											×					×		×
l																×		×
s												×						
ɬ				×	×						×	×						
ȵ										×								
ɕ											×	×				×		
j										×	×							
k										×								
kh					×						×	×					×	×
ŋ											×						×	
ʔ																		
h																		
pj										×								
phj																		×
mj										×								
lj										×								
kw																		
khw																		
ŋw																		

Appendix 3
Cognate Words

Cognate words among the Dong dialects and lects (cf. (87))

Chējiāng southern, 1	Shuǐkǒu southern, 2	Shídòng northern, 1	Chinese	
ɲan⁵⁵	ɲan⁴⁴	mjan³⁵	月亮 yuè liàng	moon
pja³²³	pja³⁵	pja³³	雷 léi	thunder
pjən⁵⁵	pjən⁴⁴	mjən³⁵	雨 yǔ	rain (n)
nui⁵⁵	ni⁴⁴	ni³⁵	雪 xuě	snow (n)
mun²¹²	mun¹²	mon²²	雾 wù	fog
pui⁵⁵	pi⁴⁴	wi³⁵	火 huǒ	fire
ti³³	ti²¹	ti⁴⁴	地 dì	the world
ȶən²¹²	ȶən¹²	ȶən²²	山 shān	mountain
ɲa⁵⁵	ɲa⁴⁴	ɲa³⁵	河 hé	river
ȶin⁵⁵	ȶin⁴⁴	ȶin³⁵	石头 shí tou	stone (n)
nɐm³¹	nɐm¹¹	nəm³¹	水 shuǐ	water (n)
ta⁵⁵	ta⁴⁴	ta³⁵	眼睛 yǎn jing	eye (n)
nɐŋ⁵⁵	nɐŋ⁴⁴	naŋ³⁵	鼻子 bí zi	nose
kha³⁵	kha⁴⁴	ka¹¹	耳朵 ěr duō	ear
na³²³	na³⁵	na³³	脸 liǎn	face
pa⁵⁵	pa⁴⁴	pa³⁵	腿 tuǐ	leg
tin⁵⁵	tin⁴⁴	tin³⁵	脚 jiǎo	foot
ʔin³⁵	qhin⁴⁴	kin¹¹	手臂 shǒu bì	arm
mja²¹²	mja¹²	mja²²	手 shǒu	hand (n)
səm³⁵	səm⁴⁴	səm¹¹	心 xīn	heart

Chējiāng southern, 1	Shuǐkǒu southern, 2	Shídòng northern, 1	Chinese	
sai^{323}	sai^{35}	sai^{33}	肠子 cháng zi	intestines
kwe^{212}	kwi^{12}	wi^{22}	水牛 shuǐ niú	water buffalo
ŋu^{453}	qhu^{53}	mu^{25}	猪 zhū	pig
ŋwa^{35}	khwa^{44}	kwa^{11}	狗 gǒu	dog
pət^{55}	pət^{44}	pət^{55}	鸭子 yā zi	duck
ɲɐn^{35}	ɲhɐn^{44}	ɲən^{11}	野猫 yě māo	wildcat
mok^{21}	nok^{32}	nok^{13}	鸟 niǎo	bird
sui^{212}	sui^{12}	si^{22}	蛇 shé	snake
nui^{212}	ni^{12}	ni^{22}	虫 chóng	insect
mɐi^{31}	mɐi^{11}	məi^{31}	树 shù	tree
pɐn^{55}	pɐn^{44}	kwən^{35}	竹子 zhú zi	bamboo
naŋ^{212}	naŋ^{12}	naŋ^{22}	竹笋 zhú sǔn	bamboo shoot
ʔɐu^{31}	qɐu^{11}	ʔəu^{31}	稻谷 dào gǔ	(unhusked) rice
ma^{55}	ma^{44}	ma^{35}	菜 cài	vegetable
ɲaŋ^{13}	ɲhaŋ^{35}	ɲaŋ^{13}	草 cǎo	grass
nu^{53}	nu^{53}	nu^{55}	看 kàn	look (v)
nɐk^{35}	nhɐk^{44}	nak^{25}	睡 shuì	sleep (v)
tuŋ^{55}	tuŋ^{44}	tuŋ^{35}	煮 zhǔ	boil (v)
sɐk^{55}	sɐk^{44}	sak^{55}	洗 (衣) xǐ	wash (clothes)
mak^{323}	mak^{35}	mak^{33}	大 dà	big
thɐm^{453}	thɐm^{53}	təm^{25}	矮 ǎi	short (of stature)
ja^{453}	jha^{53}	ja^{25}	红 hóng	red
nɐm^{55}	nɐm^{44}	nəm^{35}	黑 hēi	black
sak^{13}	sak^{35}	sak^{13}	舂 chōng	pound (v)
lɐm^{35}	lhɐm^{44}	ləm^{11}	插秧 chā yāng	transplant rice seedlings
than^{35}	than^{44}	tan^{11}	摘糯禾 zhāi nuò hé	pick glutinous rice seedlings

Cognate words in the Dòng–Tái family (cf. (88))

Dòng 侗	Shuǐ 水	Mùlǎo 仫佬	Máonán 毛难	Zhuàng 壮	Bùyī 布依	Dǎi 傣	Lí 黎	
mɐn^{55}	vɐn^{13}	fen^{42}	vɐn^{42}	ŋon^{21}	ŋon^{11}	vɐn^{55}	vɐn^{53}	sun
ɲan^{55}	njen^{31}	njen^{121}	njen^{231}	dun^{24}	din^{24}	dən^{51}	nan^{53}	moon
ma^{323}	fa^{33}	kwa^{53}	fa^{51}	fu^{55}	vuɛ^{53}	fa^{13}	fa^{11}	cloud

Cognate Words

Dòng 侗	Shuǐ 水	Mùlăo 仫佬	Máonán 毛难	Zhuàng 壮	Bùyī 布依	Dǎi 傣	Lí 黎	
pjɐn^{55}	fɐn^{13}	kwɐn^{42}	fin^{42}	fun^{24}	vun^{24}	fun^{55}	fun^{53}	rain (n)
pui^{55}	vi^{13}	fi^{42}	vi^{42}	fei^{21}	vi^{11}	fei^{53}	fei^{53}	fire
kwɐn^{212}	kwɐn^{31}	kwɐn^{121}	kwɐn^{231}	hon^{21}	hɔn^{11}	xɔn^{51}	gon^{53}	chimney smoke
nɐm^{31}	nɐm^{33}	nəm^{24}	nɐm^{51}	ɣɐm^{42}	zɐm^{31}	nɐm^{11}	nɐm^{11}	water
lɐk^{55}	dɐk^{35}	lɐk^{55}	dɐk^{55}	nŭk^{55}	nŭk^{35}	nok^{35}	łok^{55}	deaf
lak^{31}	lak^{54}	lak^{11}	lak^{24}	lŭ k^{33}	lŭ k^{33}	luk^{35}	łuk^{55}	child
noŋ^{31}	nu^{35}	nuŋ^{44}	nuŋ^{44}	nuŋ^{42}	nuŋ^{31}	nɔŋ^{11}	guŋ^{53}	younger brother
ta^{55}	^{n}da^{13}	la^{42}	^{n}da^{42}	ta^{24}	ta^{24}	ta^{55}	tsha^{53}	eye (n)
ʔin^{35}	thin^{13}	khin^{42}	chin^{42}	ken^{24}	tɕen^{24}	xɐn^{55}	khin^{53}	arm
phat^{13}	phjat^{54}	phyat^{11}	phjat^{24}	luut^{33}	lit^{33}	lət^{35}	łat^{55}	blood
lak^{323}	dak^{55}	hyak^{42}	dak^{44}	dok^{35}	do^{35}	duk^{35}	vuk^{55}	bone
pjɐn^{55}	vjɐn^{31}	fɐn^{42}	—	fɐn^{21}	fɐn^{11}	fɐn^{51}	fɐn^{53}	tooth
sai^{323}	hai^{31}	khyai^{53}	sai^{51}	sɐi^{55}	sɐi^{53}	sɐi^{13}	rai^{11}	intestines
ŋwa^{35}	ma^{13}	ŋwa^{42}	ma^{42}	ma^{24}	ma^{24}	ma^{55}	pa^{53}	dog
mɛ^{55}	ʔmi^{13}	mɛ^{42}	moi^{42}	mui^{24}	muui^{24}	mi^{55}	mui^{53}	bear (n)
ŋwɐt^{35}	mɐt^{35}	mɐt^{55}	mɐt^{55}	mɐt^{55}	mɐt^{35}	mɐt^{55}	pot^{11}	flea
nɐn^{55}	nɐn^{31}	nɐn^{42}	nan^{42}	nɐn^{21}	nɐn^{11}	min^{51}	thɐn^{53}	louse
mət^{21}	mət^{53}	myət^{12}	mət^{23}	mŏt^{33}	mɐt^{33}	mot^{35}	put^{11}	ant
mɐi^{31}	mɐi^{53}	mɐi^{24}	mɐi^{24}	fei^{42}	vɐi^{31}	mɐi^{11}	tshɐi^{53}	tree
jak^{323}	ʔyak^{55}	ʔyak^{42}	ʔik^{44}	pik^{35}	puɐ^{35}	phək^{35}	gek^{55}	taro
ɕiŋ^{35}	siŋ^{13}	hiŋ^{42}	siŋ^{42}	hĭŋ^{24}	hĭŋ^{24}	xiŋ^{55}	khuŋ^{53}	ginger
mɐn^{212}	mɐn^{31}	mɐn^{121}	mɐn^{231}	mɐn^{21}	mɐn^{11}	mɐn^{51}	mɐn^{53}	potato
ta^{55}	ja^{13}	ça^{42}	hi^{42}	ha^{21}	ha^{11}	xa^{51}	za^{53}	cogon-grass
loŋ^{323}	doŋ^{33}	lŏŋ^{53}	dŏŋ^{51}	dŏŋ^{55}	dɔŋ^{31}	duŋ^{13}	doŋ^{55}	winnowing fan
ʔun^{53}	kon^{35}	kun^{44}	kun^{44}	kon^{35}	kon^{35}	kɔn^{35}	hun^{55}	in front
nai^{33}	nai^{55}	nai^{11}	nan^{213}	nei^{42}	ni^{31}	ni^{13}	ni^{53}	this
tɐp^{55}	tsup^{35}	tsəp^{55}	tsəp^{55}	kĭp^{55}	tɕĭp^{35}	kep^{55}	tĭp^{55}	pick up
tok^{55}	tok^{35}	tŏk^{55}	tok^{55}	tŏk^{55}	tɔk^{35}	tok^{55}	thok^{55}	fall (v)
ʔum^{323}	ʔum^{33}	ŋəm^{53}	ʔum^{51}	ʔŭm^{55}	ʔŭm^{31}	ʔum^{13}	ʔom^{11}	hold (v)
lam^{212}	lam^{31}	lam^{121}	lam^{231}	lŭm^{21}	lŭm^{11}	lum^{51}	lum^{55}	forget
jɐn^{55}	tɐn^{31}	cɐn^{42}	cɐn^{231}	hɐn^{24}	hɐn^{24}	xɐn^{55}	zon^{53}	crow (v)
na^{55}	ʔna^{13}	na^{42}	na^{42}	na^{24}	na^{24}	na^{55}	na^{53}	thick
kai^{55}	qai^{13}	ce^{42}	ci^{42}	kjɐi^{24}	tɕɐi^{24}	kɐi^{55}	lɐi^{53}	far

Dòng 侗	Shuǐ 水	Mùlǎo 仫佬	Máonán 毛难	Zhuàng 壮	Bùyī 布依	Dǎi 傣	Lí 黎	
nɐm⁵⁵	ʔnɐm¹³	nɐm⁴²	nɐm⁴²	dɐm²⁴	dɐm²⁴	dɐm⁵⁵	dɐm¹¹	black
ʔɐm²¹²	qɐm¹³	kɐm⁴²	kɐm⁴²	hɐm²¹	hɐm¹¹	xum⁵¹	hŏm¹¹	bitter

Cognate words in the Dòng–Shuǐ language branch (cf. (89))

Dòng 侗	Shuǐ 水	Mùlǎo 仫佬	Máonán 毛难	Zhuàng 壮	Bùyī 布依	Dǎi 傣	Lí 黎	
ja⁵³	ʔya³⁵	ya⁴⁴	ʔja⁴⁴	na²¹	na¹¹	na⁵¹	ta⁵⁵	field (n)
lai²¹²	lai³¹	lai¹²¹	lai²³¹	lɐŋ²⁴	lɐŋ²⁴	lɐŋ⁵⁵	tshŭn¹¹	back (n)
loŋ²¹²	loŋ³¹	lŏŋ¹²¹	lŏŋ²³¹	tuŋ⁴²	tuŋ³¹	tɔŋ¹¹	pok⁵⁵	belly
ma²¹²	ma³¹	ma¹²¹	ma²³¹	lĭn⁴²	lĭn³¹	lĭn¹¹	tin¹¹	tongue
mun³³	mon⁵⁵	mun¹¹	mun²¹³	lĭŋ²¹	lĭŋ¹¹	liŋ⁵¹	nok⁵⁵	monkey
sui²¹²	hui³¹	tui¹²¹	zui²³¹	ŋɯ²¹	ŋɯə¹¹	ŋu⁵¹	ła⁵⁵	snake
ʔiŋ⁵⁵	jiŋ¹³	ṇiŋ⁴²	ⁿdiŋ⁴²	ɣuut³³	zit³³	hət³³	kuup⁵⁵	bedbug
sɐn³¹	han⁵³	tan²⁴	zan²⁴	dun²⁴	din²⁴	dən⁵⁵	hwiu⁵⁵	worm
saŋ³⁵	haŋ¹³	taŋ⁴²	saŋ⁴²	yak⁵⁵	za³³	hak³³	van⁵³	root
ma⁵⁵	ʔma¹³	ma⁴²	ʔma⁴²	plɐk⁵⁵	pik³⁵	phɐk⁵⁵	tshai⁵³	vegetable
la²¹²	ʁa¹³	ŋ̊a⁴²	ᵑga⁴²	ɣɐt⁵⁵	zɐt³⁵	het³⁵	det³⁵	mushroom
pa³³	pja⁵⁵	kwa¹¹	pa²¹³	ɣɐm²¹	zɐm¹¹	hɐm⁵¹	gom⁵³	chaff
ja²¹²	ɣa³¹	ɣa¹²¹	ja⁴²	soŋ²⁴	soŋ²⁴	sɔŋ⁵⁵	łɯ¹¹	two
jap³²³	ṭap⁵⁵	jap⁴²	cep²⁴	ham⁵⁵	ham⁵³	xam¹³	hjam⁵³	stride
sui⁵³	hui³¹	tui¹¹	zui²¹³	nɐŋ³³	nɐŋ³³	nɐŋ³³	tsoŋ¹¹	sit
ṭuŋ⁵⁵	tjoŋ¹³	kyŋ⁴²	tjuŋ⁴²	ɣam²⁴	zwam²⁴	ham⁵⁵	tsham⁵³	lift (v)
ṭɐi³²³	ⁿdjɐi³³	hɣɐi⁵³	ⁿdjɐi⁵¹	ɕau⁴²	ɕɯ³¹	su¹¹	tshət⁵⁵	buy
jɐm⁵⁵	ʔjɐm¹³	jɐm⁴²	ʔjɐm⁴²	lɐk⁵⁵	lɐk³⁵	lɐk⁵⁵	łok⁵⁵	deep
kuŋ²¹²	kuŋ³¹	kyuŋ¹²¹	coŋ²³¹	lai²⁴	lai²⁴	lai⁵⁵	łoi⁵³	many
ma³²³	ʔma³³	ma⁵³	ʔma⁵¹	ʔŭn³⁵	ʔŭn³⁵	ʔon³⁵	put¹¹	soft

Postscript

We are very pleased that *The Dong Language in Guizhou Province, China* has been published, and published in English. We want to take this opportunity to explain the genesis of the book and to add a few expressions of appreciation.

The seventh five-year plan of the Philosophical and Scientific Society of Guìzhōu Province proposed to promote a series of books entitled *Descriptions of Minority Nationality Languages in Guizhou*. The Language unit of the Guìzhōu Nationality Research Institute was to be responsible for the series. Zhèng Guóqiáo (郑国乔) and I were appointed to write the book describing the Dong language. On January 7, 1988, after assuming responsibility for writing the book, we divided the work between us. Being Dong, I was well acquainted with the history of my people and with my own mother tongue. I undertook to write the introduction and the chapter on grammar. Zhèng Guóqiáo was an expert in the field of Dong teaching and research, with nearly forty years' experience, and was very familiar with the phonology and dialects of Dong. Moreover, he was one of the creators of the Dong orthography. He assumed responsibility for writing the chapters on phonology, lexicon, and orthography. The chapter on dialects was jointly written. The Zhānglǔ (章鲁) speech in appendix 1 was compiled by Zhèng Guóqiáo, the Shídòng (石洞) speech by myself. After our first efforts emerged, we exchanged manuscripts and checked one another's work several times, until a formal first draft was together agreed upon in Běijīng and presented to the publications committee in February 1990. Afterwards, because authors of all the other books in the series were unable to complete their tasks on time, our draft was laid aside. In 1992, seeking an opportunity to publish, we left the draft at the Guìzhōu Nationalities Publishing House. After over a year there, however, the manuscript was returned to us because funding for publication could not be found. In 1994, I revised and supplemented some data in the draft.

Towards the end of 1995, Dr. Norman Geary (吉志义) from Northern Ireland and his wife Ruth (孔瑞贤) from Switzerland arrived at Guìzhōu University to study the Dong language, and I had the good fortune to become acquainted with them. In fact I became their Dong language teacher, initiating them into the rudiments of the language. In the course of their language study, we happened to discuss the draft of this book. This aroused their interest. After looking at the draft, they thought it might be useful as a resource for academic research and suggested publishing it in English. At the time, I agreed to this and reported this development to Zhèng Guóqiáo in Běijīng. Thus, from July 1996, Norman Geary began the arduous work of translation. All 350,000 characters of the draft were translated by January 1997.

We wish to thank various friends and departments for their help in the publication of this book. First of all, we want to thank Professor Yáng Quán (杨权) of the Central University of Nationalities. He is a scholar renowned in the field of Dong language research, and we shall not forget the practical backing he gave to the book. His comments on the original draft were constructive, and when publication was imminent, he took time out of a very busy schedule to write a foreword. We are indebted to him. We also wish to thank Professor Jerold Edmondson (艾杰瑞), head of linguistics at the University of Texas at Arlington. He is an overseas expert in the field of Dong language research and is also our friend. He saw an early draft of the book and made some useful criticisms and suggestions.

Again we want to thank Norman and Ruth Geary. Without their endeavor, this publication may never have materialized. We admire their attention to detail and conscientious attitude to work. They suggested many improvements to the book in the course of the translation.

Thanks are also due to Mr. Xiān Sōngkuí (鲜松奎) of the Guìzhōu Nationalities Research Institute and Ms. Zhāng Mèngpíng (张梦平) of the Guìzhōu Institute of Nationalities. They also invested much energy in the book.

Finally, we wish to point out that, owing to limitations in our own ability, the book will still contain some errors. These should not be attributed to faults in the translation. We look forward to receiving criticisms and corrections from colleagues and scholars inside and outside of China.

Lóng Yàohóng (龙耀宏)
Guìzhōu Institute of Nationalities, Guìyáng
March 10, 1997